THE ART OF JUST COOKING

The Art of

JUST Cooking

by LIMA OHSAWA

with Nahum Stiskin

Illustrated by Maurice Owen

AUTUMN PRESS

ABOUT THE COVER: Daikoku and Ebisu are two of Japan's *Shichi Fukujin,* or Seven Gods of Happiness, Good Fortune and the Household. They comprise the pair of deities most often found in the kitchen of the Japanese home. Daikoku, usually shown standing atop or seated before two bales of rice, holds a treasure-filled sack on his shoulder. His hammer embodies the forces of *yin* and *yang,* in token of his divine creativity; a stroke of this hammer conveys the precious gift of health and its accompanying good fortune. His name is often interpreted to mean "great and prosperous civilization." Ebisu holds a fishing rod and a large Tai fish, emblematic of joy and celebration. In addition to being the patron diety of laughter, he is also the god of food and of honesty.

Published by
Autumn Press, Inc.
7 Littell Road, Brookline, Massachusetts 02146

Copyright in Japan, 1974
by Autumn Press, Inc.

Book design and typography by Dana Levy
Manufactured in the United States of America

Lima Ohsawa at seventy-five.

TABLE OF CONTENTS

AUTHOR'S PREFACE

I was 54 years old before venturing beyond the shores of my native Japan. It was 1953, and Georges Ohsawa and I were leaving on our first world tour. I remember feeling as naive, excited and hesitant as a young schoolgirl about to embark on her first voyage into a wide and unknown world. I knew that Georges, having previously spent some years abroad, could speak both English and French, and that I, limited to my native language, would have to rely on him to steer our course. So I firmly resolved to accept in silence whatever fate had in store for us.

We traveled by ship to Calcutta, arriving in November, and were engulfed by a surging crowd of beggars the moment we stepped ashore. Shocked and bewildered, I wondered to what kind of world my husband was so intent upon introducing me? After a month in Calcutta seeking out Yogins, philosophers and nutritional experts with whom to discuss our philosophy of living and eating, we were on the verge of our scheduled departure for New Delhi when a newly acquired Indian friend introduced us to a local entrepreneur. Together they insisted that we begin a "short" lecture series on the philosophy of the "Unique Principle." Georges reluctantly agreed, while I, true to my resolve, remained silent. We were given use of a lovely room in the large and luxurious home of our newfound patron. In one corner I set up a very small kitchen consisting of an electric hot plate, a saucepan, platter and knife, two wooden spoons, two cups and two pairs of chopsticks. This was to serve as my laboratory, apothecary and cuisine.

Georges began a busy life of writing, lecturing and receiving inquisitive visitors, while it became my responsibility to show the practical application of the nutritional and philosophical principle that my husband was propounding. Having had no experience with Indian foods, I had to begin a serious and detailed study of native vegetation; it was off to the great public markets and in to cooking school. The goal of my study was to create a macrobiotic Indian cuisine using only native foods and traditional methods of preparation that would be in harmony with India's subtropical environment, tasteful to its people, and fundamentally healthful and balanced. The local vegetable market and its hidden secrets quickly became as exciting as the Taj Mahal. Our teaching was very well received, particularly by the Hindus and Jainists who were already strict vegetarians in conformity with the teachings of their religions. Their practice, however, was not refined, and, lacking a guiding principle, they often suffered from illnesses and disorders. How happily preoccupied we became with these activities, despite the fact that our purses were almost empty and that we were often told that the beggars who accosted us might well have been in possession of much more money than we. So preoccupied, indeed, that having originally intended to stay in all of India for only six months, we remained in Calcutta for two years.

When we finally left India, late in 1955, we were on our way to Lambaréné, in central Africa, where Georges wanted to meet with Albert Schweitzer, the world's most famous physician-philosopher. From Bombay we traveled to Mombasa, then on to Nairobi, Tanganyika and Stanleyville (Kisangani). We sailed down the Congo River to Leopoldville (Kinshasa), and finally reached Dr. Schweitzer's hospital and guesthouse. We were graciously received, and Georges spent many memorable hours explaining the Oriental principle of physical well-being and spiritual health. Being vegetarian Dr. Schweitzer was always very interested in the nutritional assets of the soybean and asked me to show him different ways to prepare it. Meanwhile, I kept busy studying Africa's rich vegetation and native cooking techniques. I remember being the center of much wonder and amazement when, working side by side with native cooks in the hospital's steaming kitchen, my brow was dry when all those around me were perspiring profusely. Gesturing with my hands and twisting up my face, I tried to explain that one perspires only as much as one drinks, and that by eating foods in proper balance with the environment one could easily and painlessly control both. I saw many smiling faces nodding in agreement, but still wonder whether my friends understood that antic explanation. We took our leave of Lambaréné, crossed the Sahara and, after visiting Algeria, left Africa's shores for Europe and, later, America. Unknown to myself, I had become the first Japanese woman to cross the interior of the "dark continent."

You may wonder how a sheltered Japanese female, born in a small village and raised in the traditional fashion to become a quiet and retiring housewife, was suddenly plunged into such an adventurous and rewarding life. Ironically, I am grateful to the frailty and fatigue that plagued my childhood and persisted well into my adult years, for were it not for an early history of weakness and infirmity I would never have come to know true health and vitality.

Until my sister was born nine years after my arrival into the world, I was the only girl among five children. Being my parents' pet I was shamelessly indulged, and during those early years I ate, what seems to me now, the world's most unmacrobiotic food. As a consequence, I was a very weak child and a constant source of concern for my parents. They brought me to Tokyo where I managed to struggle through high school and train in the traditional arts of tea ceremony, flower arrangement and music. In the process, and for years thereafter, I wandered from doctor to doctor, hospital to hospital, in search of a cure for the ills and fatigue that hung like a dark cloud over my life.

I was thirty-seven years old when, one hot summer's day, I was told by a physician that a lecture sponsored by the "Macrobiotic Association" would be held in Tokyo. I attended and found the speaker to be a Mr. Ohsawa, recently returned from a long stay in France. I listened attentively to what he said that night and was particularly struck by his emphatic pronouncement that "sickness is a crime of your own making." At that moment I realized how selfishly I had been living my life, in ignorance of nature's law. I was ashamed of my life's disorder and of the years spent as a burden on my parents and family. But now I resolved to change all that by making macrobiotic philosophy the cornerstone of my life and by mastering the art of macrobiotic cooking. I met Georges Ohsawa for the first time that night; one year later I was his wife, and from that moment my life was truly revolutionized. Freed from its earlier ills, it became a constant exercise in self-discipline, self-deepening and service to others.

Living with Georges Ohsawa was a constant challenge, for he demanded that I realize the law of nature, for and by myself, and apply it in my kitchen. Yet, he never once instructed me how to cook. It was not his way to teach directly, but to prod a person's own intuitive understanding until it awoke. For several years his only comment upon my culinary efforts was "No;" indeed, I realized that I had entered a "school of No." Then, while working in my kitchen one day, I experienced an overwhelming feeling of harmony and well-being and thought that I had—for an instant—glimpsed the law of the universe. The food I placed before my husband that night was the first to receive a "Yes." I had graduated and was a totally different person.

Georges Ohsawa spent more than twenty years abroad, lecturing on the principle of the Order of the Universe and its physiological, philosophical and practical significance. At first his philosophy appeared new and mysterious to Westerners, who found it hard to understand. Now, however, more and more people all over the world have come to recognize the meaning and effectiveness of macrobiotics, the practical application of the basic principle of Oriental philosophy. I accompanied my husband on many of his lecture tours, teaching macrobiotic cooking. And now that an ever-increasing number of people want to learn, I want to help by publishing this guide.

The recipes presented here are for use in the average home. They are unlike those in an ordinary cookbook because they are based on the ancient philosophy of *Yin* and *Yang*. Indeed, macrobiotic cookery is not a new idea, but the oldest and most timeworn method of choosing and preparing food in harmony with nature. It expresses a philosophy of life that has been put into practice in a variety of ways throughout history, all over the world. If you observe the order of nature in your kitchen you can practice any style of traditional cooking, be it Japanese, French, Italian or Middle Eastern. You will find recipes in this book, therefore, from all over the world. Georges Ohsawa and I endeavored to revive this traditional practice by stressing the law of nature that underlies it, the law that binds man's health and happiness to the food he eats. For food provides the physical foundation out of which man's mind and spirit grow and develop. Today, with the pressing problems of environmental pollution, the widespread use of chemical fertilizer, and the addition of chemical colorings and preservatives to industrialized foods, I wish to offer the benefits of macrobiotic cooking and living to all my fellow human beings. I will attempt to outline our philosophy in the pages that follow, but I can offer here only a taste of its breadth and width. For those who want to study it more deeply I have listed a bibliography at the end of the book that will provide the nourishment you seek.

The original founder of the macrobiotic regimen in Japan was the late Dr. Sagen Ishizuka. Georges Ohsawa, after studying and developing its theory, formulated the philosophy he called the "Unique Principle." My husband devoted his life to helping people and to guiding them along the path to self-discovery, health and happiness. He helped me and enabled me to help others. With his passing in 1966 I dedicated myself to the furtherance of his work. Thus, as he recommended the macrobiotic diet to me more than thirty-five years ago, I now recommend it to you and sincerely hope that you discover the true significance of the food you place upon your table. If this book contributes to your happiness, its purpose will have been achieved. I look forward to hearing from its readers.

In closing, I would like to thank Mr. Nahum Stiskin for his help in preparing this volume, and Mr. Maurice Owen for his skillfully executed illustrations. Many others have helped both materially and spiritually in the composition of this book, but the limitations of space prohibit my mentioning their names. They are, however, engraved upon my heart. My deepest thanks.

Tokyo, 1974

LIMA OHSAWA

food is the body
of nature's justice
man the mind
cooking the art

THE ART OF JUST COOKING

INTRODUCTION

In Japanese, *Inochi* means life, the vital biological and physiological functions that sustain our daily existence. In Japan, as in other parts of the world, life has always been understood to draw its material and energy from food. Although often overlooked, the obvious fact that human existence depends foremost upon the foods provided for it by nature leaves no excuse for carelessness in our choice and preparation of foods, or in our manner of eating and drinking. Nevertheless, don't many of us take these activities for granted, treating them only as habits or sources of mere sensory satisfaction? We all too often forget that while food provides the vital energy capable of supporting life, it can, if improperly and excessively indulged in, put an end to life.

Practical macrobiotics begins with a studied appreciation of foods. Our philosophy first divides the available varieties into the two categories of animal *(yang)* and vegetable *(yin)*. It is a law of ecology that all animal life depends for its existence upon the vegetable kingdom, for vegetal forms transmute nature's basic chemicals into digestible foods. A "food chain," a heirarchy of eater and eaten, dictates that large fish feed upon small ones, while the latter are nourished by sea or river plants. The carnivorous creatures of the world devour the herbivorous. We humans, too, evolutionarily the most recent addition to the food chain, depend either directly or indirectly upon plant life for our nourishment. Macrobiotic philosophy, grounded in experience, teaches that although man continually proves himself capable (at a price) of eating whatever he wishes, his health and vitality improve the more completely and directly he draws his sustenance from the vegetable kingdom. For when we take our nourishment from animal sources, the basic life-giving elements we receive have been rearranged and unbalanced; some have been concentrated while others have been removed. In addition, we absorb toxic animal wastes as well as artificial chemicals introduced by industry.

The macrobiotic diet, however, is not a strict vegetarian regimen. We do not believe that if a man or woman eats vegetable foods exclusively he or she will, of necessity, achieve health or vitality, and live in harmony with the environment, or, for that matter, that every man *must* restrict himself to the vegetal realm if he wants to realize his nature. The natural order in our surroundings is both more precise and more flexible. The shape and relative number of our teeth, the gateway of food into the body, tell us more about the order in human nutrition. Of a total of thirty-two teeth, eight (one quarter of them) are incisors designed for cutting and slicing vegetables, four (one eighth) are canines designed for tearing flesh, and twenty (five eighths) are molars designed for grinding cereal grains. Guided by the structure of our digestive system, the macrobiotic diet centers around grains and vegetables and, like the teeth, emphasizes the importance of the former. Georges Ohsawa devoted fifty years of his life to proving that, for man, cereals were first in order of nutritional importance. Room is left, however, on the plate as in the mouth, for proportionately small quantities of animal food if necessary or desirable. The animal foods we recommend are the lower forms of life, or those that have been least domesticated or processed by modern man. We do advise that as few animal foods as possible be part of one's daily fare. But what I cannot emphasize enough is that the random choice and improper preparation of ideal foods, granted even that they be in proper

17

proportion, can lessen their healthful and restorative effects. There is a proper order to be maintained in their selection, cutting, combining and cooking.

The macrobiotic diet is a very subtle regimen that makes use of the broadest possible range of available ingredients. It is the culinary expression of mankind's rich individuality, and believes in nurturing and cultivating that individuality. To follow the macrobiotic diet properly, each of us must come to know himself and understand the dynamics of food to discover how best to satisfy his own particular requirements. People's needs differ according to their physical constitution and nutritional background, their age and daily activities, their geographical location and the seasonal changes in their environment. A wife and mother must understand not only her own needs but also those of the members of her family who entrust her with the responsibility of preparing their meals. The macrobiotic secrets to healthful living and eating are balance and moderation. You can be a vegetarian and derive all the vitamins, minerals, starches, oils and proteins needed for energy, growth and tissue repair from a well-balanced diet of grains, fresh vegetables, fruits and nuts. But animal foods and dairy products can also find a place in a macrobiotic meal if we prepare them properly and combine them harmoniously with the other elements included in our menu. We are free to eat whatever we wish; nothing is forbidden but ignorance and carelessness.

COOKING AS SELF-MASTERY

After the discovery of fire many thousands of years ago, mankind developed numerous methods of cooking that slowly evolved into the variety of forms we know today. Cooking's fundamental purpose is to prepare foods that sustain our physical and psychological well-being, nourish our humanity, and improve the quality of our life. Macrobiotic methods, therefore, are designed to preserve and even improve upon essential nutrients. We believe that cooking should never be merely for the indulgence of our sensory desires, but don't misunderstand me. We must never neglect or minimize the importance of flavor, aroma, texture or appearance. The ideal is that a good cook creates truly delicious and attractive meals, but also succeeds in allowing each ingredient to retain its own natural taste.

The astronomical order of nature played out on a grand scale in the heavens has its reflection in a small, delicate order embodied in the ingredients of cooking. Each natural taste—bitter, sweet, sour, salty, pungent as well as their innumerable permutations—has a characteristic effect upon us, body and mind. Ingredients in combination accentuate, modify or moderate each other. In cooking we evoke, enhance or nullify these natural flavors (and their effects) at will. This is our creative prerogative as human beings, a first step in the mastery of our destiny. If we destroy them by using artificial seasonings or by cooking foods improperly, we harmfully tamper with "nature-as-it-is," and invariably suffer for our discretion. A good cook has studied nature and knows natural taste and how to preserve it for the benefit of those whom it is meant to nourish.

It is by means of food that man's body is sustained, and it is by means of food that the quality and direction of life are determined. Preparing the food that sustains tomorrow's life is a creative act; to be successful in this art one needs deep understanding, subtle delicacy and true dedication.

Cooking therefore is a very important skill—for men as well as women. It is especially important for wives and mothers, and those who cook each day with the true welfare of others in mind. Macrobiotic cookery provides an opportunity for self-realization, and for understanding and administering the law of nature, through the self-less act of sustaining life. Cooking is a complex activity involving the synthesis of color, flavor, shape, texture and fragrance into an integrated, harmonious whole. If music and painting be fine arts, this art should be put in a class of its own, for while the others yield pleasure, cooking nourishes humanity. We consider it the supreme art, whose devoted practitioners merit the highest respect.

COOKING WITH HARMONY IN MIND

Macrobiotic cooking is the preparation of foods according to the principle we call the Order of the Universe, our modified and updated version of the ancient Oriental principle of *yin* and *yang*. This principle expresses the harmonious interplay of opposites that governs the workings of every plant and vegetable as well as of man and nature's larger realms. If we know the law and how to apply it we can balance our foods, change their quality to make them more digestible, and draw a variety of tastes and flavors from one simple ingredient. We can make our meals delicious, enticing and healthful whether our ingredients be costly or inexpensive.

When designing your daily menu, keep in mind this dialectical harmony. When serving food that comes from the sea, combine it with the appropriate food that grows on land; a serving of animal food *(yang)* should be balanced with vegetables or fruit *(yin)*; foods rich in potassium *(yin)* go best with those rich in sodium *(yang)*. Don't worry, you need not be a scientist. The macrobiotic principle is common sense and once your intuition is revitalized you will realize that you have known and used it all along, albeit only haltingly. With a little practice macrobiotic cooking will become second nature; with a bit more it may well become your primary nature. Begin with the recipes I offer in this volume and soon you will be creating your own.

THE HARMONY OF TASTE

To succeed in making meals that are consistently delicious and tempting, nurture a gentle touch and delicate sensibility. Never season with a heavy hand. There is a proper time in the process of preparing a food when a seasoning should be introduced. Salt, for example, can be added fairly early to keep vegetables firm during cooking, but *miso* (soybean paste) should be added later. If it's overcooked it loses much of its nutritional value and flavor.

To maximize your skill in handling ingredients, regain an appreciation and sensitivity for natural taste. Harmoniously combining these flavors is an exciting challenge and one of the most important goals of macrobiotic cooking. If your palate has been dulled by chemically processed or sugar-rich foods, it will take you a week or two before you become noticeably resensitized. Have patience. The effort is well worth it.

THE HARMONY OF APPEARANCE

Place foods on a dish in consideration of the harmony of their colors, textures and shapes. Light foods should be served with heavy; the pungency of finely grated *daikon*, for example, enlivens fried *omochi* (rice cake), while the cool green stems of chopped scallion give a bowl of *soba* (buckwheat noodles) a bright lift.

Food should always be presented in a way that appeals to the eye. Don't cut vegetables as you would firewood. Here are several ways to slice and shape natural ingredients so that each piece maintains an integral harmony of *yin* and *yang:*

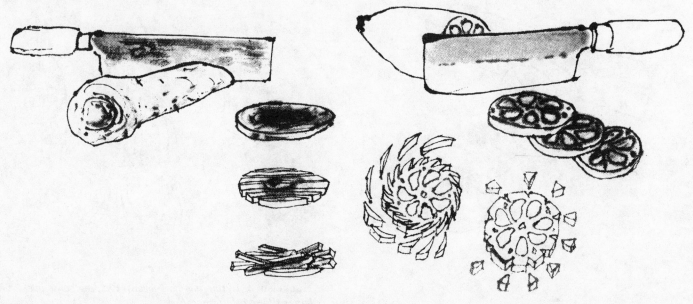

Hasugiri, *or slicing on the diagonal. Cut diagonally, on the bias.*
Sengiri, *or slivering. Cut each bias section into matchstick-size pieces.*

Koguchigiri, *or cutting into bite-size pieces. Cut into thin rounds.*

Koguchigiri Hanagata, *or cutting into bite-size flowered pieces. Cut into thin rounds; then cut small wedges.*

Rangiri, *or cutting into irregular wedges. Cut into large diagonal wedges.*

Wagiri, *or cutting into thick rounds. Cut into rounds, thicker than koguchigiri.*

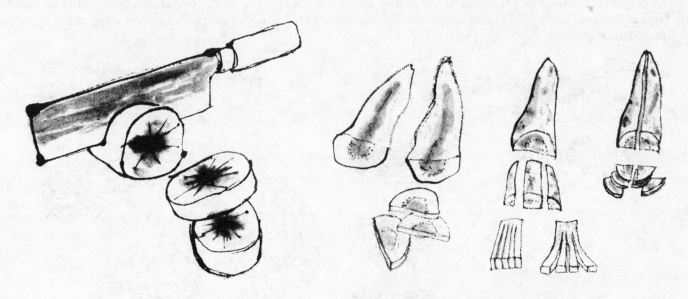

Hangetsu, *or cutting into half-moons. Cut lengthwise into halves. Then cut* koguchigiri.

Ichogiri, *or cutting into gingko leaves. Cut lengthwise into halves. Cut each half full-length again, then cut* koguchigiri.

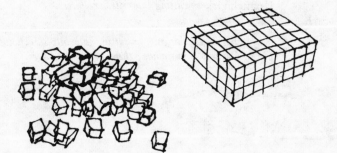

Sainome, *or dicing. Cut vegetables into ⅓-inch dice.*

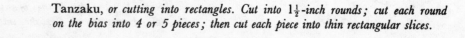

Tanzaku, *or cutting into rectangles. Cut into 1½-inch rounds; cut each round on the bias into 4 or 5 pieces; then cut each piece into thin rectangular slices.*

Kikukagiri, *or cutting chrysanthemum style. Cut into even pieces across vegetable, keeping pieces attached at base. Cut across opposite pole to same depth and thickness. Soak in ice-cold water to open up like a flower.*

Mawashigiri, *or cutting into half-moon/crescents. Cut vegetable lengthwise into halves. Turn on axis and cut vertically into thin moon-shaped slices.*

Mijingiri, *or onion-dicing. Cut into halves about $\frac{1}{8}$ inch from root end. Cut thin sections down to the same point across entire vegetable; then slice in the opposite direction, keeping same distance from root end. Next dice into small pieces.*

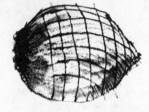

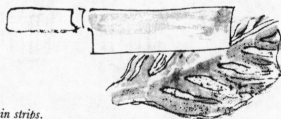

Cutting leaves into strips. Separate full leaves, stack together, and cut into thin strips.

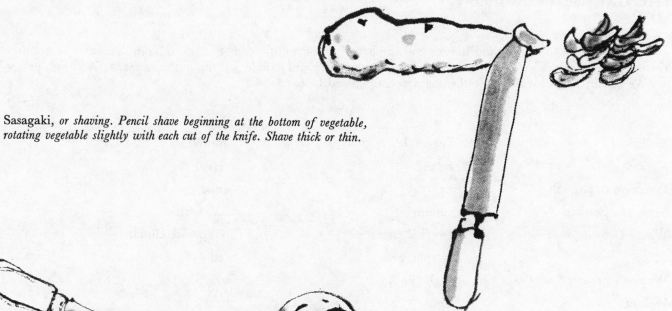

Sasagaki, *or shaving. Pencil shave beginning at the bottom of vegetable, rotating vegetable slightly with each cut of the knife. Shave thick or thin.*

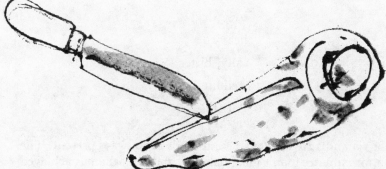

Hanagata, *or cutting into flower shapes. Cut small thin wedges full-length of vegetable 4 or 5 times around the vegetable. Then cut into rounds.*

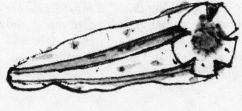

THE UNIQUE PRINCIPLE

The tool we use to understand nature and the art of preparing foods is the law of complementary opposites. *Yin* and *yang* are the poles of contraction and expansion, male and female, winter and summer, activity and passivity. We classify foods according to the characteristics listed below.*

	Yin	*Yang*
Biological	vegetable	animal
Agricultural	salad	cereal
Direction of Growth	up	down
Season of Growth	summer	fall, winter
Where Grown	tropical climate	temperate climate
Color	purple, green	red
Water Content	high (juicy)	low (dry)
Weight	light	heavy
Taste	sweet, sour, spicy	salty, bitter
Element	potassium	sodium
Vitamin	C	A,D,K

Every food in nature contains a unique balance of *yin* and *yang* elements; both kinds are always present. The ratio of *yin* to *yang* in whole brown rice (5:1) closely approximates man's ideal balance, and one who has achieved this perfectly healthful state could theoretically derive full nutritional sustenance from this one grain, if it were cooked properly. He would not need to balance it with anything else. All other foods are either more *yin* or more *yang* in relation to man's ideal balance. By applying the principle to their preparation and presentation, we broaden man's nutritional horizons by "yangizing" foods that are *yin* in their raw state and jarring to his healthful balance, and "yinizing" foods that are *yang* in their raw state and equally jarring. In our cooking and combining we delicately alter nature to suit our needs and maximize our freedom while remaining within the bounds of biological and ecological justice.

*A listing of foods according to *yin/yang* can be found on p. 41.

The *yin* or *yang* characteristics of a food are never good or bad in themselves. It is the balance we create that tells. That balance depends upon the quantity and quality of our ingredients and, most important, upon our skill in cooking. We must come to know our foods and discover the combinations and methods of preparation that best meet our individual requirements.

The four fundamental techniques of macrobiotic cooking—the use of salt, fire, pressure and time—neutralize acidic content or remove excess liquid from raw foods. In other words, cooking makes our food more *yang*. We use our knowledge of the *yin* or *yang* qualities of an ingredient when deciding upon its preparation and seasoning, and when selecting other foods to combine with it. *Yang* vegetables (roots, for example) require less salt and lower heat than do *yin*. If we overcook we can make our food too *yang;* if we undercook it can remain too *yin*. Seasoning with salt, *miso* or *shoyu* "yangizes" our food, while eliminating salt and increasing the volume of water in our cooked foods "yinizes" them. *Yang* vegetables generally go best with *yin* vegetables; they complement each other. By applying these simple principles in our kitchens we change the quality of raw foods, making *yin* ingredients more *yang* and *yang* ingredients more *yin*.

We eat balanced meals to remain in healthful harmony with our environment and joyfully carry on our daily lives. Wintry or cloudy surroundings are *yin;* we keep in dialectical balance with them by becoming relatively *yang,* choosing the appropriate ingredients for our diet, and cooking and seasoning them well. Grains may comprise from 50 to 70 percent of our daily menu. A summerlike, hot and dry environment is *yang;* we must adjust our balance toward the *yin,* eating moist, lightly cooked and sparingly salted dishes. Here, grain may account for only 20 to 50 percent of our daily menu, with light green leafy vegetables and fruits making up the rest. Observe the periodic changes of season and the daily changes in both the weather and your physical condition in order to choose your ingredients and method of preparation correctly.

LIVING ECOLOGY

Translated literally from the Greek, "Macrobiotics" means great life. Macro refers to the macrocosmic universe, the infinite womb out of which springs the Bios, or biological evolution. Macro-bios implies the law that knits the entire universe into a oneness. Living according to this law (expressed as *yin* and *yang*) is the way to achieve health, happiness and fulfillment. Practical macrobiotics is the attempt to grasp this elusive order in nature and to enable every man and woman to administer and use it in everyday life. By so doing we strive to create a civilization of free and happy people in harmony with the environment around them. We understand man to be nourished by sunlight, air, water and earth, in addition to the vegetal forms absorbed directly through the digestive system. We stress the importance of choosing and eating foods that are native to our terrain and climate, those that grow within a radius of 500 miles of our homes. Here are seven simple guidelines that summarize the macrobiotic approach to cooking and eating. They are all based on an Oriental principle of ecology traditionally expressed in the phrase, *Man and Earth are not-Two*.

(1) Primary Food

Grains are our primary food. Short-grain brown rice is ideally balanced, particularly for people living in temperate climates and at sea level. In mountainous regions, increase the proportions of wheat or buckwheat in your diet. Use a rich variety of staples (rice, buckwheat, wheat, millet, barley, rye, oats and corn), selecting what grows locally and has been traditionally enjoyed in your part of the world. Ideally, the grains you eat should be organically grown, free of chemical fertilizer and poisonous spray.

Whatever grain you choose should be used in its whole form. The rich deposits of vitamins and minerals in its outer layers play an essential role in digesting the carbohydrate that makes up its bulk. Milling or otherwise processing a grain results in an incomplete food, one robbed of its full value, that strains the body's delicate adjustive mechanisms and is ecologically wasteful. And, in addition to vitamins and minerals, we lose the unanalyzable essence of wholeness. Plant a whole kernel in the earth and a stalk will grow yielding many more. Bury a milled kernel and, cultivate it as you will, it will never sprout. It has lost its life.

(2) Secondary Food

Our second staple consists of fresh, locally grown vegetables and fruits. They are secondary in that their quantity will vary in proportion to the amount of grain in your meal, your primary consideration. Use all the parts of a vegetable and whenever possible see that it, too, has been naturally fertilized and tended. Choose what is native to your locale from among both cultivated produce and wild grasses. Sea vegetables are rich in iodine and other essential minerals and can be included in your diet even if you live far from the sea. We each carry an ocean with us in the form of bloodstream and body fluid. It may take a little time, but once you have accustomed yourself to the unique tastes of the various seaweeds they will gradually seem more and more delicious. Learn to use them every day.

When we enter our kitchens, cooked grains and vegetables are uppermost in our mind and our daily menu revolves around them. But in a given meal we may wish to include a soup or salad, some animal food, or a fruit. Soups are a fine way of drinking liquid, and *miso* soup is an excellent source of protein and energy. Beans, too, are a rich source of valuable proteins that complement those present in grains. Fresh or pressed salads are delightfully refreshing in summer and can help, during any season, to balance a side dish of fish or fowl.

Remember that no foods are forbidden except when your body tells you so. Learn to recognize the signals it gives you. If you choose to prepare animal food, remember that its proportion to the rest of your meal should be secondary. Most important, prepare it properly and serve it together with the appropriate food. Because fish and other seafood are *yin* compared to land-roving animals, they are easier to balance and are, therefore, considered preferable to meats. When such animal food forms a small part of a meal in which grains and vegetables are primary, it is often invigorating. When using eggs, try to see that they come from hens that were raised on organic feed. Fowl may be enjoyed occasionally but, being very *yang,* it requires careful balancing. Meats, like eggs, should be as free as possible from the contamination of artificial chemicals. And dairy products, particularly goat's cheese and goat's milk—*yang* entries in this generally *yin* food category—can also find a place in a macrobiotic meal, if balanced properly.

Enjoy native fruits when fresh and in season. Apples and strawberries are ideal, while berries and melons can be wonderfully refreshing on a hot summer day.

(3) Seasonings

Macrobiotic seasonings consist predominantly of natural sea salt, *miso* (soybean paste), *shoyu* (natural soy sauce) and unrefined vegetable oils. A balance of five parts oil to one part salt in our meals is theoretically ideal; the intake of 2 tablespoons of oil per day is the recommended maximum.

Our use of seasonings must accord with the weather, our geographical location and our individual activities and needs. We season with a dash more salt and oil in cold, northerly regions than in warm, southerly climes. We need more of both oil and salt if doing hard, physical labor. Adults whose bodies contain too much potassium and a deficiency of sodium require more salt, while those with too much sodium and not enough potassium require less or, in extreme cases, even none at all. Never underestimate the importance of salt in your diet, especially natural sea salt which is much stronger than ordinary table salt. A deficiency may lead to fatigue; an excess to a rigid, nervous feeling and inability to sleep.

(4) Preparing Vegetables and Fruits

Naturally fertilized, unsprayed vegetables and fruits require only a light rinsing under running cold water. Scrub them with a natural bristle brush *(tawashi)* as you rinse. Peel them only if they have been waxed to preserve their shelf life in the supermarket. Use all their parts, wasting nothing. Cut and cook them with balance in mind.

(5) The Tao of Eating

Chew your food well, each mouthful from fifty to one hundred times. Proper mastication is indispensable in the digestion of grains because their major constituent, carbohydrate, is digested by an enzyme that flows in the mouth (ptyalin). For better digestion, proceed from *yang* to *yin*: begin with soup and/or a few bitefuls of grain, then alternate grain with the most *yang* food before you. When savored, go on to the next, always returning to grain as your central focus. Follow the meal with dessert and beverage. Never eat to full capacity. Always leave the table with room left for just a little more.

(6) Following the Path of Nature

Modern methods of cultivating, processing, preserving and distributing foods have diluted our awareness of the importance of seasonality and of our ties to the earth and water around us. *Refining* a food has come to mean removing essential nutrients; when packaged, chemicals are added to preserve its life (although not necessarily *ours*), and colorings to make it more appealing to the eye. We can serve tomatoes and cucumbers at parties celebrating the New Year despite the fact that in temperate climates these are summer foods. They have either been brought from far away or grown in artificial environments. I never cease to wonder at the many people who try so hard to "return to nature" in mountains and forests, only to draw frozen vegetables, meats and chocolate candies out of their rucksacks.

To preserve your health and happiness, and to live in true harmony with the natural environment, avoid industrialized foods, refined flour products and refined sugar. These denatured foods strain and deplete the body's resources in its efforts to maintain an alkaline balance in the blood and adjust them to its real needs. As a rule, abstain from the extremes of *yin* and *yang*: refined sugar, artificial chemicals and drugs on the one hand, and meat on the other. It is true that taken together they constitute a balance, but not an ideal or healthful one. If you are addicted, free yourself from coffee which acts solely as a stimulant and has no food value, and avoid commercial teas containing artificial dyes that may be carcinogenic. To gain a more thorough understanding of why these foods can be harmful, refer to the works listed in the bibliography.

Whether you live in city or country, you will be amazed at how quickly and spontaneously your mind and body will be reattuned to the cycles of nature simply by eating locally grown, whole foods macrobiotically chosen and prepared.

(7) Enjoying your food

The law of nature is change. Macrobiotic living, eating and cooking must flow with the stream of time. Our body and each of its cells change from season to season, day to day and even moment to moment. Our nutritional requirements change with them. Vary your diet from meal to meal according to your needs. Don't be rigid in your cooking or eating; enjoy life and be creative. I invite you to begin with the recipes in this book but caution you that they are meant only as gentle prods to your own creative self-expression. After trying them once or twice, adjust them to fit your personal taste and the requirements of your family. Be free to be yourself in harmony with nature's justice.

PRACTICAL HINTS

(1) Outfitting your Kitchen

A well outfitted kitchen invites success. After carefully choosing your ingredients, have the tools on hand to prepare them properly for cooking: a fine mesh strainer for washing grains, beans or seeds; a natural bristle brush (*tawashi*) for scrubbing vegetables; a 1-inch-thick (at least) unvarnished cutting board, and a heavy all-purpose Japanese knife (*hocho*) for cutting vegetables neatly, quickly and easily; a *suribachi*, or serrated earthenware mortar, for grinding seeds and making purées; and a stainless-steel or porcelain grater with a fine section for grating *daikon* or gingerroot.

Cookware made of *yang* materials (earthenware, cast iron, stainless steel, baked enamel) gives the best results. A stainless-steel or porcelain-enamel pressure cooker is indispensable in a macrobiotic kitchen. One or two cast-iron skillets and heavy saucepans are best for sautéing and dry-roasting. A large soup pot or Dutch oven with a tight-fitting lid serves well for soups and noodles, or for steaming vegetables. Asbestos pads slipped between a pot and flame prevent scorching and keep food from sticking and burning. A wok or Chinese cooking pot is good for deep-frying and fast cooking, while an oil strainer aids in removing pieces of vegetable or fish *tempura* from the cooking oil. A bamboo or metal colander is handy for draining noodles or lightly boiled greens. Casserole dishes, bread pans, a cookie sheet and pastry brush will be essential for baking.

Wooden implements are best for stirring foods while they cook because they don't scratch or otherwise harm the surface of pots and pans. They can also be used for serving. Have several pairs of long chopsticks, a bamboo rice paddle, and wooden spoons of varying sizes near at hand.

(2) Stocking Up on the Basics

Keep well stocked with the basic ingredients; it's so unpleasant to find yourself out of supply when unexpected guests arrive:

Brown Rice and Other Grains. Short-grain brown rice is best, because it is more *yang* than the long-grain variety. Have other grains (buckwheat, millet, rolled oats, etc.) on hand as well to add to the array of your meals.

Flour. You will need flour for breads, crêpes and sauces. Whole-wheat flour is indispensable, while a few pounds of corn, rice and buckwheat will add color, flavor and aroma to your baked goods.

Noodles. Several packages of whole-wheat and buckwheat noodles (made without eggs) in your cupboard will make for quick and easy meals to please the hungriest of unexpected visitors.

Beans. Legumes are high in proteins that complement those present in grains. Tiny, red *adzuki* are the most *yang*, and have a unique, delicious flavor. Keep well stocked with your favorites.

Seaweeds. Sea vegetables are dried before packaging and therefore store easily. Black, stringy *hijiki* is said by many Westerners to be the most enjoyable to those first getting accustomed to seaweeds. Purple *nori* comes in sheets that need only be lightly toasted. *Wakame* is delicious in soups and salads, while *kombu* is essential for soup stock.

Dried Fruits, Nuts and Seeds (whole or in butters). These delicacies are handy for desserts or snacks. Make sure that the fruits are sun-dried, free of sulfur dioxide.

Bancha Tea. This is a green Japanese tea. Undyed, it is the most important and widely used beverage in macrobiotics.

Kuzu. *Kuzu* is a white thickening agent used in sauces, soups and desserts. Arrowroot starch may be substituted, but it is more *yin*.

Kanten. *Kanten*, or agar, is a sea gelatin used as a thickener in desserts.

Chirimen. These are tiny dried fish used as a flavoring agent in soup stocks. They may also be ground up in a *suribachi* and eaten as a condiment with rice and vegetables.

Condiments and Seasonings

Sea Salt. Use unrefined, white sea salt, best because it contains all the trace minerals left after sea water has evaporated. Store in an airtight container.

Miso. *Miso* paste is a mixture of cooked soybeans, grain and salt, fermented by an enzyme for four days and then aged for at least $1\frac{1}{2}$ years (except *Kome-miso* which is aged less). *Hatcho-miso* is the strongest: it is dark brown and very salty, and is best used during winter. *Mugi-miso*, made with barley, is lighter than *Hatcho* and is ideal for year-round use. *Kome-miso* is made with rice and much less salt. It is ideal for summer use and good for children and older adults.

Shoyu. This is traditionally made soy sauce, made with natural ingredients (soybeans, fermented, parched wheat, salt and water). *Shoyu* is aged naturally for at least eighteen months. Salty and strong tasting, it is used as a seasoning agent and table condiment.

Umeboshi. These are small plums pickled in salt brine for two years or more. The plums themselves and their juice (p. 207) are used as seasoning agents in place of salt.

Oil. Use unrefined, natural sesame, corn germ, soya or sunflower oil. Deep bodied and aromatic, these cold-pressed high-quality oils give the best results in cooking and baking.

Gomashio. *Gomashio* (p. 154) is a mixture of toasted sesame seeds and salt, ground together in a *suribachi*. It's perfect with rice or other grains, and goes well with almost anything.

Spices and Herbs. Because spices are rather *yin*, they are used only sparingly in the macrobiotic diet. Naturally, they are not completely excluded, and a touch of cinnamon or saffron can give a wonderful accent to a meal. Herbs such as basil and thyme can also find a place in a macrobiotic preparation.

(3) Economizing

Macrobiotic meals should, in principle, cost as little as possible. Learn to prepare just enough so that there are no leftovers or waste. Shop wisely and buy the nonperishables you intend to store when they are in season and inexpensive. Never allow a flame to burn idly, and be efficient with your time.

(4) Preparing Ahead Wisely

Before starting to cook have a fully formed menu and a step-by-step plan of preparation in mind. Place the ingredients in order of use and keep your cooking utensils in easy accessibility. Do not light your fire until your ingredients are ready, and don't allow water to boil unnecessarily.

See to it that pots and pans are cleaned thoroughly after each use, dried well, and made as bright as new. Taking good care of sturdy tools increases their life-span. Besides, you can't be a successful cook if you use a scorched pot or one with remnants of burned food stuck to its sides.

Keep your kitchen neat and clean. Storage areas should express your personal sense of order. Be able to reach into a cupboard and find a pot or pan, knife or condiment in its fixed place. Keep your vegetable knife clean and sharp if you want to do your best work. When a knife is dull, its chopping block soon wears out. A good cook creates an environment of gentle orderliness and care in which to work.

HEALTHFUL LIVING

My husband devised seven measures to evaluate a man's or woman's health and the progress made in mastering macrobiotics. If you practice our regimen correctly, they should describe you.

(1) *No Fatigue*–Having worked through the night you can leap to work again the next morning.

(2) *Good Appetite*–You can thoroughly enjoy the simplest food and take deep pleasure in but a drop of water.

(3) *Good Sleep*–Your sleep is deep and you enter it within minutes after putting your head on the pillow. You neither thrash about nor dream, and you can awake spontaneously at a predetermined hour without the help of an alarm clock. You awake fully refreshed after four or five hours sleep.

(4) *Good Humor*–From morning until night living is a joy for which you feel deep gratitude. You fear nothing and are grateful for everything. Out of misfortune you create joyful promise and opportunity.

(5) *Good Memory*–You never forget and, as you age, your ability to remember the names of an ever-increasing number of friends improves.

(6) *Good Judgment and Smart Action*–You make all decisions confidently and quickly. Your movements are swift and graceful.

(7) *A Striving for Justice*–You keep your promises and are always faithful. You neither lie nor deceive, and you value deeds above words. You live an unselfish life in pursuit of beauty, truth and justice. Living this way you are happy.

The first three measures are physiological; the second three are psychological. If you realize only these, however, you have yet to really succeed in mastering the macrobiotic way of life. But if you are truthful to yourself, admitting your shortcomings, there is a good possibility that you will eventually succeed at them all. For true mastery of macrobiotics is not limited to physical and psychological characteristics. True health is gauged by the seventh, unlimited measure. It is a spiritual state reflected in an unselfish attitude toward our fellowman and in the quality and direction of our life. Achieving this state depends upon the quality of mind which, in turn, depends upon the condition of body. The food we eat creates and sustains both. While we emphasize its importance, always remember that our goal is wisdom, humanity, harmony and joy. If you devotedly pursue the law of nature, cultivate gratitude for both hardship and ease, and desire to realize your finest potentialities as a human being, you can succeed in macrobiotics. It is never too late.

HOW TO BEGIN

The change in nutritional emphasis from natural, vegetable foods to processed, animal foods has occurred gradually over the past two or three hundred years. Similarly, a return to more traditional patterns of eating centered around cereals and vegetables should also be gradual. A digestive system that is accustomed to the usual Western diet is often incapable of immediately deriving full nutritional benefit from grains and vegetables. Thus, make the change to the macrobiotic regimen slowly.

Begin by eliminating meat and substituting fish or fowl, reducing your intake as your needs and tastes change. Attempt to eliminate industrialized foods and drugs, refined sugar, coffee and artificially dyed teas from the outset. In their place enjoy fresh vegetables, grain coffees, and natural herb or grain teas. If you crave a sweetening agent, use honey. Remember, though, that honey is an animal product, a concentrated sugar produced in the bee's body, and discontinue its regular use once you find yourself no longer craving it.

Excessively *yang* people (red-faced, husky, agressive) are best advised to adjust their daily menu toward the *yin*, reducing the amount of animal food in proportion to vegetables and fruit. Very *yin* people (pale, frail, inactive and passive) can become more *yang* by initially including a relatively greater amount of animal foods and a lessened quantity of fruits in their diet. Create a new mental and physical balance for yourself by regulating your intake of a broad array of natural foods selected and prepared properly according to the law of *yin* and *yang*. You will be well on your way to regaining health, vitality, and an ecstatic sense of harmony.

Drink enough to satisfy your thirst. The best measure of the propriety of daily fluid intake is the frequency of urination. Our standard is males three times and females four times per day. If you find yourself drinking too much reduce the amount of salt in your cooking and reflect upon any other *yang* ingredients you may be using to excess.

If you remember to chew each biteful of food from fifty to one hundred times and don't overeat, you need not count calories in your menu. Macrobiotic foods, when properly prepared and enjoyed, will keep you at your body's natural weight.

Keep active. Daily physical exercise is indispensable for regaining bodily strength and stamina. Daily mental exercise is necessary for sharpening our judgment and achieving fuller spiritual awareness. The macrobiotic diet is an opportunity for you to achieve a deepened sensitivity to yourself and an enlivened awareness of your environment. For most people it is an invaluable and indispensable first step along the path to health, happiness and self-realization. But it does not happen by itself; make a conscientious effort to harmonize your thoughts, feelings and actions with the natural flow of life's energy. Laziness, physical or mental, is taboo. Use your reinvigorated energy to greatest advantage.

Finally, as you begin the diet, and later as you become more and more attuned to it, remember that all extremes change into their opposites and that flexibility is the key to success. Let us eat to regain and preserve our health, our happiness and, above all, our freedom to enjoy truly and deeply even the simplest pleasures afforded us by nature.

WHERE THE ESSENTIALS COME FROM

A well-balanced diet of grains, beans, fresh vegetables, seeds and fruits provides us with all the nutritional essentials we need. Here are the best* sources of vitamins, minerals, proteins, oils and starches found in our principle foods:

VITAMINS
Vitamin A: Green leafy vegetables, dandelion greens, carrots, parsley, kale, lettuce, watercress, spinach
Vitamin B_1:   Almonds, kelp, soybeans, brown rice, beans, lentils
Vitamin B_2:   Sunflower seeds, rice bran, soybeans, peanuts, pinto beans, millet, wheat, rye, sesame seeds
Vitamin C: Parsley, watercress, cabbage, beets, carrot tops
Vitamin D: Dried fish, some vegetables (Sunlight is the best source of this vitamin)
Vitamin E: Rice and all whole cereals, nuts, beans, green leafy vegetables
Vitamin F: Vegetable oils, olive and sesame oils
Vitamin K: Green leafy vegetables(cabbage, parsley, spinach), brown rice(also produced by the intestinal flora).

MINERALS
Calcium: Sesame seeds, seaweed, green vegetables (watercress, dandelion), nuts, sunflower seeds
Magnesium: Seaweed, soybeans, lentils, green leafy vegetables
Phosphorus: Cereals, seaweeds, nuts, beans
Potassium: Seaweed, soybeans, dried fruits, nuts, vegetables
Iron: Seaweeds, sesame seeds, green vegetables, beans, brown rice
Iodine: Seaweed, green vegetables
Sodium: Seaweeds, green leafy vegetables, dried fruits

PROTEINS
Cereals, beans, nuts and assorted vegetables contain all the essential amino acids we need. *Miso* and *shoyu*, pure soybean products, are particularly rich in these essential nutrients.

FATS AND OILS
In the macrobiotic diet our principle oils and fats are the unsaturated type. We derive most of our fats from the unrefined vegetable oils we use in cooking and baking. Among the cereal grains, oats have the highest amount of fat, while small amounts are found in almost all vegetables.

STARCHES (CARBOHYDRATES)
Natural sugars are found in abundance in cereals and vegetables, fruits and nuts.

*by weight of edible food portion

SUGGESTED MENUS

Fall & Winter

I.

BREAKFAST
Golden Porridge
Lightly Sautéed Leafy Vegetables
Whole-wheat Bread
Bancha Tea

LUNCH
Mori Soba with Vegetables
Steamed Broccoli
Beverage

DINNER
Chawanmushi
Brown Rice with Mushrooms
Black Bean *Ni*
Acorn Squash à la Mode
Pressed Salad
Beverage

II.

BREAKFAST
Buckwheat Cream with Sautéed Onions
Puri
Rice Tea

LUNCH
Quick *Ozoni*
Koya-Dofu Sandwiches
Beverage

DINNER
Oden
Inarizushi
Daikon Leaf *Nitsuke*
Bancha Tea

III.

BREAKFAST
Brown Rice Porridge with *Gomashio*
Steamed Vegetables
Ohsawa Loaf
Grain Coffee

LUNCH
Vegetable Soup
Panfried *Musubi*
Takuwan
Beverage

DINNER
Soba Gaki in Clear Broth
Bulgur with Vegetables
Salmon Croquettes
Boiled Salad
Winter Gelatin
Bancha Tea

IV.

BREAKFAST
Wakame Miso Soup with *Tofu*
Oatmeal
Cabbage Sesame-*Ae*
Barley Tea

LUNCH
Fried *Soba* with Vegetables
Furofuki Daikon
Bancha Tea

DINNER
Gyoza in Clear Broth
Chao Fan
Renkon Yuzu-su
Fresh Salad
Beverage

V.

BREAKFAST
Whole-wheat Cream
Onion *Nitsuke* with *Miso*
Chapati
Bancha Tea

LUNCH
Leavened Bread
Fresh-ground Peanut Butter
Pressed Salad
Beverage

DINNER
Sake-no-Kasu Jiru
Kasha Croquettes
Tofu with *Kuzu* Sauce
Sautéed Vegetables
Beverage

INTRODUCTION

VI.

BREAKFAST
Buckwheat Pancakes
Apple Butter
Grain Coffee

LUNCH
Fried Rice
Steamed Leafy Vegetables
Beverage

DINNER
Soldier Bean Potage
Brown Rice Pie
Burdock, Carrot and Lotus Root *Kimpira*
Wakame and Cucumber Salad
Beverage

VII.

BREAKFAST
Oneri
Sautéed Vegetables with
   Mock Béchamel Sauce
Spiral *Karinto*
Rice Tea

LUNCH
Daikon Udon
Chinese Cabbage Pickles
Beverage

DINNER
Zucchini *Miso* Soup
Millet Burgers with *Kuzu* Sauce
Steamed Cauliflower and Broccoli
Fresh Salad with Mayonnaise Dressing
Beverage

Spring & Summer

I.

BREAKFAST
Grain Flakes with Onions and *Gomashio*
Steamed Broccoli
Chapati
Barley Tea

LUNCH
Curry *Udon* with Vegetables
Pressed Salad
Beverage

DINNER
Mugi Miso Soup
Brown Rice with *Adzuki* Beans
Daikon Nitsuke
Mustard *Ohitashi*
Chinese Cabbage Pickles
Beverage

II.

BREAKFAST
Rice Cream (Unroasted)
Sautéed Zucchini
Ohsawa Loaf with *Tahini*
Grain Coffee

LUNCH
Musubi with *Umeboshi*
Ninjin Shiro-Ae
Takuwan and Cucumber Pickles
Beverage

DINNER
Happosai
Bulgur
Baked Fish with Mock Béchamel Sauce
Steamed Acorn Squash
Fresh Salad
Chestnut-Apple Pie
Bancha Tea

III.

BREAKFAST
Cornmeal Mold
Endive with Sesame *Nitsuke*
Wakame Miso Soup with *Tofu*
Rice Tea

LUNCH
Chick-Pea Salad
Ohsawa Loaf with *Tahini*
Beverage

DINNER
Bouillabaisse of Vegetables
Brown Rice with Chestnuts
Chinese Cabbage Rolls
Carrot with Green Beans and *Tofu*
Beverage

IV.

BREAKFAST
Buckwheat Crêpes with *Adzuki*-Chestnut
  Jam
Dandelion Coffee

LUNCH
Norimaki
Scallion and *Aburage Nitsuke*
Beverage

DINNER
Soybean Potage
Corn on the Cob
Fresh Salad
Ohsawa Loaf with Sesame Butter
Beverage

V.

BREAKFAST
Ohsawa Loaf with Pumpkin-Peanut
  Spread
Coltsfoot *Nitsuke*
Grain Coffee

LUNCH
Okonomi Yaki
Boiled Salad
Beverage

DINNER
Clear Broth with Rice Dumplings
Brown Rice
Harumaki
Scallion Sesame-*Ae*
Chrysanthemum Onions
Beverage

VI.

BREAKFAST
Brown Rice Porridge with Corn
Cabbage and Carrot *Nitsuke*
Wholewheat Toast
Bancha Tea

LUNCH
Summer *Soba*
Steamed Leafy Vegetables
Beverage

DINNER
Mugi Miso Soup with Vegetables
Brown Rice with Pinto Beans
Turnip Gratin
Pressed Salad
Beverage

VII.

BREAKFAST
Barley Porridge
Cucumber with *Miso* and Sesame
Karinto
Bancha Tea

LUNCH
Cold Borscht
Ohsawa Loaf
Fresh Salad
Beverage

DINNER
Couscous with Vegetables
Hijiki with Sesame
Dandelion *Nitsuke*
Beverage

A TABLE OF DAILY FOODS

▽▽▽ = Very Yin
▽▽ = More Yin
▽ = Yin
Very Yang = △△△
More Yang = △△
Yang = △

CEREALS
corn ▽
rye
barley
oats
wheat
rice △
millet
buckwheat △△

VEGETABLES
eggplant ▽▽▽
tomato
sweet potato
potato
Japanese mushroom
  (*shiitake*)
beans (except *adzuki*)
cucumber
spinach
asparagus
artichoke
bamboo sprouts
mushroom
snow peas ▽▽

celery
cauliflower
broccoli
purple cabbage
beet
green cabbage
dandelion leaves △
lettuce
endive
kale
turnip
radish
coltsfoot
onion
garlic
parsley
pumpkin △△
carrot
burdock
watercress
dandelion root
jinenjo △△△

FISH
oyster ▽
clam
octopus
carp
mussels
halibut
lobster

trout
sole
salmon △
shrimp
herring
sardine
red snapper
caviar △△

ANIMAL FOODS
snail ▽▽
frog
pork
beef
horsemeat
hare
chicken ▽
pigeon △
duck
turkey
eggs △△
pheasant △△△

DAIRY PRODUCTS
yogurt ▽▽▽
sour cream
sweet cream
cream cheese
butter
cow's milk ▽▽
Camembert

Gruyère
Roquefort △
Edam
goat's milk △△

FRUITS
pineapple ▽▽▽
mango
grapefruit
banana
fig
orange
pear
peach ▽▽
lime
melon
almond
peanut
cashew
hazelnut
olive ▽
cherry
strawberry △
chestnut
apple △△

BEVERAGES
synthetically dyed
  tea ▽▽▽
coffee
artificially sweetened
  drinks

fruit juice
champagne
wine
beer ▽▽
mineral water
carbonated water
water
thyme tea
mugwort △
bancha
chicory
grain coffee
dandelion coffee
burdock tea
Mu tea △△
ginseng △△△

MISCELLANEOUS
sugar ▽▽▽
honey
molasses
margarine
coconut oil ▽▽
peanut oil
olive oil
soya oil
sunflower oil ▽
corn oil
sesame oil
safflower oil

I. WHOLE GRAINS AND FLOURS

GRAINS: THE PRIMARY FOOD

A palate sensitive to the body's needs is one of nature's greatest gifts. If taste buds find denatured, artificial foods desirable and delicious, they are working at cross-purposes with the real interests of the being they are meant to serve. When taste is in healthful harmony with the body's true needs, the foods nature intended for us are always the most delicious. A healthy palate is within everyone's reach but must be cultivated and nurtured. Take the first step by gradually changing your nutritional habits and this precious sense will be reawakened to the infinite subtleties of nature and become a trustworthy compass guiding you through the world of food.

Yin or *yang,* simmered or pressure cooked, the grains you prepare should always turn out delicious and be just right for the day's needs. The better you come to know yourself and the people for whom you cook, and the more you refine your judgment of foods and methods of preparation, the more your cooking style will fit a unique, pleasing pattern. The day's cereals should fit this pattern while accommodating the season, the day's weather and your activities. As you deepen your self-awareness and become more sensitively attuned to the environment, all these factors join into an unspoken Oneness. When they are expressed spontaneously in the foods you prepare you will have taken a giant step toward becoming a master cook and will no longer need to refer to this book.

The first skill to develop is in the tasteful preparation of brown rice. Of course, anyone can cook a pot of rice, but not everyone can cook it well. If your rice was too chewy yesterday and too soft today, take a hard lesson in the lack of consistency and simple mastery in your life, but don't lose heart. For steady results carefully measure your water and regulate your heat. Of equal importance is your attitude: enter your kitchen with a calm mind, cleared of distractions, and concentrate as you would for any other act of meditation. Develop a sense of dedication to the art, for from that dedication not only you and your family but all of mankind will benefit. Make your kitchen, the center of your home, radiate creativity and joy.

BROWN RICE

Learn to use a pressure cooker in preparing rice. Pressure cooking is fast and conserves on whatever fuel you use. It also allows for greater control of the consistency of the cooked grain. Less water is required than in simmering, and mistakes are less likely to be made. Perhaps most important, cooking under pressure brings out the full, delicious flavor of the grain.

In the recipes that follow you will be instructed to use high heat to bring pressure rapidly up to full. Pressure cookers are fitted with a regulator of appropriate weight, yielding 5, 10 or 15 pounds pressure. When the regulator jiggles, full pressure has been reached. Slip an asbestos pad under the pot, reduce heat to low, and simmer until done, always making sure that pressure is maintained throughout the cooking time. When pressure has returned to normal, uncover and gently stir the rice. The kernels that cooked close to the heat are more *yang* than those that cooked farther away. Mix the two together, then let the rice stand undisturbed for several minutes to achieve a quiet, peaceful balance.

Climate is a factor that influences the way a pressure cooker is used. In Japan the climate is moist and humid, and the rice grows in wet paddies. Compared to the dry rice grown in the drier climates of America and Europe, the Japanese variety is *yin* and requires less water in its preparation. In addition, the pressure cooker is allowed to stand for less than a minute after being removed from the heat. The pressure regulator is then quickly removed to allow the steam to escape so it does not settle back into the grain. In America and Europe, the pressure may be allowed to return slowly to normal, permitting the cooling steam to add moisture to the grain. Try both techniques and judge their appropriateness for yourself.

The more water you add per cup of rice (or any other grain), the softer the rice (or grain) will be. The less water you add, the harder and chewier it will be. After many years of experience I have found that a proportion of $1\frac{1}{3}$ parts water for each part rice (cooked under pressure) serves as a useful standard. Remember, though, that in reality a mathematical formula gives us only a rough approximation. Freshly harvested rice, for example, will always contain more moisture than rice that has been stored for a time, and for that reason requires less water in its preparation. Remember, too, that when cooking only 1 or 2 cups of rice, your cooking water will come quickly to a boil and evaporate before the grain may have a chance to absorb enough moisture. Lest the rice turn out too hard when cooking small quantities, it is advisable to use a little more water ($1\frac{1}{2}$ cups per cup of rice). When the rice you are cooking more than half fills your pot, the greater quantity of water you add will come to a boil slowly and the rice kernels may absorb more than you had intended, turning out too soft. When cooking large quantitites of rice, therefore, gradually lessen the amount of water used per cup until a minimum of equal parts rice and water is reached. A good working knowledge of the rate at which your pressure cooker absorbs and retains heat is very helpful. You can gain that knowledge from patient, careful observation.

Add salt to rice (and all grains) lightly to bring out the grain's full flavor. Each person can garnish a serving with *gomashio* if he or she wants a saltier taste. But once it's served, we cannot make a dish less salty, so season with a light hand.

Children and elderly adults are best served a soft, moist and lightly salted rice. Young and middle-aged adults usually enjoy a chewier, saltier variety. If you are cooking for a family you need not prepare separate pots for each of its members. Experiment to find the ideal mean.

Always wash rice (and other grains, as well as seeds and beans) before using. Place the rice in a fine-mesh strainer and, stirring lightly, rinse in a stream of cold water until the water drains clear. Or place the rice directly into the pot and cover it with water. Swirl lightly with your hand, removing hulls or other particles that may rise to the surface, and drain through a strainer. Three or four such rinsings should be enough. When cooking one grain in combination with another, or together with seeds or beans, always wash each ingredient separately before combining in the pot.

Some recipes will call for dry-roasting or sautéing a grain or flour to make it sweeter and more *yang*. When dry-roasting you may start with a cold skillet or saucepan. When you sauté, preheat your pot or pan until a drop of water sprinkled upon its surface will dance before evaporating; then coat the pot evenly with oil. By the time the oil is spread evenly over the surface of the pan and you have reached for your ingredients, the oil should be hot enough to cook with. If the oil smokes, both oil and pan are too hot.

After cooking rice, the bottom of your pressure cooker will be slightly scorched. The yellowish rice that forms a layer directly above it is the most *yang* and rich in minerals that settled during cooking. The scorching will wash out easily if you pour cold water into the pot immediately after serving.

You may find that you prefer the taste and texture of simmered rather than pressure-cooked rice. It is not necessary that grains always be cooked under pressure and you will find recipes for simmering or baking the grain in the pages that follow. Trust in your developing sense of taste, and don't limit yourself to any one way of cooking. Each has its appropriate time and place, climate and season. Enjoy the adventure of discovery in this subtle and delicate art by experimenting broadly and accepting both successes and failures, for this is the only way we learn.

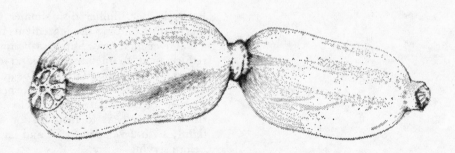

WHOLE GRAINS

Brown Rice *(Pressure Cooked)*   SERVES 4

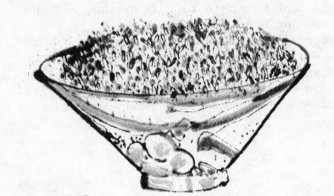

2 cups brown rice, washed
3 cups water
¼ teaspoon sea salt, or 1 *umeboshi*, or
   1 tablespoon *shoyu*

Combine the ingredients in a pressure cooker, cover, and over high heat bring rapidly to full pressure. Slip an asbestos pad under the pot, reduce heat to low, and simmer for 40 minutes. Remove from heat and allow pressure to return to normal. Uncover and mix gently with a wooden spatula or rice paddle lightly moistened in cold water to prevent sticking. Re-cover and let stand for 5 minutes before serving.

Brown Rice *(Simmered)*   SERVES 4

2 cups brown rice, washed
4 cups water
¼ teaspoon sea salt

For a lighter, fluffier dish simmer the rice in a heavy saucepan. Combine the ingredients and bring rapidly to a boil over high heat. Slip an asbestos pad under the pan, reduce heat to medium-low, and cover with a tight-fitting lid. Cook for 20 minutes, or until most of the water has been absorbed, then reduce heat to very low and simmer for 30 minutes more. Before removing pan from stove, return heat to medium for a count of 10. Toss lightly with 2 wooden forks, and let stand for 5 minutes before serving.

For a drier variety, place a thin cloth that will absorb moisture over the mouth of the pan, with the ends of the cloth extending slightly over the sides, before fitting on the lid.

If using the saucepan as a substitute for a pressure cooker, place a 1-pound weight on the lid of the saucepan.

Brown Rice *(Baked)* SERVES 4

> 2 cups brown rice, washed
> 3 cups cold or boiling water
> ¼ teaspoon sea salt, or 1 tablespoon *shoyu*

Preheat your oven to 350°F. Place the rice in a heavy skillet and roast over medium heat, stirring constantly, until the rice is dry and deep brown. Transfer to a casserole dish; add water and salt. Cover and bake for 50 minutes. Mix gently and let stand for 5 minutes before serving.

Roasted Rice SERVES 5 OR 6

> 3 cups brown rice, washed
> 3 cups water
> ½ teaspoon sea salt

Roast the rice in a pressure cooker until it turns a rich brown, stirring constantly to prevent scorching. Add water and salt, and bring rapidly to full pressure over high heat. Slip an asbestos pad under the pot, reduce heat to low, and simmer for 40 minutes. Remove from stove, allow pressure to return to normal, and uncover. Mix gently, re-cover, and let stand for 5 minutes before serving.

To make this dish even more *yang,* roast the rice in 1 tablespoon corn or sesame oil before combining with the remaining ingredients.

Brown Rice Cream SERVES 5

> 1 cup brown rice, washed
> 10 cups water
> ½ teaspoon sea salt

Dry-roast the rice in a heavy saucepan until rich brown, stirring constantly to assure even heating. Add water and salt, and bring rapidly to a boil over high heat. Slip an asbestos pad under the pan, turn heat to medium-low, and cover with a tight-fitting lid. Simmer for 2 to 3 hours. Remove from heat and allow to cool. Spoon the lukewarm rice onto the center of a 2-foot-square of unbleached muslin, then draw up the cloth by the corners and join them to form a sack. Holding it over a saucepan, squeeze to express the broth. When the sack's contents have been squeezed dry, open and remove the grains, setting them aside for later use in fried *musubi* (p. 50).

To prepare under pressure, combine 1 cup rice, ½ teaspoon salt and 5 cups water. Bring rapidly to full pressure, and simmer over an asbestos pad for 45 minutes to 1 hour. Remove regulator to release pressure rapidly. Uncover, and stir in 5 more cups water. Still uncovered, bring just to a boil. Remove from stove and allow to cool, then spoon the lukewarm rice onto the center of the unbleached muslin. Drawing the corners together to form a sack and holding it over a saucepan, squeeze to express the broth.

To make a soup of the broth, stir in 4 to 5 cups water and bring just to a boil. Season with salt to taste, and serve topped with croutons and garnished with a sprig of parsley.

To make a thin cream or tea, add 10 cups water and bring to a boil.

This dish can be made more *yang* by preroasting the rice in 1 tablespoon oil and using only a pinch of salt. It can be made more *yin* by refraining from roasting the rice at all.

VARIATION: A prepackaged rice cream powder is available at natural-food stores and macrobiotic outlets. Combine 1 cup of the powder with 4 cups water, stirring constantly to prevent lumping, and add ¼ teaspoon salt; or sauté the powder in ½ teaspoon oil, allow it to cool, and then gradually stir in cold water. Stir and bring to a boil over high heat, then reduce heat to low and cover with a tight-fitting lid. Simmer over an asbestos pad for 30 to 40 minutes, or pressure-cook for 20 minutes. Serves 4.

Musubi *(Brown Rice Patties)*

5 cups brown rice, washed
7 cups water
1 teaspoon and a dash of sea salt
2 tablespoons soya flour
2 sheets of *nori*
Parsley sprigs

Combine rice, water and 1 teaspoon salt in a pressure cooker and bring to full pressure over high heat. Slip an asbestos pad under the pot, reduce heat to low, and simmer for 40 minutes. Remove from heat and quickly remove pressure regulator to allow steam to escape. Mix gently with a moistened rice paddle, re-cover, and let stand undisturbed until rice has cooled to room temperature.

Moisten your hands in cold water (to prevent sticking) and shape 7 cups of the cooked rice into 14 triangular wedges, approximately $\frac{1}{4}$-inch thick. Form remaining 3 cups rice into 6 or 7 square or round patties.

Set seven of the wedges aside. Add a dash of salt to the soya flour and roll the other 7 wedges in the flour, coating thoroughly.

Toast the *nori* lightly by waving it over low heat for several seconds until just crisp. Cut each sheet of *nori* into 4 strips, and wrap 1 strip around the center of each square or round *musubi*. (Remember to keep your hands lightly moistened at all times.) Now arrange all the *musubi* attractively on a large platter, decorate with sprigs of parsley, and serve. Wonderful for parties, picnics or box lunches.

VARIATIONS: A. Form each cup of cooked rice into 2 balls, place an *umeboshi* in the center of each ball, and wrap in lightly toasted *nori*.

B. Cooking uncovered over medium heat, brown the triangular *musubi* in a heavy skillet coated lightly with corn or sesame oil.

Brown Rice with Sesame Seeds   SERVES 5 OR 6

$\frac{1}{4}$ cup white sesame seeds
3 cups brown rice, washed
$3\frac{2}{3}$ cups water
$\frac{1}{4}$ teaspoon sea salt

Wash the sesame seeds in a strainer. Drain, then dab the strainer with a dry sponge to draw off any excess water. Put the seeds in a heavy skillet and roast over medium-high heat, stirring the seeds constantly and shaking the pan to warm them evenly. When the seeds turn light brown and release their fragrance, remove from heat and combine in a pressure cooker with rice, water and salt. Bring to full pressure over high heat, then slip an asbestos pad under the pot and simmer for 40 minutes. Remove from heat, allow pressure to return to normal, and uncover. Stir gently with a lightly moistened rice paddle, re-cover, and let stand for 5 minutes before serving.

VARIATION: Prepare pressure-cooked rice. Begin toasting the sesame seeds about 10 minutes before removing pressure cooker lid. Remove seeds from heat when they are light brown and with a heavy knife chop them very fine. Now uncover the rice and stir gently. Using a pair of long wooden chopsticks, mix in the seeds. Re-cover and let stand for 5 minutes. Served hot, this dish gives off a wonderful aroma. Adjust the proportion of seeds and rice to taste.

Brown Rice with Chestnuts   SERVES 6

3 cups brown rice, washed
$\frac{1}{2}$ cup chestnut meats
$4\frac{1}{2}$ cups water
$\frac{1}{2}$ teaspoon sea salt

Use either fresh or dried chestnut meats. Combine all ingredients in a pressure cooker and bring rapidly to full pressure over high heat. Slip an asbestos pad under the pot, reduce heat to low, and simmer for 40 minutes. Remove from heat and allow pressure to return to normal. Uncover and mix gently with a lightly moistened rice paddle or wooden spatula. Re-cover and let stand for 5 minutes before serving.

Brown Rice with Barley   SERVES 4

$1\frac{1}{2}$ cups brown rice, washed
$\frac{1}{2}$ cup barley, washed
$2\frac{2}{3}$ cups water
$\frac{1}{4}$ teaspoon sea salt

Combine the ingredients in a pressure cooker and bring rapidly to full pressure over high heat. Slip an asbestos pad under the pot, reduce heat to low, and simmer for 40 minutes. Remove from heat and allow pressure to return to normal. Uncover and mix gently with a lightly moistened rice paddle or wooden spatula. Re-cover and let stand for 5 minutes before serving.

VARIATION: One-half cup fresh corn kernels may be substituted for the barley. The proportions of water and salt used above remain the same.

Brown Rice with Millet   SERVES 6

3 cups brown rice, washed
1 cup millet, washed
5 cups water
1 teaspoon sea salt

Combine all ingredients in a pressure cooker and bring to full pressure over high heat. Slip an asbestos pad under the pot, reduce heat to low, and simmer for 40 minutes. Remove from heat and allow pressure to return to normal. Uncover and mix gently with a lightly moistened rice paddle. Re-cover and let stand for 5 minutes before serving.

Brown Rice with Whole Kernels of Wheat
SERVES 4

1½ cups brown rice, washed
½ cup whole kernels of wheat, washed
 and soaked overnight
5 cups water
¼ teaspoon sea salt

Combine the ingredients in a pressure cooker and bring to full pressure over high heat. Slip an asbestos pad under the pot, reduce heat to low, and simmer for 1 to 1½ hours. Remove from heat and allow pressure to return to normal; or remove pressure regulator and allow steam to escape. Mix gently with a moistened rice paddle, cover, and let stand for 5 minutes before serving.

VARIATION: Substitute ½ cup whole oats (soaked overnight) for the wheat berries and proceed as above.

Brown Rice with Adzuki Beans
SERVES 10

5 cups brown rice, washed
½ cup *adzuki* beans, washed
7 cups water
¾ teaspoon sea salt

Combine the ingredients in a pressure cooker and bring rapidly to full pressure over high heat. Slip an asbestos pad under the pot, reduce heat to low, and simmer for 40 minutes. Remove from heat and allow pressure to return to normal; or, for a drier variety, remove pressure regulator and allow steam to escape. Uncover and mix gently with a lightly moistened rice paddle or wooden spatula. Re-cover and let stand for 5 minutes before serving.

To prepare in a saucepan, first simmer the beans in 1½ cups water until their skins wrinkle, about 20 minutes. Drain, then combine with the rice, adding 10 cups water and ¾ teaspoon salt. Bring rapidly to a boil over high heat, slip an asbestos pad under the pan, and reduce heat to low. Cover with a tight-fitting lid and simmer for 40 to 50 minutes. Remove from heat and toss lightly with 2 wooden forks. Let stand for 5 minutes before serving.

Brown Rice with Pinto Beans
SERVES 6

½ cup pinto beans, washed
3 cups brown rice, washed
4 cups water, approximately
1 teaspoon sea salt

Simmer the beans in 2 cups water for 30 minutes, or until slightly tender and wrinkled. Drain through a strainer placed over a bowl, reserving any cooking water. Combine the rice, beans and salt in a pressure cooker, adding whatever liquid may have been left over from boiling the beans plus enough fresh water to equal a total of 4 cups. Over high heat bring rapidly to full pressure, then slip an asbestos pad under the pot, reduce heat to low, and simmer for 40 minutes. Remove from heat and allow pressure to return to normal. Mix gently with a lightly moistened rice paddle, cover, and let stand for 5 minutes before serving.

VARIATION: Substitute ½ cup chick-peas for the pinto beans. Soak the chick-peas overnight or pressure-cook in 3 parts water for 40 minutes before combining with the rice, then proceed as above.

Brown Rice with Soybeans   SERVES 10

> 5 cups brown rice, washed
> ½ cup soybeans, washed and soaked
>   overnight
> 6½ cups water
> 1 teaspoon sea salt

Combine the ingredients in a pressure cooker and bring rapidly to full pressure over high heat. Slip an asbestos pad under the pot, reduce heat to low, and simmer for 40 minutes. Remove from heat and allow pressure to return to normal; or remove pressure regulator and permit steam to escape. Mix gently with a moistened rice paddle, cover, and let stand for 5 minutes before serving.

Brown Rice with Hokkaido Pumpkin   SERVES 6

> 3 cups brown rice, washed
> 4 ounces Hokkaido pumpkin (or acorn
>   squash), peeled and cubed
> 3½ cups water
> ½ teaspoon sea salt
> 2 teaspoons minced parsley

Combine the first four ingredients in a pressure cooker and bring rapidly to full pressure over high heat. Slip an asbestos pad under the pot, reduce heat to low, and simmer for 40 minutes. Remove from heat and allow pressure to return to normal; or remove pressure regulator and allow steam to escape. Mix gently, cover, and let stand for 5 minutes. Serve topped with mock Béchamel sauce (p. 162) and a sprinkling of minced parsley.

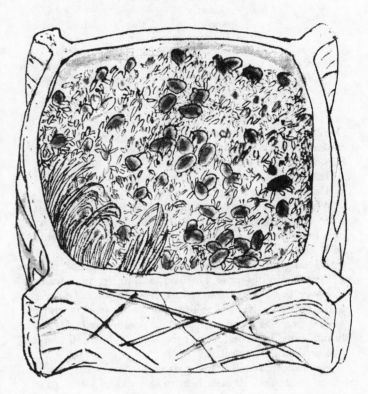

Brown Rice with Vegetables   SERVES 10

5 cups brown rice, washed
6½ cups water
1½ teaspoons and a dash of sea salt
2 tablespoons sesame oil
1 small carrot, slivered
1 cup thin gingko leaves of lotus root
½ cup equal parts water and *shoyu*
Greens from 1 carrot
1 sheet of *nori*

Combine rice, water and ½ teaspoon salt in a pressure cooker and bring rapidly to full pressure over high heat. Slip an asbestos pad under the pot, reduce heat to low, and simmer for 40 minutes. When done, remove from heat and allow pressure to return to normal.

While the rice is cooking, heat a heavy skillet and coat with 1 tablespoon sesame oil. Sauté the carrot slivers over medium heat, stirring constantly to coat them evenly with oil and prevent scorching. After 2 or 3 minutes, sprinkle lightly with a dash of salt, cover pan, and cook for 1 to 2 minutes more. Uncover, add just enough water to cover the slivers, and reduce heat to low. Re-cover and simmer for 10 to 15 minutes, or until carrot is tender and water has been absorbed or evaporated. If any liquid remains when carrot is done, remove lid and simmer until evaporated.

Heat another skillet and coat with remaining 1 tablespoon sesame oil. Reduce heat to low and add lotus root. Sauté for 1 or 2 minutes, stirring lightly, then add equal parts water and *shoyu* to cover. Cover skillet and simmer for 15 minutes, or until lotus is tender and liquid has been absorbed or evaporated.

Bring a small pan of water to a boil over high heat and add 1 teaspoon salt. Drop in the carrot greens, return to the boil, and cook for 1 or 2 minutes, or until stems are tender. Transfer greens to a basin of cold water to stop the cooking and set their color, then drain in a colander. Chop fine.

Uncover the rice and stir lightly. Using a pair of long, wooden chopsticks gently mix in the carrot slivers, lotus slices and chopped carrot greens. Re-cover and let stand for 5 minutes.

A moment before serving, toast 1 side of the *nori* by waving it over low heat for several seconds until just crisp. Crumble and serve as a garnish, sprinkled over individual portions of the vegetable-rice.

Brown Rice with Mushrooms   SERVES 4

2 cups brown rice, washed
¼ teaspoon sea salt
3¼ cups water
4 *shiitake* (dried Japanese mushroom),
    soaked in cold water for 20 minutes, or
    8 to 10 fresh mushrooms rinsed in
    lightly salted water
1 teaspoon sesame oil
½ tablespoon *shoyu*

Combine rice, salt and 3 cups water in a pressure cooker and bring rapidly to full pressure over high heat. Slip an asbestos pad under the pot, reduce heat to low, and simmer for 40 minutes. Remove from heat and allow pressure to return to normal.

After soaking the *shiitake*, remove their hard stems and slice their broad caps fine. If using fresh mushrooms, slice fine through crown and stem. After removing pressure cooker from stove, heat a heavy skillet and coat with 1 teaspoon sesame oil. Sauté the *shiitake* or mushrooms over medium heat for 3 minutes, stirring lightly. Add remaining ¼ cup water and ½ tablespoon *shoyu*, cover pan, and reduce heat to low. Simmer for 5 minutes, then uncover and simmer until all liquid has evaporated.

Uncover rice and mix gently. Using a pair of long, wooden chopsticks, mix in the sautéed *shiitake*, re-cover, and let stand for 5 minutes. Serve while still warm and fragrant.

Inarizushi

(Brown Rice and Vegetables in Aburage)

3 cups brown rice, washed
4½ cups water
1¼ teaspoons and a dash of sea salt
10 pieces of *aburage* (fried bean curd)
1 cup *shoyu*
10 green beans, rinsed and trimmed
1 tablespoon sesame oil
1 small carrot, slivered

Combine rice, water and ¼ teaspoon salt in a pressure cooker and bring to full pressure over high heat. Slip an asbestos pad under the pot, reduce heat to low, and simmer for 40 minutes. When done, remove from heat and allow pressure to return to normal.

Cut each piece of *aburage* into halves and pull open its center to make a pouch. Stand the pouches close together in the bottom of a saucepan, and add enough water to cover. For each cup of water added stir in 2 to 3 tablespoons *shoyu*. Cover with a tight-fitting lid, or insert the lid of a smaller saucepan so that it fits directly above the pouches and will keep them in place. Bring to a boil and cook until all liquid has been absorbed or evaporated and the pouches are well flavored. Drain the *aburage* in a colander and allow to cool.

Bring a small pan of water to a boil over high heat and add 1 teaspoon salt. Drop in the green beans, return to the boil, and cook for 4 or 5 minutes, or until beans are bright green and tender but still crisp. Transfer beans to a basin of cold water to stop the cooking and set their color, and drain in a colander. When cool, slice fine on the diagonal.

Heat a heavy skillet and coat with the oil. Sauté the carrot slivers over medium heat for 2 or 3 minutes, stirring constantly. Sprinkle with a dash of salt, add just enough water to cover, and bring to a boil. Cover pan, reduce heat, and simmer for 10 minutes, or until the slivers are tender. If any liquid remains when carrot is done, remove lid and simmer until evaporated.

Uncover rice and stir lightly. Using a pair of long, wooden chopsticks, mix the vegetables into the freshly cooked rice. Now use the mixture to half-fill each of the *aburage* pouches, then fold over the lip of each pouch to form a flap. Serve hot.

Brown Rice with Shrimps

2 cups brown rice, washed
3 cups water
¼ teaspoon sea salt
1 tablespoon sesame oil
1 small onion, minced
4 medium-size raw shrimps, shelled,
   deveined and chopped
1 tablespoon *shoyu*

Combine rice, water and salt in a pressure cooker and bring rapidly to full pressure over high heat. Slip an asbestos pad under the pot, reduce heat to low, and simmer for 40 minutes.

About 10 minutes before rice is done, heat a heavy skillet and coat with 1 tablespoon sesame oil. Sauté the onion over medium heat, stirring gently, for 4 or 5 minutes, or until lightly browned. Add shrimps and sauté together for 1 or 2 minutes more. Season with *shoyu* before turning off heat.

When the rice is done, turn off heat and immediately remove pressure regulator to permit steam to escape. Leaving the pot on the stove, uncover and mix lightly. Gently stir in the shrimp-and-onion mixture, then replace both lid and pressure regulator. Allow to stand undisturbed for 5 minutes to absorb the heat retained in the metal burner and asbestos pad. This gentle steaming assures that the flavor and fragrance of the shrimps spread evenly throughout the rice.

Norimaki

(Brown Rice with Vegetables Wrapped in Nori)

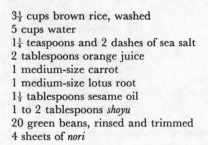

3½ cups brown rice, washed
5 cups water
1¼ teaspoons and 2 dashes of sea salt
2 tablespoons orange juice
1 medium-size carrot
1 medium-size lotus root
1⅓ tablespoons sesame oil
1 to 2 tablespoons *shoyu*
20 green beans, rinsed and trimmed
4 sheets of *nori*

Combine rice, water and ¼ teaspoon salt in a pressure cooker and bring to full pressure over high heat. Slip an asbestos pad under the pot, reduce heat to low, and simmer for 40 minutes. Remove from heat, allow pressure to return to normal, and mix gently. Transfer the hot rice to a large nonmetallic platter or wide shallow bowl. Immediately pour on the orange juice and mix thoroughly. Fan the rice to cool it quickly to room temperature.

While the rice is cooking, prepare the vegetables. Quarter the carrot and lotus root lengthwise, then cut each quarter into sticks approximately ⅓ inch thick. Heat a heavy skillet and coat with 1 teaspoon oil. Sauté the carrot sticks over medium heat for 1 or 2 minutes, stirring gently to coat them evenly with oil and prevent scorching. Add 2 tablespoons water, reduce heat to low, and cover pan. Simmer for 15 minutes, then season with a dash of salt. If any liquid remains, simmer uncovered until evaporated. Remove carrot from heat and set aside.

Heat another skillet and coat with remaining 1 tablespoon oil. Reduce heat to low and sauté lotus sticks for 2 or 3 minutes, stirring gently. Add enough water to half-cover sticks, cover pan, and simmer for 10 minutes. Now uncover, season with *shoyu*, and continue to simmer until all liquid has been absorbed or evaporated. Remove lotus from heat and set aside.

Bring a small pan of water (just enough to cover the

green beans) to a boil over high heat and add 1 teaspoon salt. Drop in the beans, return to the boil, and cook for 4 or 5 minutes, or until the beans are bright green and tender but still crisp. Transfer to a basin of cold water to stop the cooking and set the color, then drain in a colander. Sprinkle with a dash of salt.

To assemble the ingredients, wave the sheets of *nori* over low heat, on one side only, for several seconds. Place 1 sheet of *nori* on a *sudare* or bamboo mat. Divide the rice into 4 portions and spread one portion over most of the *nori* sheet, leaving a 1-inch edge at the near and far ends of the *nori* exposed. Place a double row of carrot sticks across the center of the rice and lay 5 green beans and a double row of lotus sticks on top of the carrot. Lightly moisten both the exposed edges of the *nori* sheet and the vegetables with water, then roll up the mixture in the mat, pressing the ingredients together into a firm cylinder approximately $1\frac{1}{2}$ inches in diameter. Remove the bamboo mat and repeat with the remaining ingredients until all are used.

Using a sharp knife slice each *norimaki* into 1- to $1\frac{1}{2}$-inch rounds. For neat slices wipe the knife after each cut with a clean damp cloth. Serve as part of a meal in place of plain rice, or as an accompaniment.

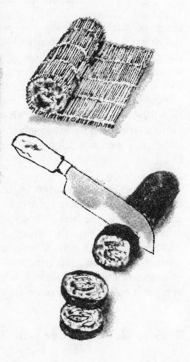

BROWN RICE

Brown Rice Porridge

SERVES 4

1 cup brown rice, washed
4 cups water
½ teaspoon sea salt

Combine the ingredients in a pressure cooker and bring to full pressure over high heat. Slip an asbestos pad under the pot, reduce heat to low, and simmer for 30 to 40 minutes. Remove from heat and allow pressure to return to normal. Lest the contents boil over do not remove lid until pot has cooled. Once uncovered it will reveal a thin layer of water resting on the surface of the rice. With a rice paddle or wooden spoon, gently stir the water back into the rice to make the porridge glisten. Serve hot.

VARIATION: Dry-roast rice in the pressure cooker until deep brown, stirring constantly. Add 2 tablespoons *adzuki* beans (washed), 4 cups water and ½ teaspoon salt, and bring rapidly to full pressure. Slip an asbestos pad under the pot, reduce heat to low, and simmer for 30 minutes. Remove from heat and allow pressure to return to normal. Uncover and stir when pot has cooled. This version is called *omedeto* or celebration.

Brown Rice Porridge with Corn

SERVES 5 OR 6

2 cups brown rice, washed
¼ cup fresh corn kernels
12 cups water
1 teaspoon sea salt

Combine all ingredients in a pressure cooker and bring to full pressure over high heat. Slip an asbestos pad under the pot, reduce heat to low, and simmer for 30 to 40 minutes. Remove from heat and allow pressure to return to normal. When pot has cooled, carefully uncover and gently stir. Reheat, if necessary, to serve.

Golden Porridge

SERVES 5 OR 6

2 cups brown rice, washed
8 ounces Hokkaido pumpkin or acorn
    squash, peeled and cubed
12 cups water
1 teaspoon sea salt

Combine all ingredients in a heavy saucepan and bring to a boil over high heat. Slip an asbestos pad under the pan, reduce heat to low, and cover with a tight-fitting lid. Simmer for 4 hours, stirring occasionally. If rice is still not tender after all water has been absorbed or evaporated, add more water and simmer longer.

To prepare this porridge more quickly, simmer under pressure for 1½ hours. Remove from heat and allow pressure to return to normal and pot to cool before carefully uncovering. Stir gently before serving. A wonderful remedy for fatigue.

Brown Rice Porridge with Vegetables and Miso

SERVES 5

2 cups brown rice, washed
10 cups water
2 tablespoons sesame oil
1 medium-size onion, cut into thin
    crescents
3 ounces *daikon*, diced
1 small carrot, diced
2 tablespoons *miso* thinned in ½ cup water

Combine rice and water in a pressure cooker and bring to full pressure over high heat. Slip an asbestos pad under the pot, reduce heat to low, and simmer for 30 to 40 minutes. Remove from heat and allow pressure to return slowly to normal and pot to cool. Begin preparation of the vegetables after removing rice from heat.

Heat a heavy skillet and coat with the oil. Sauté onion over medium heat, stirring gently, until the strong onion aroma is no longer released. Add *daikon* and sauté for 1 minute, then add carrot and mix the ingredients together. Reduce heat to low and continue to sauté for 10 to 15 minutes, stirring lightly. Add the thinned *miso*, bring vegetables and *miso* to a boil, and turn off heat.

Carefully uncover porridge and blend in the vegetables and *miso*. Re-cover, return pot to stove, and simmer for 2 or 3 minutes. Serve individual portions topped with minced watercress and crumbled toasted *nori*, or sprinkled with *gomashio*. Best served with a side dish of steamed or boiled *daikon* (p. 98) and boiled greens. This porridge will keep you warm on the coldest day of the year.

Fried Rice with Carrots and Sesame Seeds   SERVES 5

1 heaping tablespoon white sesame seeds, washed
1⅓ tablespoons corn oil
1 small carrot, slivered
¼ teaspoon sea salt, or 1 teaspoon *shoyu*
4 cups cooked brown rice
1 or 2 tablespoons minced parsley

Roast the sesame seeds in a heavy skillet over moderately high heat for several minutes, stirring the seeds constantly and shaking the pan to heat them evenly. When the seeds turn light brown and release their fragrance, remove from heat and set aside.

Reheat the skillet (if necessary) and coat with 1 teaspoon corn oil. Sauté the carrot slivers over medium heat for 2 or 3 minutes, stirring constantly to coat them evenly with oil. Season with sea salt or *shoyu*, stir in the sesame seeds, and turn off heat.

Heat another skillet and coat with remaining 1 tablespoon oil. Add the rice and sauté over medium heat for 1 or 2 minutes. Mix in the carrot and sesame seeds, cover pan, and reduce heat to low. Simmer for 20 minutes. Uncover, and simmer for 2 or 3 minutes more. Serve garnished with minced parsley.

Brown Rice with Onion Tempura   SERVES 5

5 cups cooked brown rice
1 cup minced onion
2 dashes of sea salt
Oil for deep-frying
½ cup unbleached white flour
⅓ cup water, approximately

Combine rice, onion and a dash of salt in a large bowl, mixing thoroughly. Moisten your hands lightly with water, then form each cup of the mixture into 2 egg-shaped ovals. To assure that it will cook through, flatten each oval so that it is no more than ⅔ inch thick.

Fill a heavy skillet or deep-fryer with 3 inches of oil and heat to 360°F. While the oil is heating, combine flour, water and remaining dash of salt to form a thin batter. Dip ovals into batter, coating thoroughly, then drop into the hot oil and deep-fry until crisp and golden. Drain on a wire rack or absorbent paper before serving.

Chao-Fan (*Fried Rice Chinese Style*)   SERVES 5

2 teaspoons corn or sesame oil
½ cup minced onion
¼ cup minced carrot
⅓ cup snow peas
½ teaspoon sea salt
4 cups cooked brown rice

Heat a heavy skillet and coat with the oil. Sauté the onion over medium heat for 2 or 3 minutes, or until translucent, stirring gently. Add carrot and snow peas, in that order, and sauté together for 1 or 2 minutes more. Season with the salt and add the rice, breaking up any lumps by slicing the rice into a checkerboard pattern with a wooden spoon or rice paddle. Reduce heat to very low, cover pan, and simmer for 15 minutes. Now uncover and simmer for 5 minutes more. Stir gently before serving.

Brown Rice Croquettes

MAKES 15 CROQUETTES

5 cups cooked brown rice
1 cup minced onion
1 cup diced carrot
Dash of sea salt
1 cup whole-wheat or unbleached white
    flour
Oil for deep-frying
2 cups bread crumbs or cornmeal

Place the rice in a large bowl and separate the grains with a lightly moistened rice paddle. Mix minced onion and diced carrot into the rice. Add the salt and enough of the flour (if necessary) to hold the mixture together. Form each cupful of the mixture into 2 croquettes and set aside.

Fill a heavy skillet or deep-fryer with 3 inches of oil and heat to 330°F. Roll the croquettes in bread crumbs or cornmeal, coating thoroughly, then drop immediately into the hot oil. Deep-fry for 3 to 5 minutes, or until cooked through, crisp and golden. Drain on a wire rack or absorbent paper before serving.

VARIATION: Coat a preheated skillet with a ⅓-inch layer of corn or sesame oil and brown the croquettes over medium heat. Do not cover pan.

Brown Rice Pie

SERVES 4

3 cups whole-wheat flour
¾ teaspoon sea salt
8 tablespoons sesame oil
1½ cups water, approximately
1 tablespoon white sesame seeds, washed
3 cups cooked brown rice

Combine the flour and ½ teaspoon salt in a large bowl, mixing thoroughly. Add 7 tablespoons of the oil, rubbing the mixture through your palms to blend evenly. Gradually add enough of the water for dough to hold together, and knead lightly for 8 to 10 minutes. Separate the dough into 2 portions, one slightly larger than the other. Roll out the larger piece on a floured board into a circle slightly larger than an 8-inch pie pan. Lightly oil the pan and gently fit the pastry into it. Roll out the rest of the pastry and cut it into narrow strips to make a lattice top.

Put the sesame seeds in a heavy skillet and roast over moderately high heat, stirring constantly, until they turn light brown and release their fragrance. Remove from heat and chop fine with a heavy knife. Put the chopped seeds into a small bowl and add ¼ teaspoon salt, mixing well.

Heat another skillet and coat with remaining 1 tablespoon oil. Add the rice and sauté for 3 minutes, stirring to coat the grains evenly with oil. Turn off heat and sprinkle rice with sesame-seed and salt mixture, then stir to blend evenly.

Preheat oven to 350°F. Fill pie shell with rice. Arrange the pastry strips on top to form a lattice, and pinch the edges of the lattice to seal it to the lower pastry. Brush pastry lightly with oil and bake pie for 30 minutes, or until nicely browned. Remove pie from plate and allow to cool slightly before serving.

Sweet Brown Rice with Adzuki Beans

SERVES 10

5 cups sweet brown rice*, washed
½ cup *adzuki* beans, washed
2 tablespoons white sesame seeds, roasted
5 cups water
1½ teaspoons sea salt

Combine all ingredients in a pressure cooker and bring to full pressure over high heat. Slip an asbestos pad under the pot, reduce heat to low, and simmer for 20 minutes. Turn off heat and allow pressure cooker to remain undisturbed for 10 minutes more, gently steaming. Remove from stove and allow pressure to return to normal; or remove regulator and permit steam to escape. Mix gently, cover, and let stand for 5 minutes. Serve with black-sesame-seed *gomashio*. A wonderful party dish or delicacy for special occasions.

*Sweet brown rice kernels are short, stout and very glutinous. This variety of the grain has a much stickier consistency than regular brown rice. In Japan it is reserved traditionally for holidays and celebrations. Sweet brown rice is also used in the making of rice wine *(sake)* and *omochi*.

Omochi *(Rice Cakes)*   MAKES 2 POUNDS

6 cups sweet brown rice†, washed
5½ cups water
½ to 1 teaspoon sea salt

Combine the ingredients in a pressure cooker and bring to full pressure over high heat. Slip an asbestos pad under the pot, reduce heat to low, and simmer for 20 minutes. Remove from heat and allow pressure to return to normal. Transfer rice from pressure cooker to a large wooden bowl, if available. Using a large wooden pestle *(surikogi)* or baseball bat, pound the rice vigorously for 1 hour or more, until the outer skin breaks and a paste forms. Sprinkle the rice mass and the bottom of the pestle or bat with cold water to prevent sticking. From time to time, grind the rice with a heavy circular motion. When individual grains can no longer be distinguished, the dough is ready.

With moistened hands form each cup of *omochi* dough into 2 cakes 3 by 2 inches and ¼ inch thick, or form each cup of dough into 4 balls. If too moist, add just enough sweet brown rice flour to hold the dough together. Serve fresh or pan-toasted, seasoned with *shoyu* to taste; or add to soups about 5 minutes before the soups are done. Refrigerate or dry to store.

A happy food, *omochi* fits in perfectly at parties and get-togethers, and makes a quick lunch as well.

VARIATION: *Ohagi* (rice dumplings) are quicker and easier to make than *omochi*, for not all the rice need be pounded to a paste. Follow the recipe for making *omochi*, but pound the rice only until approximately half has been turned to a paste. Using a moistened paddle, mix whole grains and paste together. With moistened hands form each cup of the *ohagi* dough into 4 balls. These may then be rolled in a mixture of soya flour and salt, or coated with *adzuki* jam (p. 168). They are delicious covered with a purée of pumpkin or sweet potato, or rolled in sesame paste seasoned lightly with *shoyu*. For parties serve many of each kind, arranged attractively on a large platter.

†*see footnote in preceding recipe*

Soya Omochi   SERVES 5

5 cups fresh *omochi* dough
Sesame oil
3 tablespoons soya flour
Dash of sea salt

With moistened hands form each cup of the *omochi* dough into 2 cakes 3 by 2 inches and ¼ inch thick. Brown the rice cakes in a covered heavy skillet brushed lightly with sesame oil; or grill the cakes over an open flame.

Combine the flour and salt, mixing thoroughly. Dip the toasted rice cakes into hot water, then roll in the flour to coat thoroughly. Serve 2 per person.

Daikon Omochi   SERVES 10

5 cups fresh *omochi* dough
5 tablespoons finely grated *daikon*
2½ teaspoons *shoyu*

With lightly moistened hands form each cup of the *omochi* dough into 4 balls. Pour the *shoyu* on the grated *daikon* and mix thoroughly. Place small mounds of the mixture, about ½ tablespoon, on each of 10 individual serving dishes. Serve 2 *omochi* balls per person and use the *daikon* for dipping.

Walnut Omochi
SERVES 5

2½ cups fresh *omochi* dough
10 walnut meats
2 or 3 tablespoons water
1 teaspoon *shoyu*

Lightly moisten your hands with water and form each cup of the *omochi* dough into 4 balls. Roast the walnut meats in a heavy skillet over medium heat, stirring constantly, until lightly toasted and fragrant. With a heavy knife, sliver the nut meats and place them in a *suribachi*. Grind to a paste, adding water and *shoyu*. Cover the *omochi* balls with the paste and serve 2 per person.

VARIATION: Form the *omochi* dough into 5 cakes 3 by 2 inches and ¼ inch thick. Embed 1 or 2 toasted whole walnuts in each cake. Serve and allow each person to season the rice cake with *shoyu* to taste.

Black Sesame Omochi
SERVES 5

5 cups fresh *omochi* dough
3 tablespoons black sesame seeds, washed
2 tablespoons water
2 teaspoons *shoyu*
1 sheet of *nori*

With lightly moistened hands, form each cup of the *omochi* dough into 2 cakes 3 by 2 inches and ¼-inch thick, and reserve.

Put the sesame seeds into a heavy skillet and roast over moderately high heat, stirring constantly, for several minutes, or until lightly toasted and fragrant. Place in a *suribachi* and grind lightly so as to crush the seeds but not express their oil. Add water and *shoyu* and blend into a thin paste.

Toast 1 side of the *nori* by waving it over low heat for several seconds until crisp. Using scissors, cut the sheet into halves, place the halves together, and cut crosswise into 3 strips.

Cover the rice cakes with the crushed seeds and *shoyu*. Wrap 1 strip of *nori* around the center of each rice cake, and serve 2 cakes per person.

Quick Ozoni
SERVES 5

5 cups fresh *omochi* dough
Sesame oil
4 cups *kombu dashi* (p. 136)
2 tablespoons *shoyu*
2 tablespoons *chirimen iriko* (small dried fish)
1 scallion, sliced into thin rounds

With moistened hands form each cup of the *omochi* dough into 2 cakes, 3 by 2 inches and ¼ inch thick. Brown the cakes in a covered heavy skillet brushed lightly with oil, and set aside.

Bring the stock to a boil and season with *shoyu*. Return just to a boil and turn off heat. Place 2 toasted rice cakes in each of 5 serving bowls. Divide the *chirimen* among the bowls, pour in the hot broth, and serve topped with scallion rounds.

VARIATION: Divide 10 toasted rice cakes among 5 serving bowls, and add 1 teaspoon *gomashio* to each bowl. Pour in boiling water, and serve topped with crumbled toasted *nori*.

Seaweed Omochi SERVES 5

5 cups fresh *omochi* dough
Sesame oil
2 sheets of *nori*

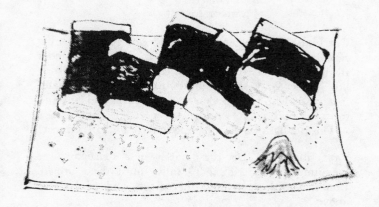

With moistened hands form each cup of the *omochi* dough into 2 cakes 3 by 2 inches and $\frac{1}{4}$ inch thick. Brown the rice cakes in a covered heavy skillet brushed lightly with sesame oil; or grill the cakes over an open flame.

Lightly toast 1 side of each *nori* sheet by waving it over low heat for several seconds until crisp. Using scissors, cut the sheets into halves, place the halves together, and cut crosswise into 3 strips. Wrap 1 strip of *nori* around the center of each toasted rice cake, and serve.

These lightly toasted rice cakes make excellent box lunches on outings. Retoasted over a picnic fire, they taste fresh and delicious.

VARIATION: Blend 3 tablespoons sesame butter *(tahini)*, 2 tablespoons water and 1 teaspoon *shoyu* to a paste. Spread on the toasted rice cakes before wrapping them in the toasted *nori* strips.

OTHER GRAINS

To give nutritious variety to your meals alternate your use of grains. Serve lighter preparations during the *yang* seasons and heavier ones during the *yin*. Chew well, savoring the unique flavors of the various types of grain, and be ever grateful for the special sustenance they provide us.

Barley   SERVES 5

> 1 cup barley, washed
> 3 cups water
> ½ teaspoon sea salt

Combine the ingredients in a heavy saucepan and bring rapidly to a boil over high heat. Slip an asbestos pad under the pan, reduce heat to low, and cover with a tight-fitting lid. Simmer for 30 to 40 minutes. Remove from heat, and toss lightly with two wooden forks. Re-cover and let stand for 5 minutes before serving.

This is a light *yin* dish, especially refreshing in summer.

VARIATIONS: A. Dry-roast barley in a saucepan over medium heat, stirring constantly, until deep brown. Combine with remaining ingredients and proceed as above.

B. To make barley porridge, combine 1 cup barley with 4 to 5 cups water and 1 teaspoon sea salt in a heavy saucepan, and simmer for 1½ hours. Stir gently before serving.

Buckwheat Groats *(Kasha)*   SERVES 5

> 1 tablespoon sesame oil
> 2 cups buckwheat groats, washed
> 3 cups boiling water
> ¼ teaspoon sea salt

Heat a heavy saucepan or deep skillet and coat with the oil. Sauté the groats over medium heat for 5 minutes if they have been preroasted, or for 10 minutes if they have not. Stir constantly to heat evenly. Add boiling water and salt, and cover. Slip an asbestos pad under the pan, reduce heat to low, and simmer for 15 minutes. Turn off heat and toss lightly with a wooden fork. Let stand undisturbed for several minutes more. Serve with *gomashio* and lightly boiled greens.

VARIATION: To make buckwheat porridge, combine 1 cup sautéed buckwheat groats with 3 cups boiling water and ¼ teaspoon salt. Simmer in a covered pan for 20 minutes. Mix gently before serving.

Soba Gaki   SERVES 5

> 1 cup buckwheat flour
> 1¼ to 1½ cups boiling water

Pour the water into the flour while stirring vigorously with 4 long wooden chopsticks (to keep sticking to a minimum). Shape the mixture into 10 small balls approximately 1 inch in diameter. Drop balls into a small pan of boiling water and cook for 2 or 3 minutes. Serve as a side dish, to be seasoned with *shoyu* to taste.

VARIATION: Prepare a clear soup by bringing 4 cups *kombu dashi* to a boil and seasoning with 2 tablespoons *shoyu*. Place 2 *soba gaki* in each of 5 serving bowls, and pour in the soup. Serve garnished with chopped scallion rounds and bits of toasted *nori*.

Kasha Croquettes

3 small *shiitake*, or 6 fresh mushrooms
5 green beans, rinsed and trimmed
½ teaspoon and 2 dashes of sea salt
1 medium-size onion, minced
2 cups cooked buckwheat groats
¾ cup unbleached white flour
Oil for deep-frying
½ cup water, approximately
2 cups bread crumbs or cornmeal

Soak the *shiitake* in cold water for 20 to 30 minutes; remove hard stems and slice the caps fine. If using fresh mushrooms, rinse them in lightly salted water, then slice fine. Bring a small pan of water (just enough to cover the green beans) to a boil and add a dash of salt. Drop in the beans, return to the boil, and cook for 3 to 5 minutes, or until beans are bright green and tender but still crisp. Drain beans in a colander and allow to cool, then slice fine on the diagonal.

Combine *shiitake*, beans and minced onion with buckwheat groats, mixing thoroughly. Add ½ teaspoon salt and enough flour (if necessary) to hold the mixture together. Form the mixture into 8 croquettes and set aside.

Fill a heavy skillet or deep-fryer with 3 inches of oil and heat to 350°F. Combine remaining flour with enough water to form a thin batter, and add a dash of salt. Dip croquettes into the batter, then roll in bread crumbs, coating thoroughly. Drop immediately into the hot oil and deep-fry for 3 to 5 minutes, or until cooked through, crisp and golden. Drain on a wire rack or absorbent paper before serving.

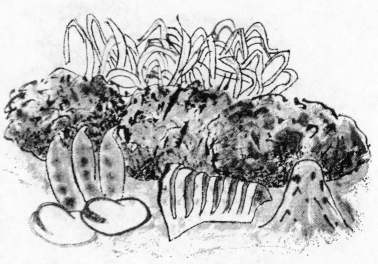

6 pieces of *aburage* (fried bean curd)
12 strips (2 inches long) of *kampyo* (gourd)
1 tablespoon corn or sesame oil
⅓ cup minced onion
⅓ cup minced lotus root
Dash of sea salt
2 cups cooked buckwheat groats
5 cups *kombu dashi* (p. 136)
4 tablespoons *shoyu*
6 thin strips of lemon peel

Pour boiling water over the fried bean curd to rid it of excess oil. Drain, cut pieces into halves, and pull open the center of the pieces to make pouches. Set aside. Rinse the gourd strips in lightly salted water, squeeze them dry, and set aside.

Heat a heavy skillet and coat with the oil. Sauté the onion over medium heat, stirring constantly, until its strong aroma is no longer released. Add the lotus root and sauté together for 1 minute more. Add just enough water to cover. Bring to a boil, cover pan, and reduce heat to low. Simmer for 15 minutes, or until the vegetables are tender and almost all the cooking water has been absorbed or evaporated. Uncover, season with the salt, and stir in the buckwheat groats, mixing thoroughly. Replace lid and simmer together for 5 minutes. Half-fill each bean-curd pouch with the groats and vegetables. Draw pouch edges together and tie with a gourd strip to form a sack.

Bring the *kombu dashi* to a boil and season with the *shoyu*. Place the pouches carefully into the *dashi* and simmer for 20 minutes. Remove pouches and place 2 in each of 6 individual serving bowls. In each bowl place a strip of lemon peel, then gently pour in the stock. Serve immediately.

Buckwheat Cream
SERVES 2

1 teaspoon sesame oil
2 heaping tablespoons buckwheat flour
2 cups water
¼ teaspoon sea salt, or 1 teaspoon *shoyu*
1 tablespoon finely chopped scallion rounds

Heat a heavy skillet and coat with the oil. Sauté the buckwheat flour over medium heat for 1 or 2 minutes, stirring constantly. Remove from heat and allow to cool, then return pan to stove and gradually stir in the water while bringing to a boil. Stirring constantly, simmer for 10 minutes while the cream thickens; then season with salt or *shoyu*. Serve topped with scallion rounds.

VARIATION : For added sweetness stir ¼ cup sautéed onion into the cream while it simmers.

Bulgur *(Steamed Wheat)*
SERVES 5

3 tablespoons sesame oil
2 cups bulgur, washed
4 cups boiling water
⅓ teaspoon sea salt

Heat a heavy saucepan and coat with the oil. Sauté the bulgur over medium heat, stirring constantly, for 3 to 5 minutes. Stir in boiling water, season with salt, and cover with a tight-fitting lid. Slip an asbestos pad under the pan, turn heat to low, and simmer for 15 minutes. Remove from heat, toss lightly with 2 wooden forks, and let stand for several minutes. Delicious served with a sauce of carrot and onion, seasoned with a dash of curry powder.

Quick and easy to make, this delicious dish is perfect for those hungry but unexpected guests.

Bulgur with Vegetables
SERVES 5

2 cups bulgur, washed
4 cups water
1 teaspoon and 2 dashes of sea salt
Pinch of thyme (optional)
1 tablespoon corn or sesame oil
1 small onion, cut into thin half-moons
½ small carrot, diced
½ medium-size red turnip, cubed
2 tablespoons chopped parsley

Dry-roast the bulgur in a heavy saucepan over medium heat, stirring constantly, for 3 or 4 minutes. Remove from heat and allow to cool, then stir in water and add a dash of sea salt and (if used) a pinch of thyme. Bring to a boil over high heat, slip an asbestos pad under pan, and reduce heat to low. Cover with a tight-fitting lid and simmer for 20 minutes.

While the bulgur is simmering, heat a skillet and coat with the oil. Sauté the onion over medium heat, stirring lightly, until it no longer releases its strong aroma. Add the carrot and sauté together for 1 or 2 minutes more. Add water to cover and a dash of salt, then cover pan and reduce heat. Simmer for 20 minutes, or until the vegetables are tender and the cooking water has been absorbed or evaporated. If any liquid remains when the vegetables are done, uncover and simmer until dry.

Bring a small pan of water to a boil and add 1 teaspoon sea salt. Drop in the turnip cubes, return to the boil, and cook for 10 minutes, or until tender. Drain turnip cubes in a colander.

When bulgur is ready, uncover and toss lightly with a fork. Blend in the sautéed vegetables and red turnip, and serve sprinkled with chopped parsley.

OTHER GRAINS

Bulgur Croquettes   MAKES 10 TO 12 CROQUETTES

3 cups cooked bulgur
½ cup minced onion
¼ cup minced carrot
¼ teaspoon and a dash of sea salt
½ cup whole-wheat flour
Oil for deep-frying
1 cup unbleached white flour
⅔ cup water, approximately
2 cups bread crumbs or cornmeal

Combine bulgur, onion and carrot, mixing thoroughly. Add a dash of salt and enough of the whole-wheat flour (if necessary) to hold the mixture together. Form each cupful of the mixture into 3 or 4 croquettes and set aside.

Fill a heavy skillet or deep-fryer with 3 inches of oil and heat to 350°F. Combine unbleached flour with enough water to form a thin batter, and add ¼ teaspoon salt. Dip croquettes into the batter, then roll in bread crumbs, coating thoroughly. Drop immediately into the hot oil and deep-fry for 3 to 5 minutes, or until cooked through, crisp and golden. Drain on a wire rack or absorbent paper before serving.

Bulgur Gratin   SERVES 2 OR 3

4 tablespoons sesame oil
1 cup bulgur, washed
2 cups boiling water
1½ teaspoons and a dash of sea salt
1 medium-size onion, minced
10 green beans, washed and trimmed
2 tablespoons unbleached white flour
1 cup cold water

Heat 1 tablespoon of the oil and sauté the bulgur in a heavy saucepan over medium heat, stirring constantly, for 3 or 4 minutes. Stir in boiling water and season with ¼ teaspoon salt. Bring to a boil over high heat, slip an asbestos pad under pan, and reduce heat to low. Simmer covered for 20 minutes, and turn off heat.

Heat a heavy skillet and coat with 1 tablespoon oil. Sauté the onion over medium heat, stirring gently, for 4 or 5 minutes, or until lightly browned. Sprinkle lightly with a dash of salt, turn off heat, and set aside.

Bring a small pan of water (enough to cover the beans) to a boil over high heat, and add 1 teaspoon salt. Drop in the beans, return to the boil, and cook for 5 minutes, or until the beans are bright green and just tender. Scoop out the beans with a slotted spoon and dip them into a basin of cold water to stop the cooking and set the color. Drain in a colander. When cool, slice thin on the diagonal.

Prepare a mock Béchamel sauce. Heat another skillet and coat with remaining 2 tablespoons oil. Stir in the flour and cook for 30 seconds, stirring constantly to heat evenly. Remove from heat and cool, then return to stove and add ½ cup cold water, stirring until smooth. Bring to a boil while adding remaining water, then reduce heat and simmer for 10 minutes, stirring constantly. When done, season with ¼ teaspoon salt, or to taste.

Preheat oven to 350°F. Place the bulgur into a lightly oiled gratin dish and cover with the onion and beans. Pour on the sauce and sprinkle the top with 2 or 3 drops of oil. Bake for 20 minutes, or until nicely browned.

Corn on the Cob   SERVES 5

5 medium-size ears of corn, husks and silks
    removed
Water
Dash of sea salt

Cover the bottom of a pot with 2 to 3 inches of water and bring to a boil. Add the corn, return to the boil, and season with a dash of sea salt. Cover and simmer for 10 minutes, or until tender. Turn off heat and allow to stand for several minutes before serving.

To cook under pressure, use less than 1 inch of water in the bottom of the pot. Add a dash of sea salt and the ears of corn, then cover. Bring rapidly to full pressure, slip an asbestos pad under the pot, and reduce heat to low. Simmer for 3 minutes, turn off heat, and allow pressure to return slowly to normal.

To bake, preheat oven to 450°F. Replace ears into husks after removing silk, or wrap in aluminum foil. Bake for 10 to 15 minutes.

Morning Cereal

SERVES 4

1 teaspoon corn oil
1 cup cornmeal
4 cups boiling water
¼ teaspoon sea salt

Heat a heavy saucepan and coat with the oil. Sauté the cornmeal over medium heat for 5 minutes, or until golden and fragrant. Stir constantly to heat evenly. Gradually stir in the water, season with the salt, and cover with a tight-fitting lid. Slip an asbestos pad under the pan, reduce heat to low, and simmer for 30 minutes. Stir gently and allow to stand for several minutes before serving.

Cornmeal Mold

SERVES 6 TO 8

1 tablespoon corn oil
2 cups cornmeal
8 cups *kombu dashi* (p. 136)
1 teaspoon sea salt

Heat a heavy saucepan and coat with the oil. Sauté the cornmeal, stirring constantly, for 5 minutes, or until golden and fragrant. Remove from heat and allow to cool, then return to stove and gradually add the *kombu dashi*, stirring until smooth. Stir and bring to a boil over moderately high heat. Season with the salt, and cover with a tight-fitting lid. Slip an asbestos pad under the pan, reduce heat to low, and simmer for 40 minutes to 1 hour, stirring occasionally. If the polenta thickens early, stir in more *dashi* or water.

When done, pour into a rinsed mold and allow to cool and harden. When firms, tap out carefully and cut into slices. Serve spread with sesame butter for a delicious side dish.

I discovered this simple delicacy in the Italian countryside.

Oneri

SERVES 5 TO 7

(*Japanese Country-Style Cornmeal*)

2 cups cornmeal
5 cups *kombu dashi* (p. 136)
1 teaspoon sea salt
2 tablespoons *shoyu*
1 scallion, sliced into thin rounds

Dry-roast the cornmeal in a heavy saucepan, stirring constantly, for 5 to 10 minutes. Allow to cool, the gradually pour in the *dashi*, stirring until smooth. Stir and bring to a boil over moderately high heat. Season with the salt and *shoyu*, and cover with a tight-fitting lid. Slip an asbestos pad under the pan, reduce heat to low, and simmer for 40 to 45 minutes, stirring occasionally. If the cornmeal thickens early, stir in a little water. After 40 minutes the cornmeal should be thick enough to spoon out. Turn off heat and serve as a side dish, topped with scallion rounds.

Millet Omedeto

SERVES 5

⅓ cup *adzuki* beans, washed
7 cups water
1 cup millet, washed
½ teaspoon sea salt

Simmer the *adzuki* beans in 1 cup water for 20 minutes, or until wrinkled. Combine with the millet, the remaining 6 cups water, and the salt in a heavy saucepan, and bring rapidly to a boil. Slip an asbestos pad under the pan, reduce heat to low, and cover with a tight-fitting lid. Simmer for 1 hour. Stir gently and let stand for several minutes before serving.

OTHER GRAINS

Couscous

SERVES 5

(Steamed Wheat with Vegetables)

1 cup dried chick-peas, soaked in water
  overnight
6 cups water
3 teaspoons and a dash of sea salt
2 cups couscous
3 tablespoons olive oil
2 small onions, cut into thick half-moons
1 small carrot, cubed
2-inch square of *kombu,* wiped clean with a
  dry cloth
2 bay leaves (optional)
8 Brussels sprouts
½ small cauliflower, separated into
  flowerets
Parsley sprigs

Combine the chick-peas and 3 cups water in a pressure cooker and bring rapidly to full pressure over high heat. Slip an asbestos pad under the pot, reduce heat to low, and simmer for 40 minutes. Remove from heat and allow pressure to return to normal.

Bring remaining 3 cups of water to a boil in a heavy saucepan, add a dash of salt, then gradually stir in the couscous. Simmer for 4 or 5 minutes, cover, and turn off heat. Allow pan to remain on stove for 10 minutes, gently steaming. Uncover, toss grains lightly with 2 wooden forks, and set aside.

To cook under pressure, combine equal parts couscous and water in a pressure cooker and add a dash of salt. Bring rapidly to full pressure, slip an asbestos pad under the pot, and reduce heat to low. Simmer for 5 minutes, remove from heat, and allow pressure to return to normal. Toss lightly, re-cover, and set aside.

Heat a heavy skillet and coat with the oil. Sauté the onions over medium heat, stirring gently, for 5 minutes. Add the carrot cubes and cooked chick-peas, mix the ingredients together, and sauté for 1 or 2 minutes more. Place a strip of *kombu* in the pan, add slightly more than enough water to cover, and bring to a boil. Season with 1 teaspoon sea salt, reduce heat to low, and (if used) drop in the bay leaves. Cover pan and simmer for about 30 minutes, or until vegetables and chick-peas are fully tender. If preferred, the *kombu* may be removed from pan after simmering for 5 minutes.

Bring a small pan of water to a boil over high heat and add 1 teaspoon sea salt. Drop in the Brussels sprouts, return to the boil, and cook for 3 to 5 minutes, or until sprouts are bright green and just tender. With a slotted spoon, remove Brussels sprouts and dip them into a basin of cold water to stop the cooking and set the color. Drain in a colander. Bring another small pan of water to a boil, add 1 teaspoon salt, and drop in the cauliflowerets. Return to the boil and cook for 3 minutes, or until tender but still crisp. Remove flowerets, plunge into cold water, and drain in a colander.

When the chick-peas and vegetables are ready, mix in the sprouts and cauliflowerets. Season with sea salt to taste, bring just to a boil, and turn off heat.

To serve, spread out the couscous on a large platter and cover with the vegetables and broth. Garnish with sprigs of parsley.

Kokoh *(Grain Milk)*

SERVES 4

1 teaspoon corn or sesame oil
1 cup *kokoh**
5 cups water
½ teaspoon sea salt
3 tablespoons croutons
Parsley sprigs

Heat a heavy saucepan and coat with the oil. Sauté the *kokoh* over medium heat until fragrant. Stir constantly to heat evenly. Remove pan from stove and allow to cool, then gradually stir in the water, and season with salt. Stir while bringing rapidly to a boil, and cover with a tight-fitting lid. Slip an asbestos pad under the pan, reduce heat to low, and simmer for 30 to 40 minutes, stirring occasionally. Serve topped with croutons and garnished with sprigs of parsley.

*Kokoh, a nutritious mixture of roasted and finely ground rice, sweet rice, oatmeal, soybeans and sesame seeds, is available prepackaged at macrobiotic outlets and natural food shops. It can be served as a morning cereal or tea, and is used as a base for desserts and in baking.

Millet   SERVES 5

    1 teaspoon sesame oil
    1 cup millet, washed
    4 cups water
    ¼ teaspoon sea salt

Heat a heavy saucepan and coat with the oil. Sauté the millet over medium heat, stirring constantly, until lightly browned and fragrant. Remove pan from stove and allow to cool, then gradually stir in water. Season with salt and bring rapidly to a boil. Cover, and simmer over an asbestos pad for 30 minutes. Stir gently and let stand for 5 minutes before serving.

Millet is a very *yang* grain that is best served in winter.

VARIATION: For added sweetness, stir ¼ cup sautéed onion into the grain and simmer together.

Beignets de Millet   SERVES 4 OR 5

    ½ cup millet flour
    ½ cup whole-wheat flour
    Dash of sea salt
    2 tablespoons sesame oil
    1 small onion, minced
    ½ cup water, approximately
    Oil for deep-frying
    Parsley sprigs

Combine the first 3 ingredients in a large bowl, mixing thoroughly. Add the oil and blend it in evenly by rubbing the mixture through your palms. Mix in the onion and add enough water to form a thick batter.

Fill a heavy skillet or deep-fryer with 3 inches of oil and heat to 360°F. Drop the batter by the tablespoonful into the hot oil and deep-fry until crisp and pale golden. Drain on a wire rack or absorbent paper. Serve 2 or 3 pieces per person, and accompany each serving with a tablespoon of finely grated *daikon* seasoned lightly with *shoyu*, for dipping, and garnish with parsley.

This simple dish can provide us with great stamina and vitality.

Millet Burgers   SERVES 5
with Kuzu Sauce

    3 cups cooked millet
    1 medium-size onion, minced
    ½ small carrot, minced
    Dash of sea salt
    ½ cup whole-wheat flour
    Corn or sesame oil
    1 tablespoon *kuzu*
    ½ cup water
    1 cup *kombu dashi* (p. 136)

Combine the first three ingredients, mixing thoroughly. Sprinkle with salt and add enough flour (if necessary) to hold the mixture together. Form the mixture into 10 burgers. Cover the bottom of a heavy skillet with a layer of oil approximately ⅓ inch deep, and panfry the burgers over medium heat. Do not cover pan.

Dissolve the *kuzu* in the water and combine with the *dashi* in a small saucepan. Simmer for 3 to 4 minutes, stirring constantly, until thick. Serve over the burgers.

OTHER GRAINS

Grain Flakes

SERVES 4

1 cup oat flakes (or flakes of millet, rye, wheat, or rice)
2 tablespoons corn or sesame oil
1 small onion, minced
3 cups boiling water
½ teaspoon sea salt

Dry-roast the flakes, or, if desired, use 1 tablespoon of the oil to sauté the flakes, in a heavy saucepan over medium heat for 5 minutes, or until lightly browned. Stir the flakes and shake the pan to heat evenly and prevent scorching. Remove pan from stove and allow to cool.

Heat a heavy skillet and coat with the remaining tablespoon of oil. Sauté the onion, stirring gently, for 3 or 4 minutes. Add onion to flakes, pour in the water, and season with salt. Bring to a boil over moderately high heat, stirring constantly. Cover with a tight-fitting lid, slip an asbestos pad under the pan, and reduce heat to low. Simmer for 30 minutes. Serve with *gomashio*.

Whole-Wheat Cream

SERVES 4

1 tablespoon corn or sesame oil
1 cup whole-wheat flour
4 cups water
¼ teaspoon sea salt

Heat a heavy saucepan and coat with the oil. Sauté the flour over medium heat, stirring constantly, until fragrant. Remove from heat and allow to cool. Gradually stir in water, season with salt, and bring to a boil. Slip an asbestos pad under the pan, turn heat to low, and cover with a tight-fitting lid. Simmer for 30 minutes, stirring occasionally.

When cooking under pressure, dry-roast or sauté the flour in the pressure cooker. When it has cooled, add water and salt. Bring rapidly to full pressure, slip an asbestos pad under the pot, and reduce heat to low. Simmer for 15 minutes. Remove from heat and allow pressure to return to normal. Mix gently before serving.

VARIATION: Drop 5 or 6 leaves of spinach or 1 or 2 small beets into a pan of boiling salted water. Return to the boil and cook until tender. Purée in a *suribachi*, then add to the cream during the last 10 minutes of cooking.

Harudi *(Semolina)*

SERVES 4 OR 5

3 tablespoons sesame oil
1 cup semolina
2½ cups water
1 medium-size sweet potato
Dash of sea salt
2 tablespoons white sesame seeds
4 or 5 camellia or chrysanthemum leaves

Heat the oil in a heavy saucepan. Add the semolina and sauté over medium heat for 10 to 15 minutes, or until golden and fragrant. Allow to cool, then gradually stir in water and bring to a boil. Slip an asbestos pad under pan and reduce heat to low. Simmer covered, stirring occasionally, for 35 minutes.

Peel the sweet potato, and steam it over high heat for 10 minutes. Purée it and season lightly with sea salt. When semolina is done, blend in sweet potato and simmer together for 1 or 2 minutes before removing from heat.

Roast the sesame seeds in a heavy skillet over medium heat until lightly browned and fragrant, stirring constantly. Sprinkle the seeds in the bottom of a gratin dish or mold, pour in the semolina, and press firm with the back of a wooden spoon. Allow to cool and become firm, then invert the dish and tap out carefully. Serve individual portions on leaves of camellia or chrysanthemum.

I discovered this dish in India where the grain is boiled in the milk of water buffalo and sweetened with sugar.

NOODLES

Flour is most digestible when in the form of noodles. Noodles lend themselves to a wide variety of uses: added to fresh salads or to soups, or mixed with sautéed vegetables, they add flavor and texture to whatever we serve. Noodles can be served steaming hot or, in summer, ice cold. Here are a few basic recipes for you to elaborate on.

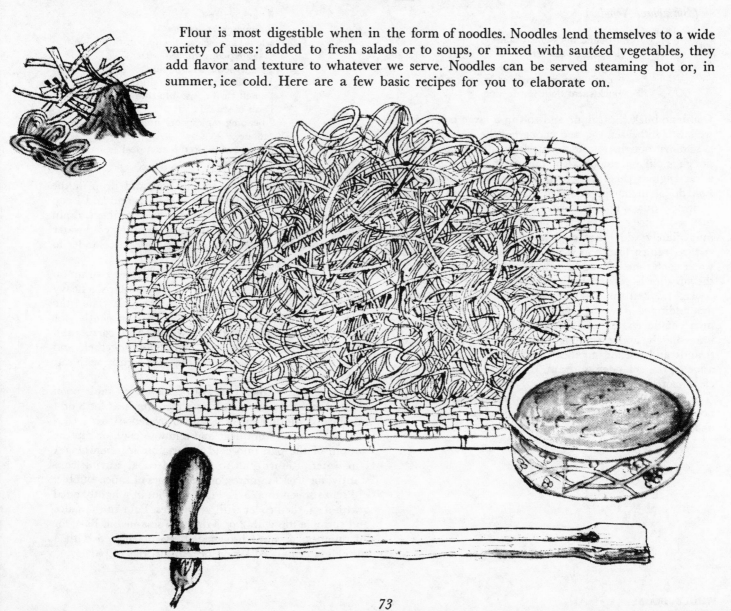

Homemade Soba

SERVES 4 TO 5

(Buckwheat Noodles)

1 pound buckwheat flour
1 teaspoon sea salt
1 egg, beaten
½ cup water, approximately
Buckwheat flour for dusting

Combine buckwheat flour and salt in a large bowl; mix well. Stir in beaten egg and enough of the water to form a semidry dough. Knead for at least 20 minutes, until dough is stiff and smooth. Roll out on a floured board into a rectangular sheet $\frac{1}{10}$ inch thick, and dust thoroughly. Fold dough in fourths, and slice crosswise into thin strands.

Bring 2 quarts unsalted water to a rolling boil and drop in noodle strips. Over high heat return to a boil and immediately add 1 cup cold water. Repeating this procedure, return to a boil twice more, adding 1 cup cold water each time. (By adding cold water the inner core of the noodles is cooked before the outer surface is overcooked.) When the noodles reach their third boil (after first adding cold water), turn off heat and drain noodles in a colander, reserving cooking water. Rinse noodles immediately under running cold water, separating the strands and cooling noodles thoroughly. Now set them aside in the colander to drain, patting them dry with a clean cloth if desired.

Season the cooking water with *shoyu* and pour over the noodles; or reserve the liquid for baking and serve the noodles with *tsuke-jiru* sauce (p. 163) for dipping.

Mori Soba Gratin

SERVES 5

6 cups water
8 ounces *soba* noodles
½ loaf Chinese *dow-foo*, or substitute 5 tablespoons minced *seitan*
2 tablespoons sesame oil
1 small onion, cut into thin crescents
½ small carrot, cut into thin gingko leaves
Dash of sea salt
2 heaping tablespoons unbleached white flour
1 teaspoon minced lemon peel
Parsley sprigs

Bring 4 cups water to a rolling boil and drop in the noodles. Return to the boil over high heat and add 1 cup cold water. When water boils again, turn off heat, drain noodles in a colander, and rinse under running cold water until thoroughly cooled. Set noodles aside in colander to drain.

If using Chinese *dow-foo*, deep-fry until crisp, drain on absorbent paper, and slice it into thin strips. Heat a heavy skillet and coat with 1 tablespoon of the oil. Sauté the onion crescents over medium heat, stirring gently, for 5 minutes, or until lightly browned. Add carrot and Chinese *dow-foo* or *seitan*, mix ingredients together, and sauté for 2 or 3 minutes more. Sprinkle lightly with salt and turn off heat.

Heat another skillet, coat with remaining 1 tablespoon oil, and add the flour. Cook over medium heat for 3 or 4 minutes, or until flour is lightly browned, stirring constantly. Remove from heat and allow to cool, or dip the bottom of the pan into cold water. Stir in remaining 1 cup water. Return pan to heat and cook, stirring constantly, for 1 or 2 minutes, or until edges of sauce bubble.

Preheat oven to 425°F. Place noodles in a lightly oiled gratin dish, then cover with vegetables. Pour in the sauce and sprinkle top with 2 or 3 drops of sesame oil. Bake for 20 minutes, or until browned. Serve garnished with a sprinkling of minced lemon peel and sprigs of parsley.

Mori Soba with Vegetables
SERVES 5

1 pound *soba* noodles*
5 *maki-yuba*† (optional)
3 cups *kombu dashi* (p. 136)
3 tablespoons *shoyu*
1 teaspoon sea salt
20 green beans, rinsed and trimmed
1 small carrot, cut into fine diagonal slices
3 scallions, cut into 1-inch diagonal lengths

Bring 2 quarts unsalted water to a rolling boil and drop in the noodles. Over high heat return to a boil and immediately add 1 cup cold water. Repeating this procedure, return to a boil twice more, adding 1 cup cold water each time. When the noodles reach their third boil (after first adding cold water), turn off heat and drain noodles in a colander. Rinse noodles immediately under running cold water, separating the strands and cooling noodles thoroughly. Set them aside in the colander to drain.

Soak the *maki-yuba* in cold water for 5 minutes, then combine in a saucepan with enough of the *kombu dashi* to cover. Lightly season *dashi* with *shoyu*, bring to a boil, and cook for 5 minutes. Drain *maki-yuba* and set aside.

Bring a small pan of water to a boil over high heat and add ½ teaspoon salt. Drop in the beans, return to the boil, and cook for 3 or 4 minutes, or until beans are bright green and tender but still crisp. With a slotted spoon, scoop out beans and dip them into a basin of cold water to stop the cooking and set the color. Drain, then slice the beans crosswise into halves. Set beans aside in a colander.

Bring another small pan of water to a boil, add remaining ½ teaspoon salt, and drop in the carrot slices. Return to the boil and cook for 2 or 3 minutes. Plunge carrot slices into a basin of cold water and drain in a colander.

To reheat the noodles, douse them with a kettle of hot water. Place individual portions of noodles into serving bowls and top with the vegetables and *maki-yuba*. Garnish with scallion slices and serve with *tsuke-jiru* dipping sauce (p. 163).

*Prepackaged Japanese noodles are quite salty and need not be boiled in salted water.
†*Maki-yuba*, strips of soybean gluten wound into a little cake, is available at Oriental food shops and macrobiotic outlets.

Yaki Soba
SERVES 4

Oil for deep-frying
4 *maki-yuba* (optional)
4 handfuls of cooked soba noodles
1 tablespoon corn oil
1 medium-size onion, cut into thin crescents
1 small carrot, slivered
2 tablespoons *kuzu*
1 tablespoon *shoyu*
2 tablespoons chopped parsley

Fill a heavy skillet or deep-fryer with 3 inches of oil and heat to 360°F. Drop in the *maki-yuba* and deep-fry until swollen and crisp. Drain on absorbent paper. Now deep-fry the noodles by the handful until golden and crisp. Drain on absorbent paper and set aside in a warm oven (120°F.).

Heat a heavy skillet and coat with the oil. Sauté the onion over medium heat, stirring gently, for 2 or 3 minutes. Add the carrot and *maki-yuba*, and sauté together for 3 minutes more. Add water to cover and bring to a boil. Cover pan, reduce heat to low, and simmer for 10 to 15 minutes, or until the vegetables are tender.

Dissolve the *kuzu* in ¼ cup water, stirring until smooth. Two or 3 minutes before turning off heat under the simmering vegetables, stir in the *kuzu* and season with the *shoyu* (or to taste). Stir while simmering for several minutes more as the *kuzu* thickens; turn off heat.

Place 1 piece of noodle *tempura* on each of 4 serving dishes, and cover with the *kuzu* sauce. Serve sprinkled with chopped parsley.

Tempura Soba

SERVES 5

1 pound *soba* noodles
¾ cup *shoyu*
3 or 4 leaves of spinach
Oil for deep-frying
1 cup whole-wheat flour
2 dashes of sea salt
1 small carrot, slivered
¾ cup thin gingko leaves of lotus root
3 or 4 scallions, sliced diagonally into 1-inch lengths
1 piece of *kombu*, 2 inches square
5 thin strips of fresh orange or lemon peel

Bring 2 quarts unsalted water to a rolling boil and drop in the noodles. Over high heat return to a boil and immediately add 1 cup cold water. Repeating this procedure, return to a boil twice more, adding 1 cup cold water each time. When the noodles reach their third boil (after first adding cold water), turn off heat and drain noodles in a colander. Rinse noodles immediately under running cold water, separating the strands and cooling noodles thoroughly. Set them aside in the colander to drain.

Bring a small pan of water to a boil and add 1 or 2 tablespoons *shoyu*. Drop in the spinach leaves, return to the boil, and cook for 2 or 3 minutes, or until stems are tender. Drain spinach in a colander. When cool, squeeze the leaves between your palms, and chop fine.

Fill a heavy skillet or deep-fryer with 3 inches of oil and heat to 360°F. Combine the flour with a dash of salt and enough water (about ½ cup) to form a thick batter. Mix carrot, lotus root and scallions into the batter. Scoop out 3 or 4 tablespoons of the batter and place on a spatula; the batter should be thick enough to adhere to the spatula's surface. Shape the batter into a round patty and using chopsticks nudge it off the edge of the spatula into the hot oil. Deep-fry until crisp and golden, then drain on a wire rack or absorbent paper.

Put the *kombu* in a saucepan and cover with 5 cups water. Bring to a boil and add a dash of salt and as much of the remaining *shoyu* as desired. Return to the boil and turn off heat.

To reheat the noodles, douse them with a kettle of hot water, or place them in a strainer and dip them into a pot of boiling water. Divide the noodles among 5 serving bowls, and top each portion with 1 or 2 pieces of vegetable *tempura* and chopped spinach. Garnish with lemon or orange peel and pour in the hot *shoyu* broth. Serve immediately.

Summer Soba

SERVES 3

2 pieces of *daikon*, each 1½ inches long and of uniform width
8 ounces *soba* noodles
1 sheet of *nori*

Prepare *daikon* sheets by paring each piece of *daikon* to half its width in a long continuous strip. Cut the *daikon* sheets lengthwise into thin, noodle-length strips. Soak the strips in cold water for 20 minutes.

Bring 1 quart of water to a boil over high heat and add the noodles. Return to a boil and add 1 cup cold water. Repeating this procedure, return to a boil twice more, adding 1 cup cold water each time. When the noodles reach their third boil, turn off heat and drain noodles in a colander. Rinse noodles immediately under running cold water, separating the strands and cooling noodles thoroughly.

Toss noodles and *daikon* strips together, and divide the mixture among individual serving bowls. Lightly toast the *nori* sheet by waving it over low heat for several seconds until just crisp. Using scissors, cut the sheet into halves, put the halves together, and cut crosswise into thin strips. Top each portion of noodles with the crisp *nori* and serve with *tsuke-jiru* dipping sauce (p. 163).

NOODLES

Homemade Udon (*Wheat Noodles*)   SERVES 5

1 cup whole-wheat flour
3 cups unbleached white flour
1 teaspoon sea salt
⅔ cup water, approximately
White flour for dusting
Shoyu

Combine the first three ingredients in a large bowl; mix thoroughly. Gradually add enough of the water to form a semidry dough. Knead for at least 20 minutes, until dough is stiff and smooth. Roll out on a floured board into a rectangular sheet $\frac{1}{10}$ inch thick, and dust thoroughly. Fold dough in fourths, and slice crosswise into strands.

Bring 2 quarts unsalted water to a rolling boil and drop in the noodle strips. Over high heat return to the boil, then reduce heat and cook for 10 minutes, or until the noodles are tender but still crisp at the core. Drain noodles in a colander, reserving the cooking water. Rinse noodles immediately under running cold water, separating the strands and cooling noodles throughly. Set noodles aside in the colander to drain.

Season the cooking water with *shoyu* and pour over the noodles: or reserve the liquid for baking and serve the noodles with *tsuke-jiru* sauce (p.163) for dipping.

VARIATIONS: A. *Daikon Udon:* Lightly toast 1 sheet of *nori* by waving it over low heat for several seconds until just crisp. Using scissors, cut the sheet into halves, put the halves together, and cut crosswise into thin strips. Grate enough *daikon* to make 5 tablespoons and cut enough scallions into rounds to make 2 tablespoons. Divide the noodles among 5 serving bowls. Add 1 tablespoon grated *daikon* to each bowl, then divide 4 cups *tsuke-jiru* dipping sauce among the bowls. Top with scallion rounds and toasted *nori.*

B. *Tempura Udon:* Place 1 or 2 pieces of vegetable-batter *tempura* over individual servings of boiled *udon.* Serve in bowls of *tsuke-jiru* broth, and garnish with grated *daikon* and scallion rounds.

C. *Kitsune Udon:* Douse 1 piece of *aburage* with boiling water to rid it of excess oil; drain. Put the *aburage* into a saucepan with just enough water to cover, bring to a boil, and season with *shoyu.* Cook covered until all the water has been absorbed or evaporated, and the *aburage* is well flavored. Drain, then slice the *aburage* lengthwise into thin strips. Placed cooked *udon* noodles into individual serving bowls, cover with strips of the *age,* and pour in a hot broth. Serve garnished with grated *daikon* and chopped scallion rounds.

D. *Curry Udon:* Prepare a *kuzu* sauce with your favorite vegetables and a dash of curry powder. Pour hot over individual servings of *udon,* and serve.

E. *Kama Age Udon:* Keep a large pot of water or *dashi* simmering over a gas ring or alcohol burner at the center of the table. Serve a large platter of cooked *udon* noodles together with several small bowls of chopped scallion and toasted *nori* strips. Provide each person with a bowl of *tsuke-jiru* dipping sauce topped with toasted and finely chopped sesame seeds and garnished with scallion and *nori.* Let each guest heat bitefuls of noodles in the simmering pot, then dip the noodles in the sauce.

Oda Maki (*Steamed Udon*)   SERVES 5

5 *maki-yuba,* deep-fried (optional)
10 slices of flowered carrot, lightly boiled
2 handfuls of cooked *udon* noodles
1 leek, sliced diagonally into 1-inch lengths
4 cups *kombu dashi* (p. 136)
2 eggs, hard-cooked and sliced
2 tablespoons minced parsley

Divide the noodles among 5 custard cups, and attractively arrange the *maki-yuba,* carrot slices and leek pieces around the *udon.* Carefully pour in enough *kombu dashi* to cover. Cover the cups and steam over high heat for 20 minutes. Serve topped with egg slices and a sprinkling of minced parsley.

BREADS, SNACKS AND OTHER GOOD THINGS FROM FLOUR

Breads that use yeast as a leavening agent are rather *yin* and are usually reserved for special occasions. Unleavened bread is heavier and needs to be chewed very well, but is all the more delicious for the effort. Use a wide variety of flours in your baking, experimenting with and enjoying their various combinations. Remember that no two cups of flour are exactly alike in the amount of moisture they will absorb. For batter breads, add enough water to make a thick batter; kneaded dough should be elastic and fall readily away from the sides of the bowl.

Ohsawa Loaf *(Unleavened Bread)*   MAKES 1 LOAF

2½ cups whole-wheat flour
1½ cups millet flour
1 cup brown rice flour
½ tablespoon sea salt
5 tablespoons corn or sesame oil
3 cups water, approximately

This is a batter bread that requires no kneading. Preheat oven to 325°F. Combine the flours and salt in a large bowl, mixing thoroughly. Add the oil and blend it in evenly by gently rubbing the mixture through your palms. Stir in the water, making sure that it is absorbed evenly. Lightly oil a loaf pan 9 by 5 by 3 inches and preheat. Turn the batter into the pan, aerating it. With a moistened spatula gently smooth the top of the batter and pull it away from the sides of the pan. Bake for 1 hour, or until nicely browned, then remove bread from pan and cool on a rack before slicing.

VARIATIONS: A. Add 1 or 2 cups leftover cooked grain, freshly sautéed vegetables or a purée of sweet potato, squash or apples to the batter.

B. Add 1 teaspoon ground cinnamon to batter and sprinkle top with sesame seeds.

C. Add peanuts, almonds, cashews, raisins, currants, etc.

Leavened Bread   MAKES 2 LOAVES

1 envelope (¼ ounce) dry yeast, or 1 cake (.6 ounce) compressed yeast
¼ cup water
5 cups brown rice flour
4 cups whole-wheat flour
1 cup unbleached white flour
½ tablespoon sea salt
5 tablespoons sesame or corn oil
3 cups water, approximately

Soften dry yeast in warm water (110°F.) or cake yeast in lukewarm water (85°F.). Combine flours and salt. Add oil and rub the mixture between your palms to blend evenly and to be sure that no lumps remain. Mix in the yeast, and add water gradually to form a dough. Knead for 10 to 15 minutes, until smooth and elastic. Shape into a ball, wrap in a damp cloth, and set aside in a warm place for several hours, or until doubled in bulk.

Punch down. Cut dough into 2 portions and shape each into a smooth ball. Cover and let rest for 10 minutes.

Shape into loaves, and place in lightly oiled loaf pans (8½ by 4½ by 2½ inches). Let rise until doubled, about 1¼ hours. Bake in a preheated 350°F. oven for 1 hour. Cover with foil for last 20 minutes if the crust is done before the center of the loaves.

Chapati

5 cups unbleached white flour
½ teaspoon sea salt
1¼ cups water, approximately
Corn oil

Combine flour and salt in a large bowl, mixing well. Stir in water gradually to form a semidry, elastic dough. Knead for 10 to 15 minutes until smooth. Divide dough into 15 parts, and roll out each one on a floured board into a 3-inch round. Rounds should be as thin as possible.

Preheat separately both a heavy skillet and an asbestos pad over medium-low heat. Brown *chapati* in the heated skillet for 1 or 2 minutes, or until the edges curl. Turn over quickly and brown again for 1 minute. Now remove *chapati* from pan and place on the asbestos pad until puffed up. Remove from pad and brush with corn oil. Repeat with remaining ingredients until all are cooked.

VARIATION: To make *puri*, knead the dough for 20 to 30 minutes. Roll out on a floured board into a rectangular sheet ¹/₁₀ inch thick, then cut dough into 2-inch rounds with a jar top or cookie cutter.

Pour 3 inches of oil into a heavy skillet or deep-fryer and heat to 360°F. Drop the *puri* into the hot oil and deep-fry, holding the *puri* under the surface with a pair of long chopsticks. When puffed up, turn *puri* over carefully (do not puncture the surface) and deep-fry again. Drain, on absorbent paper before serving.

Chick-Pea Muffins

MAKES 15 MUFFINS

3 cups whole-wheat flour
2 teaspoons sea salt
½ teaspoon ground cinnamon
4½ cups water, approximately
4 cups cooked chick-peas, mashed

Preheat oven to 350°F. Combine flour, salt and cinnamon, and stir in water until well mixed. Lightly oil muffin tins and half fill with muffin batter. Add a layer of chick-peas, then cover with more batter until mold is four-fifths full. Bake for 40 to 50 minutes, or until muffins are puffed up and nicely browned.

VARIATIONS: A. Substitute cornmeal or buckwheat flour for whole-wheat.

B. Instead of chick-peas use 1 cup squash, sweet-potato or chestnut purée, or apple butter, raisins or nuts (whole or as butters).

Karinto

MAKES 12 TO 16

Oil for deep-frying
1 cup unbleached white flour
½ teaspoon sea salt
1 tablespoon sesame oil
6 to 8 tablespoons water
Flour for dusting

Fill a heavy skillet or deep-fryer with 2 to 3 inches of oil and heat to 360°F.

Combine flour and salt, mixing well. Add the tablespoon of oil, rubbing mixture through palms to blend evenly. Gradually and water to form a dough. Dust with flour and knead lightly for about 3 minutes, until smooth and elastic. Roll out on a floured board. Cut into strips ⅔ by 2 inches and cut a short slit in the middle of each strip. Thread one end of strip through slit. Drop into the hot oil and deep-fry until puffed up, crisp and lightly golden, 3 to 4 minutes. Drain on absorbent paper before serving.

VARIATIONS: A. Use the following combinations and proceed as above:

1 cup whole-wheat flour	½ cup whole-wheat flour
½ cup buckwheat flour	½ cup rice flour
½ teaspoon sea salt	½ teaspoon sea salt
1 tablespoon sesame oil	1 tablespoon sesame oil
⅓ to ½ cup water	6 to 8 tablespoons water

1 cup oat flour
½ cup unbleached white flour
½ teaspoon sea salt
1 tablespoon sesame oil
⅓ to ½ cup water

B. Knead the following combinations for 8 to 10 minutes, or until stiff. If desired, add unroasted black sesame seeds while kneading, then proceed as above. Shape in imaginative ways to delight family or guests.

1 cup buckwheat flour	½ cup millet or corn flour
1 teaspoon sea salt	½ cup unbleached white
1 tablespoon sesame oil	flour
½ cup water	½ teaspoon sea salt
1 tablespoon black	1 tablespoon sesame oil
sesame seeds	½ cup water

Tazuna Karinto   MAKES 18

Oil for deep-frying
1 cup whole-wheat flour
½ teaspoon sea salt
⅓ teaspoon ground cinnamon
1 tablespoon sesame oil
6 to 8 tablespoons water
Flour for dusting

Fill a heavy skillet or deep-fryer with 2 to 3 inches of oil. Bring to 360°F. over slow heat.

Combine dry ingredients, mixing well. Add oil, rubbing mixture through palms to blend it evenly. Gradually add water to form a dough. Knead lightly for about 3 minutes, until smooth and elastic. Roll out on a floured board into a rectangular sheet approximately $\frac{1}{10}$ inch thick. Dust with flour, then cut into strips $\frac{2}{3}$ by 2 inches. Holding both ends of strip, twist up and drop into hot oil. Deep-fry until puffed up, crisp and pale golden, 3 or 4 minutes. Drain on absorbent paper before serving.

Spiral Karinto

Oil for deep-frying
A. 1 cup unbleached white flour
½ teaspoon sea salt
1 tablespoon sesame oil
6 to 8 tablespoons water
B. ⅔ cup unbleached white flour
⅓ cup *yannoh* (grain coffee)
½ teaspoon sea salt
1 tablespoon sesame oil
6 to 8 tablespoons water

Fill a heavy skillet or deep-fryer with 2 to 3 inches of oil. Bring to 360°F. over slow heat.

Combine dry ingredients in A, blend in oil, and gradually add water to form a dough. Knead lightly for about 3 minutes, until smooth and elastic, then roll out on a floured board. Repeat with ingredients in B.

Place B dough on top of A dough, matching edges. Roll into a tight cylinder and cut it into 12 slices. Drop each slice into hot oil. Deep-fry until crisp and lightly golden, 3 or 4 minutes. Drain on absorbent paper before serving.

Rice Snacks

2 cups brown rice flour
½ teaspoon sea salt
1 tablespoon sesame oil
½ cup water, approximately

Combine flour and salt, mixing well. Add oil, rubbing mixture through palms to blend it evenly. Gradually add water to form a dough. Knead lightly for 1 or 2 minutes, until smooth and very elastic. Pinch off and roll into balls. Press balls between palms to flatten, then, using a chopstick, draw a floral design on each. Brown in a lightly oiled skillet over medium heat, or bake in a preheated 350°F. oven for 20 to 25 minutes.

Millet Snacks

1 cup millet flour
1 cup unbleached white flour
½ teaspoon sea salt
1 teaspoon ground cinnamon
2 tablespoons sesame or corn oil
⅓ cup chopped peanuts
½ cup water, approximately
Flour for dusting

Preheat oven to 350°F. Combine dry ingredients, mixing thoroughly. Add oil, rubbing mixture through palms to blend it evenly. Add peanuts and enough water to form a dough. Knead lightly for 3 or 4 minutes, until smooth and elastic. Roll out on a floured board into a ¼-inch-thick sheet, and dust with flour. Place on a lightly oiled cookie sheet, then cut into squares with a roller or heavy knife. Brush lightly with oil. Bake for 25 minutes, or until nicely browned.

Soba Snacks

1 cup buckwheat flour
1 teaspoon sea salt
⅓ teaspoon ground cinnamon
1 tablespoon sesame oil
½ cup water, approximately
10 almonds

Preheat oven to 350°F. Combine dry ingredients, mixing thoroughly. Add oil, rubbing mixture through palms to blend it evenly. Gradually add water to form a smooth, thick batter. Drop onto a lightly oiled cookie sheet by the spoonful and top each piece with an almond. Bake for 25 minutes, or until nicely browned.

Buckwheat Pancakes with Adzuki-Chestnut Jam

½ cup *adzuki* beans, washed
½ cup chestnut meats
6 cups water, approximately
1 teaspoon and a dash of sea salt
2 cups buckwheat flour
1 egg, beaten
Corn or sesame oil for frying

To prepare jam, boil *adzuki* beans in 1½ cups water for 20 to 30 minutes, or until wrinkled. In another pan, cook the chestnuts in 1½ cups water. Combine beans and chestnuts and simmer together for 40 minutes to 1 hour, or until pasty. Season with 1 teaspoon of salt to bring out the ingredients' sweetness.

Add remaining dash of salt to buckwheat flour, and stir in the beaten egg and remaining 3 cups water to form a thick, smooth batter. Heat a heavy skillet, brush lightly with oil, and reduce heat to medium-low. Ladle in just enough batter to cover surface of pan. Fry until set: using a thin spatula, carefully turn pancake and fry the other side. Spread 1 heaping tablespoon of *adzuki*-chestnut jam over surface of pancake, then fold pancake into fourths. Transfer to a platter and serve as a main dish.

VARIATION: To make crêpes, combine 1 cup buckwheat flour with ¼ teaspoon salt and ¼ teaspoon ground cinnamon. Stir in 1 well-beaten egg and 4 cups water to form a thin, smooth batter. Proceed as above, turning the pan as you add the batter to spread it as thinly as possible. Fry on both sides. To serve as a dessert, spread the crêpe with a purée of pumpkin, sweet potato or chestnut, or with apple butter or *tahini*. Makes 12.

Sarasin Yaki

2 cups buckwheat flour
1 teaspoon sea salt
2 tablespoons sesame or corn oil
2 cups boiling water

Preheat oven to 350°F. Combine flour and salt: mix well. Add oil, and rub mixture through palms to blend it evenly. Add boiling water while stirring vigorously with 4 long wooden chopsticks (to keep sticking to a minimum). When well mixed, form dough into flattened rounds approximately $\frac{1}{3}$ inch thick. Decorate in one of the following ways:

*Shape into floral, leaf or fan designs.
*Indent and fill with an almond, peanut or cashew.
*Sprinkle with sesame seeds.

Place on a lightly oiled cookie sheet and bake for 25 minutes, or until nicely browned.

Okonomi Yaki

MAKES 15 PANCAKES

1 tablespoon sesame oil
1 cup onion crescents
$\frac{3}{4}$ cup shredded cabbage
$\frac{1}{4}$ cup slivered carrot
1 teaspoon and a dash of sea salt
$\frac{1}{2}$ cup buckwheat flour
$\frac{1}{2}$ cup unbleached white flour
4 cups water
Oil for frying

Heat a heavy skillet and coat with 1 tablespoon oil. Sauté onion over medium heat for 2 or 3 minutes, stirring gently, until its strong aroma is no longer released. Add cabbage, then carrot, and sauté together for 2 or 3 minutes more. Mix ingredients together, sprinkle with a dash of salt, and turn off heat.

Combine buckwheat and unbleached flour and remaining 1 teaspoon salt, mixing well. Add water to form a batter, stirring until smooth. Heat a heavy skillet and brush lightly with oil. Ladle in enough batter to cover surface of pan, and immediately sprinkle sautéed vegetables over surface of batter. Fry until set; turn carefully with a thin spatula, and brown second side for less than 1 minute. Roll or fold. Serve with a mock Béchamel or clear *kuzu*-vegetable sauce.

KOFU: WHEAT GLUTEN

Kofu is a valuable source of protein that may be eaten during any season. It has always been popular among vegetarian peoples throughout the world. First introduced to Japan from China by Buddhist monks, *kofu* became a very popular food in Zen temples. It is delicious in soups and stews and mixed with sautéed vegetables. *Kofu* cutlet looks, feels, and tastes like meat.

Homemade Kofu *(Wheat Gluten)*   MAKES 5 CUPS

> 10 cups whole-wheat flour
> 4 cups unbleached white flour
> 2 teaspoons sea salt dissolved in 5 cups cold water

Combine the flours in a large bowl; mix well. Add salted water to form a dough. Knead vigorously for 20 to 30 minutes until dough is smooth and soft. Set dough aside in a large dry bowl and let stand, uncovered, for 40 minutes.

Cover dough with $2\frac{1}{2}$ quarts cold water, and knead vigorously. When water clouds with a cream-colored sediment (starch), drain off liquid and reserve for use in baking. Add 10 more cups fresh water, knead, and drain. Repeat this procedure 5 more times, or until water is only lightly sedimented. After final draining, knead dough well until stiff.

Wrap gluten dough in a damp cloth and steam over high heat for 30 minutes; or pinch off small pieces, about 1 inch square, drop them into $2\frac{1}{2}$ quarts boiling water, and cook until they rise to the surface. Drain, then cool the gluten thoroughly under running cold water. Refrigerate to store.

The gluten may be eaten as is, seasoned with *shoyu* to taste; or it may be prepared in either of the following ways:

Kofu Loaf:
> $2\frac{1}{2}$ cups what gluten
> $1\frac{1}{2}$ cups sweet brown rice flour
> $1\frac{1}{2}$ cups whole-wheat pastry flour

Combine the ingredients in a large bowl, mixing well. Knead vigorously for 20 to 30 minutes until dough is smooth. Pat out into a rectangular loaf 5 by 6 inches and 2 inches thick. Bring 1 quart water to a boil and drop in the loaf. Return to a boil, reduce heat, and simmer for 20 minutes; or steam the loaf over high heat for 30 minutes. Drain loaf and allow to cool thoroughly.

Seitan:
> 1 tablespoon sesame oil
> 1 tablespoon minced gingerroot
> 1 to 2 cups *shoyu*
> 5 cups cold wheat gluten, separated into small pieces

Heat a heavy saucepan and coat with the oil. Sauté gingerroot over medium heat for 3 or 4 minutes, stirring gently. Pour in *shoyu* and bring to a boil. Drop in the pieces of wheat gluten, reduce heat and simmer, covered, stirring frequently, for 3 hours. Uncover and continue to simmer until all liquid has been absorbed or evaporated.

Refrigerate to store for long periods.

Kofu Cutlet

Oil for deep-frying
½ pound *kofu* loaf, cut lengthwise into
    halves
4 cups *kombu dashi* (p. 136)
1 teaspoon and a dash of sea salt
6 tablespoons *shoyu*
1 cup unbleached white flour
⅔ cup water, approximately
2 cups bread crumbs or cornmeal
1 tablespoon sesame oil
4 medium-size cabbage leaves, shredded
¾ cup slivered carrot
Parsley sprigs
5 red radishes, cut into flowers

Fill a heavy skillet or deep-fryer with 3 inches of oil. Bring to 360° F. over slow heat. Drop the two *kofu* halves into the hot oil and deep-fry for 3 to 5 minutes. Drain *kofu* and slice crosswise into strips about ⅓ inch wide.

Bring the *dashi* to a boil and add 1 teaspoon salt and the *shoyu*. Drop in the *kofu* strips, return to the boil, and cook until all liquid has been absorbed or evaporated and the *kofu* is well flavored. Drain, then dip *kofu* into a thin batter made of the white flour and ⅔ cup water. Roll strips in bread crumbs, coating thoroughly, then drop into hot oil once again and deep-fry for 5 minutes, or until nicely browned and crisp. Drain on absorbent paper.

Heat a heavy skillet and coat with the sesame oil. Sauté the cabbage and carrot over high heat, stirring constantly, for 5 minutes. Season with a dash of salt. Arrange vegetables on serving dishes to form a bed for the cutlet strips. Serve garnished with sprigs of parsley and red radish flowers.

II. VEGETABLES FROM LAND AND SEA

DAILY VEGETABLE DISHES

There are many ways to cook vegetables: we can boil, bake, steam, deep-fry or sauté. Vegetable *nitsuke* is the most widely used method of preparing vegetables in the macrobiotic diet. There are two ways to make *nitsuke*. The first method is quick and the vegetables are crisp when done. Cut the vegetables into slivers or very thin pieces and sauté in a little corn or sesame oil over medium heat for 5 minutes. Reduce heat and sauté for 10 minutes more, stirring constantly. Season with salt or *shoyu* and remove from heat.

The second method uses water; the vegetables are more tender when done and can be cut into thicker slices at the outset. Sauté the vegetables in oil over medium heat, then add enough water to cover either the surface of the pan or the vegetables themselves, depending upon your ingredients. Cook until the vegetables have reached the desired degree of tenderness. Add water occasionally if necessary to prevent burning. Season with salt when the vegetables first begin to soften or midway in the cooking. Add *shoyu* or *miso* at the end. If water remains when the vegetables are done, uncover and simmer until evaporated.

Vegetables that contain a great deal of moisture, like green leafy heads, can cook in their own fluids or just a little water.

Burdock, Carrot and Lotus Root Kimpira

SERVES 5

1½ tablespoons corn or sesame oil
1 cup slivered burdock root*
½ cup thin gingko leaves of lotus root
½ cup slivered carrot
Dash of sea salt
2 tablespoons *shoyu*, approximately

Heat a heavy skillet and coat with oil. Add the burdock slivers (they should sizzle softly as soon as they touch the surface of the pan) and sauté over medium heat until they no longer release their strong aroma. Stir constantly to coat the slivers evenly with oil and prevent burning. Add lotus slices, then the carrot slivers, mixing the ingredients together. Sauté for 1 or 2 minutes longer, then add enough water to cover bottom of pan. Season with a dash of salt, cover pan, and reduce heat. Simmer for 25 to 30 minutes, or until the vegetables are tender, adding water occasionally if necessary.

Uncover, season with *shoyu* to taste, and simmer until dry while gently shaking the pan (stirring will make the burdock sticky). Serve 2 to 3 tablespoons per person.

VARIATIONS: A. Change the proportions of the vegetables to make lotus root the major ingredient. Used traditionally in the Orient in the treatment of respiratory ailments. The burdock may be shaved as well as slivered.

B. Make delicious *kimpira* using other combinations of vegetables.

*The nutritious burdock root, cultivated in Japan, plays an important roll in the macrobiotic diet.

Burdock with Sesame

SERVES 5

1 burdock root (¾ inch thick)
1½ tablespoons corn or sesame oil
Shoyu
3 tablespoons toasted white sesame seeds

Scrub the burdock with a natural fiber brush *(tawashi)*, then cut into logs that will fit your skillet. Heat the oil and sauté the burdock until its strong aroma is no longer released. Add slightly more than enough water to cover and bring to a boil. Cover pan and cook until burdock is tender and no longer resistant to the insertion of a food pick or skewer. Add water during cooking if necessary. Season with *shoyu* to taste, and simmer until dry.

Cut the logs into ⅔-inch lengths and serve upright, topped with a sprinkling of toasted sesame seeds.

Burdock with Miso and Lemon Peel

SERVES 5

2 tablespoons sesame oil
2½ cups thin rounds of burdock root
1 to 2 tablespoons *miso*
3 to 6 tablespoons water
3 tablespoons white sesame seeds, toasted
1 teaspoon minced lemon peel

Heat a heavy skillet and coat with oil. Sauté the burdock rounds until their strong aroma is no longer released. Add water to cover, bring to a boil, and cover pan. Cook until tender, adding water occasionally if necessary.

Thin *miso* in 3 parts water and add to the pan when burdock is ready. Stir and simmer over very low heat until all liquid has evaporated. Add sesame seeds and lemon peel, and sauté together for 1 or 2 minutes more.

For balance, serve with lightly boiled green beans, spinach or trefoil.

Deep-Fried Burdock Roll

SERVES 5

Oil for deep-frying
2 cups grated burdock root
1 cup grated carrot
½ cup minced onion
½ cup unbleached white flour
Shoyu

Pour 3 inches of oil into a heavy skillet or deep-fryer and heat to 330° F. Combine burdock, carrot and onion, and add enough of the flour to hold the mixture together. Put 1 heaping tablespoon of the mixture at the edge of a spatula and form into a log approximately ½ inch in diameter. Using chopsticks, nudge the log into the hot oil and deep-fry until lightly browned and crisp. (If the oil is too hot, the logs will burn.) Drain on absorbent paper. Apportion the burdock rolls among 5 individual serving dishes and allow each person to season them to his taste with *shoyu*.

Isomaki Gobo *(Burdock Wrapped in Nori)*   SERVES 5

Oil for deep-frying
2 cups grated burdock root
1 teaspoon grated gingerroot juice
¼ cup unbleached white flour
1 sheet of *nori*
1 tablespoon *miso*
2 tablespoons *tahini* (sesame butter)
Water

Pour 3 inches of oil into a heavy skillet or deep-fryer and heat to 330°F. Combine burdock and gingerroot juice, and add enough of the flour to hold the mixture together. Form into a log and place at one edge of the *nori*. Combine 1 tablespoon of the unused flour with 1 tablespoon water to form a thin paste. Roll the *nori* into a cylinder. Seal the edge of the cylinder with the flour paste and drop into the hot oil. Deep-fry until crisp, and drain on absorbent paper. Slice while still warm.

Grind the *miso* and *tahini* together in a *suribachi*. Thin with water to the desired consistency and serve over the *nori*-roll slices.

Gobo Age *(Deep-Fried Burdock in Pastry)*   SERVES 5

1 cup whole-wheat flour
½ teaspoon sea salt
3 tablespoons sesame or corn oil
¼ to ½ cup water, approximately
5 burdock logs (3 inches long)
Shoyu
Oil for deep-frying

Combine flour and salt, mixing well. Add 2 tablespoons oil, rubbing the mixture between palms to blend evenly. Add water gradually to form an elastic dough, and knead lightly for several minutes until smooth. Form into a ball, wrap in a damp cloth, and let stand in a cold place for 30 mintues.

Heat remaining 1 tablespoon oil in a heavy skillet. Sauté the burdock until its strong aroma is no longer released. Add water to cover, bring to a boil, and cover pan. Cook for 30 minutes, or until burdock is tender and no longer resistant to the insertion of a food pick or skewer. Season generously with *shoyu* so that it permeates the logs and simmer until dry.

Pour 3 inches of oil into a heavy skillet or deep-fryer and heat to 350°F. Roll out the dough on a floured board into a thin rectangular sheet 3 inches wide. Place 1 burdock log at the edge of the dough and roll to cover. Cut roll away from the sheet and seal the roll's seam with a few drops of water. Repeat until all ingredients are used. Drop the rolls into the hot oil and deep-fry until golden and crisp. Drain on absorbent paper, then slice on the diagonal into 1-inch pieces.

DAILY DISHES

Broccoli and Radish with Miso Dip   SERVES 5

2 teaspoons sea salt
1 small broccoli, separated into flowerets
1½ cups *daikon* cubes
3 to 5 tablespoons *shoyu*
1 heaping tablespoon *miso*
Pinch of pepper

Bring 6 cups of water to a boil and add 1 teaspoon salt. Drop in the broccoli flowerets, return to the boil, and cook for 5 minutes, or until flowerets are bright green and just tender. Dip flowerets into a basin of cold water to stop the cooking and set the color, and drain in a colander.

Bring 3 cups water to a boil in a separate pan and add remaining 1 teaspoon salt. Drop in the *daikon* cubes, return to the boil, and cook for 5 to 10 minutes, or until tender. Season lightly with *shoyu* and simmer for several minutes more. Drain and allow to cool.

Grind the *miso* in a *suribachi*, adding a pinch of pepper and a little water to achieve a thick, creamy consistency. Arrange 2 or 3 broccoli flowerets and 5 or 6 *daikon* cubes on a serving dish with a small mound of *miso* cream for dipping. Serve at room temperature.

Broccoli Cream Ni   SERVES 5

½ teaspoon sea salt
½ small broccoli, separated into
   flowerets
Mock Béchamel sauce (p. 162)
Parsley sprigs

Bring a small pan of water to a boil and add the salt. Drop in the broccoli flowerets, return to the boil, and cook for 5 minutes, or until bright green and just tender. Dip into a basin of cold water to stop the cooking, and drain in a colander.

Prepare the mock Béchamel sauce. Approximately 5 minutes before the sauce is done, add the broccoli flowerets and simmer together. Serve garnished with parsley.

Cabbage and Carrot Nitsuke

SERVES 5

2 tablespoons sesame oil
4 or 5 leaves of cabbage, chopped
½ small carrot, slivered
½ teaspoon sea salt, approximately

Heat the oil in a heavy skillet. Add the cabbage and sauté briskly over high heat, stirring constantly. After 1 or 2 minutes, add the carrot slivers and sauté together. Cover pan, reduce heat to very low, and simmer for 10 to 15 minutes. Season with salt to taste.

Cabbage Sesame-Ae

SERVES 5

1 teaspoon and a dash of sea salt
4 or 5 cabbage leaves
1 tablespoon sesame oil
½ small carrot, slivered
2 tablespoons white sesame seeds, washed
1 tablespoon *shoyu*
3 tablespoons water, approximately

Bring a pan of water (just enough to cover the cabbage leaves) to a boil and add 1 teaspoon salt. Using long chopsticks, hold the stems of the cabbage leaves down in the water and cook until tender. Submerge the upper portion of the leaves for an instant, then drain and chop the leaves fine.

Heat the oil in a heavy skillet and sauté the carrot, stirring constantly, for 4 or 5 minutes, or until it begins to soften. Season with a dash of salt and remove from heat.

In a separate skillet, toast the sesame seeds over moderately high heat for 4 or 5 minutes, or until browned and fragrant. Stir constantly and shake the pan to prevent scorching. Empty seeds into a *suribachi* and grind to a paste, adding *shoyu* and water. Add cabbage and carrot slivers and toss the ingredients together.

Cabbage Rolls

MAKES 10 ROLLS

10 cabbage leaves
3 *shiitake* (dried Japanese mushrooms)
2 tablespoons sesame oil
1 small onion, cut into thin half-moons
1 small carrot, slivered
Dash of sea salt
1 piece of *kombu*, 2 inches square
4 to 6 tablespoons *shoyu*
1 cup mock Béchamel sauce (p. 162)
1 or 2 teaspoons minced parsley

Put the cabbage leaves in a colander and douse them with boiling water until they start to wilt. Drain, then trim the cores smooth and set the leaves aside. Soak the *shiitake* in lightly salted water for 20 to 30 minutes; remove tough stems and slice mushrooms fine.

Heat a heavy skillet and coat with the oil. Sauté the onion over medium heat for 5 minutes, or until lightly browned. Add carrot slivers, then mushroom slices, and mix ingredients together. Season with a dash of salt, and turn off heat.

Place 2 or 3 tablespoons of the sautéed vegetables at the end of a cabbage leaf, and roll the leaf to cover filling. Tuck in edges of leaf, roll again, and secure with a food pick. Repeat with remaining ingredients until all are used.

Put the *kombu* in a saucepan and arrange the cabbage rolls above it. Add just enough water to cover the ingredients and bring rapidly to a boil. Simmer for 10 minutes. Season with 1 tablespoon *shoyu* per cup of water used to cover, and simmer for 10 minutes more. Turn off heat, then drain cabbage rolls. Serve topped with mock Béchamel sauce and a sprinkling of minced parsley.

Rolled Cabbage Gratin MAKES 10 ROLLS

1 cup *kombu dashi* (p. 136)
2 tablespoons *shoyu*
¼ pound *kofu* (p. 85), or substitute 5 tablespoons minced *seitan*
1 ounce *biifun* (transparent noodles), or substitute 1 ounce cooked vermicelli
10 cabbage leaves
2 tablespoons corn or sesame oil
1 small onion, minced
1 small carrot, slivered
Dash of sea salt
Oil
1 cup mock Béchamel sauce (p. 162)
2 tablespoons minced parsley

Combine *dashi, shoyu* and *kofu* (or *seitan*) in a small pan and bring to a boil. Cook until all liquid has been absorbed or evaporated and the *kofu* has been well flavored. Drain *kofu,* and dice. Boil the *biifun* for 2 to 4 minutes; drain, then cut into 2-inch lengths. Put the cabbage leaves in a colander and douse them with boiling water until they start to wilt. Drain, then trim the cores smooth and set the leaves aside.

Heat a heavy skillet and coat with the oil. Sauté the onion over medium heat for 5 minutes, or until lightly browned. Add carrot slivers, then *kofu* (or *seitan*), sautéing each lightly as you add it. Season with a dash of salt, add *biifun,* and mix ingredients together. Remove from heat.

Place 2 or 3 tablespoons of the vegetable and noodle mixture at the end of a cabbage leaf, and roll the leaf to cover filling. Tuck in edges of leaf, roll again, and secure with a food pick. Repeat with remaining ingredients until all are used.

Place rolls on a generously oiled baking pan and bake in a preheated 425°F. over for 15 minutes. Serve individual portions with mock Béchamel sauce, topped with a sprinkling of minced parsley.

Chinese Cabbage Rolls SERVES 5

1½ teaspoons sea salt
9 Chinese cabbage leaves
1 bunch of watercress, or ½ pound spinach

Bring 6 cups of water to a boil and add 1 teaspoon salt. Using long chopsticks, hold the stems of the Chinese cabbage leaves in the water and cook until they are just tender. Submerge the upper portion of the leaves for an instant, then dip the leaves into a basin of cold water. Drain the leaves, then trim the cores smooth.

Bring a small pan of water (enough to cover the watercress) to a boil and add remaining ½ teaspoon salt. Drop in the watercress (or spinach), return to the boil, and cook until the stems are tender. Dip leaves into cold water to stop the cooking, then squeeze to rid them of excess water.

Place 3 cabbage leaves, their edges overlapping, on a *sudare* or bamboo mat. (Arrange the cabbage with stems and leaves overlapping alternately.) Lay the watercress or spinach in a neat double row (alternating stem and leaf) horizontally across the center. Roll from the wide edge of the mat into a tight cylinder. Squeeze roll to remove excess water, then remove *sudare,* and slice the roll into 1-inch-thick sections. Repeat with remaining ingredients until all are used. Serve with lemon or orange *shoyu* (p. 163).

VARIATIONS: A. For added color place a row of boiled carrot slivers alongside the watercress before rolling.

B. Add 3 pieces of *aburage* (fried bean curd) to the ingredients listed above. Douse the *aburage* with boiling water, and drain. Using scissors, open the pieces by cutting into 1 long and 2 short sides. Bring to a boil in water to cover, and add 2 tablespoons *shoyu* for each cup of water used. Cover pan with a tight-fitting lid and cook until all liquid has been absorbed or evaporated and the *aburage* is well flavored. Allow to cool, then place 1 piece on a *sudare* or bamboo mat. Place 3 cabbage leaves on top of the *aburage* and proceed as above.

Carrot with Green Beans and Tofu   SERVES 5

    1 teaspoon sea salt
    10 green beans, rinsed and trimmed
    1 tablespoon sesame oil
    1 small carrot, slivered
    ½ cake of *tofu*, drained and mashed (p. 173)

Bring a small pan of water (enough to cover the beans) to a boil and add ½ teaspoon salt. Drop in the green beans, return to the boil, and cook for 5 minutes, or until beans are bright green and just tender. Dip beans into a basin of cold water to stop the cooking. Drain and slice beans fine on the diagonal.

    Heat the oil in a heavy skillet. Sauté the carrot slivers for 5 minutes, stirring constantly to coat them evenly with oil. Season with remaining ½ teaspoon salt; remove from heat and allow to cool.

    Add the cooled beans and carrot slivers to the *tofu* and mix thoroughly. Serve small portions as a delicate side dish, to be seasoned with *shoyu* to taste.

Ninjin Shiro-Ae *(White Carrot Mix)*   SERVES 5

    1 ounce *shirataki* (transparent noodles)
    1 tablespoon corn or sesame oil
    1 small carrot, sliced fine on the diagonal
    ½ teaspoon sea salt
    1 tablespoon white sesame seeds, toasted
    ½ cake of *tofu*, drained and mashed (p. 173)
    Shoyu

Drop the *shirataki* into a pan of boiling water and cook for 2 or 3 minutes; drain and set aside.

    Sauté the carrot slices in the oil over medium heat for 3 or 4 minutes, or until they begin to soften. Add the *shirataki* and sauté together for several minutes more. Season with salt, remove from heat, and allow to cool.

    Add carrot-*shirataki* mixture and the sesame seeds to the *tofu* and toss together. Season with *shoyu* to taste.

Ninjin Soboro *(Carrot with Sesame)*   SERVES 5

    1 tablespoon sesame oil
    1 cup grated carrot
    ½ teaspoon sea salt
    2 tablespoons white sesame seeds, toasted

Heat the oil in a heavy skillet. Sauté the carrot over medium heat, stirring constantly, for 5 minutes. Season with salt, then stir in the sesame seeds. Sauté for several minutes more and serve.

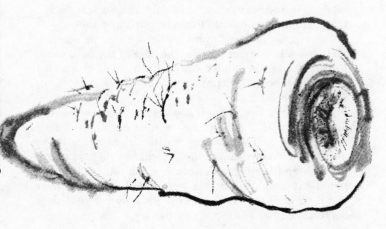

Ninjin Shinoda (*Carrot with Aburage*) SERVES 6

3 pieces of *aburage* (fried bean curd)
12 strips (3 inches long) of *kampyo* (gourd)
2 or 3 medium-size carrots
6 cups *kombu dashi* (p. 136), approximately
½ to ¾ cup *shoyu*
Parsley sprigs

Douse the *aburage* with boiling water, and drain. Using scissors, open the pieces by cutting into 1 long and 2 short sides. Soak the *kampyo* in lightly salted water until pliable, and sqeeze dry. Quarter the carrots lengthwise, then trim the carrot sticks to the length of the *aburage*.

Put 1 piece of fried bean curd on a *sudare* or bamboo mat, and pile 3 carrot sticks at the edge of the bean curd. Roll into a tight cylinder and tie with gourd strips at 4 equidistant points. Repeat with remaining ingredients until all are used.

Bring to the boil enough *kombu dashi* to cover the rolls and season with 2 tablespoons *shoyu* for each cup of *dashi* used. Put in the rolls and cover with a tight-fitting lid or one from a smaller saucepan that will rest directly above the rolls and keep them in place. Cook until half of the liquid has been absorbed or evaporated; turn rolls over and cook until dry. Drain rolls thoroughly before slicing. Serve garnished with sprigs of parsley.

Celery Nitsuke SERVES 5

1 or 2 celery stalks
1 tablespoon corn or sesame oil
Shoyu

Slice the celery stalks on the diagonal into bite-size pieces. Heat the oil in a skillet, add the celery, and sauté briskly over high heat for several minutes. Cover the bottom of the pan with a mixture of equal parts *shoyu* and water, reduce heat, and simmer to the desired degree of tenderness.

Celery Goma-Ae (*Celery with Sesame*) SERVES 5

1 celery stalk
½ teaspoon sea salt
3 tablespoons black sesame seeds, washed
1 or 2 tablespoons *shoyu*
2 tablespoons water

Shave the celery stalk into thick pieces. Bring a small pan of water to a boil and add the salt. Drop in the celery and cook for 30 seconds. Drain thoroughly and allow to cool.

Toast the sesame seeds in a heavy skillet over moderately high heat for 5 minutes, or until browned and fragrant. Empty the seeds into a *suribachi* and grind to a paste, adding *shoyu* and water. Add the celery to the *suribachi* and toss the ingredients together. A delicious side dish that goes well with fish.

VARIATION: Cut the stalk into 1½-inch lengths and drop into salted boiling water. Cook for less than a minute, then drain and slice each piece into thin strips. Toss with mayonnaise (p. 164) lightly seasoned with *shoyu*.

Cucumber with Wakame and Walnut Miso SERVES 5

1 cup *wakame*
1 cucumber
Dash of sea salt
Walnut *miso* (p. 163)

Soak the *wakame* in water for 10 to 15 minutes, or until soft and pliable. Separate the leaves from the tough stem and chop the leaves into small pieces.

Trim the tips from the cucumber and rub them against the exposed ends until a white foam is no longer released. Rinse away the foam, then slice the cucumber fine on the diagonal. Rub salt into the slices and set aside for 10 minutes. Now squeeze the slices to remove excess liquid.

Toss *wakame* leaves and cucumber together. Serve with walnut *miso* for dipping.

Cucumbers with Miso and Sesame   SERVES 5

2 cucumbers
1 teaspoon *miso*
3 to 4 teaspoons water
1 tablespoon toasted sesame seeds

Trim the tips from the cucumbers, then rub them against
the exposed ends until a white foam is no longer released;
rinse away the foam. Slice one cucumber fine on the
diagonal, then cut the other lengthwise into halves; cut
each half into large pieces and score each piece to about
three-fourths its depth. Now thin the *miso* with the water,
and dip the cucumber slices into the mixture, coating
thoroughly. Serve topped with toasted sesame seeds.

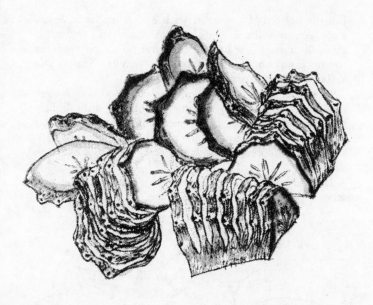

Daikon Mizunashidaki *(Daikon Nitsuke)*   SERVES 5

2 tablespoons corn or sesame oil
1½ cups thin half-moons of onion
1 cup thin half-moons of *daikon*
¾ cup thin gingko leaves of carrot
3 pieces of *aburage* (fried bean curd), cut
    into thin strips
Shoyu

Heat a heavy skillet and coat with the oil. Sauté the
onions over medium heat, stirring gently, for 2 or 3
minutes, or until translucent. Add *daikon*, carrot, and
aburage, in that order, sautéing each lightly as you add
it. Reduce heat to low, cover pan, and simmer for 15 to
20 minutes. Add a little water only if necessary to
prevent burning. Season with *shoyu* to taste.

Furofuki Daikon *(Steamed Daikon)*   SERVES 5

         Kombu dashi (p. 136)
         10 rounds (¾ inch thick) of *daikon*
         Sea salt
         3 tablespoons black sesame seeds, washed
         1 tablespoon *miso*

Fill the bottom of a steamer with 2 to 3 inches of *kombu dashi*. Arrange the *daikon* above the *dashi* and steam for 20 to 30 minutes, or until tender and no longer resistant to the insertion of a food pick or skewer. Season the *daikon* with salt to accentuate its sweetness.

Dry-roast the sesame seeds in a heavy skillet over moderately high heat, stirring constantly, until lightly toasted and fragrant. Empty seeds into a *suribachi* and grind to a paste. Blend in *miso* and thin the mixture with 2 or 3 tablespoons of the *kombu dashi* used to steam the *daikon*.

Divide the *daikon* among 5 individual serving dishes and serve topped with sesame-*miso* sauce.

VARIATION: Bring 5 to 6 cups of *kombu dashi* (enough to more than cover the *daikon*) to a boil and add 1 or 2 tablespoons *shoyu* for each cup of *dashi* used. Drop in the *daikon* and cook for 30 minutes, or until tender. Serve alone or topped with sesame-*miso* sauce.

Daikon no Ha Nitsuke   SERVES 5
(Nitsuke of Daikon Leaves)

         2 tablespoons sesame oil
         Leaves from 1 *daikon*, chopped
         2 pieces of *aburage*, slivered
         Shoyu

Heat the oil in a heavy skillet. Add the leaves and sauté over medium heat for 5 minutes, or until the leaves have wilted. Add the *aburage* and sauté together for 1 or 2 minutes more. Season with *shoyu* to taste. Delicious served with brown rice.

Kiriboshi Daikon Nitsuke   SERVES 5
(Nitsuke of Dried Daikon)

         1 ounce dried *daikon*
         2 tablespoons sesame oil
         3 pieces of *aburage*, slivered
         Shoyu

Rinse the *daikon* in cold water and cut into 1-inch lengths. Heat the oil in a skillet and sauté the *daikon* over medium heat for 5 minutes. Add the *aburage* and toss the pan to mix the ingredients together. Add water to cover, bring to a boil, and cover the pan. Cook for 30 to 45 minutes, or until the *daikon* is tender, adding a little water occasionally if necessary. Season with *shoyu* and simmer until dry.

VARIATION: The *daikon* may be soaked in cold water for 15 minutes before cooking. Use the soaking water in the cooking, and reduce cooking time accordingly.

Katsura Maki *(Daikon Rolls)*   SERVES 5

7½ inches *daikon*, cut into 5 equal lengths
Sea salt
½ bunch watercress
1 teaspoon sesame oil
10 thin diagonal slices of carrot
¼ cake of *tofu*, drained and mashed (p. 173)
1 teaspoon lemon juice

Pare each piece of *daikon* to half its width in a long continuous strip. Roll out the *daikon* sheets and sprinkle lightly with salt. Re-roll, press with palm to soften, and set aside.

Bring a small pan of water to a boil and add ¼ teaspoon salt. Drop in the watercress, return to the boil, and cook for 1 or 2 minutes, or until the stems are tender. Dip the leaves into a basin of cold water and drain in a colander. Arrange the watercress into a neat bundle, alternating leaves and stems, and cut into 1½-inch mounds.

Heat the oil in a heavy skillet and sauté the carrot slices over medium heat for 5 minutes, or until they begin to soften. Sprinkle carrot with a dash of salt and remove from heat. When cooled to room temperature, add to *tofu* and mix thoroughly.

Unroll the *daikon* sheets. Spread the *tofu*-carrot mixture at the narrow edge of each sheet and place a mound of watercress on top of the *tofu*. Now re-roll into a cylinder and tie with string at 2 points ⅓ inch distant from the ends of each roll. Cut rolls into halves, remove strings, and sprinkle each roll with 1 or 2 drops of lemon juice.

Yaki Nasu *(Sautéed Eggplant)*   SERVES 5

5 small eggplants
2 tablespoons sesame oil

Cut the eggplants lengthwise into halves. Score the outer surface in a checkerboard pattern to a depth of ⅓ inch. Heat the oil in a skillet, add the eggplant, and sauté over low heat until browned and tender. Serve with *goma miso* (p. 164).

VARIATION: Simmer whole eggplants in the oil until no longer resistant to the insertion of a food pick or skewer. Trim off eggplant tops and peel away skins. Serve with walnut *miso* (p.163).

Daikon Onamasu   SERVES 5
(Blanched Daikon with Carrot)

1½ cups slivered *daikon*
½ cup slivered carrot
Sea salt
½ to 1 teaspoon minced lemon rind
1 cup *shoyu*
1 cup water
1 teaspoon lemon juice

Sprinkle the *daikon* and carrot with sea salt and place in separate colanders. Douse each with boiling water, then press to soften and drain thoroughly. Toss the *daikon*, carrot and lemon rind together. Serve with a dipping sauce of equal parts *shoyu* and water accented with a little lemon juice. Delicious with *yang* animal food; very refreshing in summer.

Endive with Sesame Nitsuke   SERVES 5

1 tablespoon sesame oil
5 small Belgian endives
2 tablespoons *tahini* (sesame butter)
2 tablespoons *shoyu*
2 tablespoons water

Heat a heavy skillet and coat with the oil. Add the whole endives carefully and sauté over low heat for 2 to 4 minutes. Cover pan and simmer for 10 minutes more. Combine *tahini*, *shoyu* and water, and add to the pan. Simmer together for 15 minutes, or until endives are tender.

    DAILY DISHES

Onion Nitsuke with Sesame   SERVES 5

> 1 tablespoon sesame or corn oil
> 3 cups thin half-moons of onion
> 1 teaspoon sea salt
> 1 or 2 tablespoons sesame seeds, washed

Heat the oil in a heavy skillet. Sauté the onions over medium heat, stirring gently, for 5 minutes or until lightly browned. Reduce heat to low, season with salt, and continue to sauté for about 10 minutes more, or until tender.

Dry-roast the sesame seeds in another skillet over moderately high heat until toasted and fragrant. Stir the seeds into the onion, mixing well, and serve.

Onion Nitsuke with Miso   SERVES 5

> 2 tablespoons sesame oil
> 2 medium-size onions, sliced into thin half-moons
> 1 heaping tablespoon *miso*, thinned in $\frac{1}{3}$ cup water

Heat the oil in a heavy skillet. Sauté the onions over medium heat, stirring gently, for 5 minutes or until lightly browned. Add the thinned *miso*, cover pan, and simmer for 20 to 30 minutes, or until onions are tender and the liquid has evaporated. Do not stir while the mixture simmers.

Onion Goma-Miso-Ae   SERVES 5 OR 6
(Onion with Sesame-Miso)

> 2 medium-size onions
> 1 teaspoon sea salt
> 1 tablespoon *miso*
> 1 tablespoon *tahini* (sesame butter)

Slice each onion into 6 half-moons. Bring a small pan of water (enough to cover the onions) to a boil and add the salt. Drop in the onions, return to the boil, and cook for 15 to 20 minutes, or until tender. Blend the *miso* and *tahini* in a *suribachi,* and thin the mixture with 2 or 3 tablespoons of the cooking water. Add the onions and toss the ingredients together.

Kiku Onions (Chrysanthemum Onions)   SERVES 5

> 5 medium-size onions
> 4 cups *kombu dashi* (p. 136)
> 2 teaspoons sea salt
> $\frac{3}{4}$ cup pumpkin purée or lightly salted grated carrot

Quarter the onions to three-fourths their depth, but leave the bottoms intact. Combine with the *dashi* and salt in a saucepan and bring to a boil. Cook for 15 minutes, then remove onions and drain. Carefully slice each onion quarter lengthwise into halves and slowly spread the halves apart to create a chrysanthemum shape. Fill the onion centers with 2 to 3 tablespoons of pumpkin purée or grated carrot, and serve with *goma miso* (p. 164).

Eggplant Nabeshigi-yaki   SERVES 5
(Eggplant with Miso)

> 5 small eggplants
> 2 tablespoons sesame oil
> 2 or 3 tablespoons *miso*

Slice whole eggplants into thick rounds. Sauté in the oil over low heat, stirring lightly, for 2 or 3 minutes. Add enough water to half-cover, bring to a boil, and cook for 15 to 20 minutes. Add *miso* thinned in equal parts water, and simmer until dry. Lest the eggplant be bruised do not stir at the end.

VARIATION: Pour 3 inches of oil into a heavy skillet or deep-fryer and heat to 350°F. Cut the eggplants lengthwise into halves and score the outer surfaces on the diagonal. Drop into the hot oil and deep-fry for 2 or 3 minutes, or until cooked through and crisp. Drain on absorbent paper and serve with *tsuke-jiru* dipping sauce (p.163).

Scallion Sesame-Ae   SERVES 5

> 1 teaspoon sea salt
> ½ pound scallions, sliced into 1-inch lengths
> 3 tablespoons white sesame seeds, washed
> 2 tablespoons *shoyu*
> 1 or 2 tablespoons water

Bring 4 to 6 cups of water to a boil and add the salt. Drop in the scallions, return to the boil, and cook for 1 or 2 minutes, until vegetables are bright green. Dip scallions into a basin of cold water and drain thoroughly.

Dry-roast the sesame seeds in a heavy skillet over moderately high heat for 5 minutes, or until lightly toasted and fragrant. Stir constantly and shake the pan to heat evenly. Empty seeds into a *suribachi* and grind to a paste, adding *shoyu* and water. Add scallions and toss the ingredients together.

Scallion and Aburage Nitsuke   SERVES 5

> 1 tablespoon corn or sesame oil
> ½ pound scallions, sliced on the diagonal into 1-inch lengths
> 1 or 2 pieces of *aburage* (fried bean curd), slivered
> *Shoyu*

Heat a heavy skillet and coat with the oil. Sauté the scallions in the order of roots, greens, whites over medium heat, stirring constantly, for 2 or 3 minutes. Add the *aburage* slivers and sauté together for 1 minute more. Add a little water to cover the bottom of the pan and simmer for 15 to 20 minutes. Season with *shoyu* to taste and simmer until dry.

Scallion and Wakame Nuta SERVES 5

1 cup *wakame*
½ teaspoon sea salt
3 or 4 scallions, sliced into 1-inch lengths
1 tablespoon *miso*
1 tablespoon *tahini* (sesame butter)
4 to 5 tablespoons water

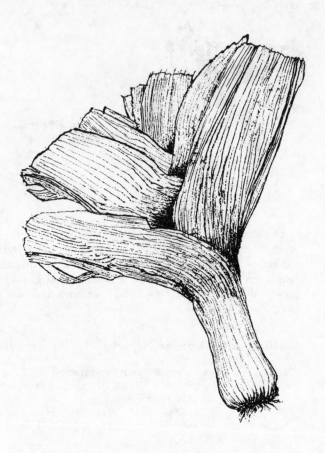

Soak the *wakame* in cold water for 10 to 15 minutes, or until soft and pliable. Separate the leaves from the tough stem and set leaves aside.

Bring a small pan of water (enough to cover the scallions) to a boil and add the salt. Drop in the scallions, return to the boil, and cook for 1 to 2 minutes, or until scallions are bright green. Dip scallions into a basin of cold water and drain thoroughly.

Grind the *miso* and *tahini* together in a *suribachi* and thin with the water. Add *wakame* leaves and scallions and toss the ingredients together.

Scallion Dengaku *(Grilled Scallions)* SERVES 5

4 or 5 scallions or leeks, sliced into 1½-inch lengths
½ cup walnut *miso* (p. 163), approximately

Skewer the scallions, 4 pieces at a time, and grill until nicely browned. Dip into walnut *miso*, grill for 1 minute more, and serve.

Renkon Yuzu-su
(Lotus Root with Lemon Juice)

SERVES 5

1 tablespoon sesame oil
2 cups paper-thin gingko leaves of lotus root
5 to 6 drops of lemon juice
½ teaspoon sea salt

Heat a heavy skillet and coat with the oil. Add the lotus slices and sauté over low heat for 5 minutes, or until the slices turn a light gray. Stir very gently. Add lemon juice and just enough water to prevent burning. Cover pan and simmer for 5 more minutes. Season with the salt, and serve.

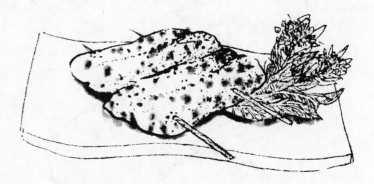

Renkon Ikada Age
with Kuzu-Lemon Sauce

SERVES 5

Oil for deep-frying
2 sheets or *nori*
2 cups grated lotus root
¾ cup grated carrot
1 small onion, minced
1 teaspoon and a dash of salt
1 tablespoon *kuzu*
1 cup *kombu dashi* (p. 136)
½ tablespoon *shoyu*
Few drops of lemon juice

Pour 3 inches of oil into a heavy skillet or deep-fryer and heat to 350°F. Using scissors, cut the *nori* into halves, then cut each half into 3 rectangular pieces. Combine lotus, carrot, onion and a dash of salt. Cover the surface of each piece of *nori* with a layer of this mixture approximately ⅓-inch thick. Quickly score the top of the mixture in a shallow grid pattern with the blade of a *hocho* or heavy knife, then press the back of the knife across the mixture's center. Nudge immediately into the hot oil from the edge of a spatula and deep-fry for 2 or 3 minutes until cooked through and crisp. Drain on absorbent paper

and skewer 2 on each of 6 bamboo skewers. Serve with *kuzu*-lemon sauce.

Dissolve the *kuzu* in the *dashi* and bring to a boil. Add remaining 1 teaspoon salt, the *shoyu* and lemon juice, and simmer for several minutes until thick, stirring constantly.

Jinenjo Age Ni

SERVES 5

Oil for deep-frying
15 thin rounds of *jinenjo*
1 or 2 tablespoons *shoyu*

Pour 3 inches of oil into a heavy skillet or deep-fryer and heat to 350°F. Drop in the *jinenjo* rounds and deep-fry until crisp and golden. Remove round from the oil and transfer immediately to a small skillet. Sprinkle with *shoyu* and simmer until dry. Delicious and very invigorating.

DAILY DISHES

Jinenjo Burgers *(Wild Mountain Potato)* SERVES 5

1 tablespoon sesame oil
1½ cups minced onions
1 small carrot, slivered
2½ cups grated *jinenjo*
½ teaspoon sea salt
½ cup whole-wheat flour, approximately
Oil for frying
1 tablespoon scallion rounds

Heat a heavy skillet and coat with 1 tablespoon oil. Sauté the onions over medium heat, stirring gently, for 2 or 3 minutes, or until translucent. Add carrot and sauté for 2 or 3 minutes more, or until carrot begins to soften. Remove from heat and add to the *jinenjo*, mixing thoroughly. Season the mixture with salt and add enough of the flour to hold it together. Form into 5 patties and brown in a well-oiled skillet. Cook for 15 to 20 minutes, until cooked through.

To 1 tablespoon oil remaining after frying add 2 tablespoons of the unused flour and cook, stirring constantly, for 4 or 5 minutes. Allow flour to cool, then stir in 1 cup water and bring just to a boil. Serve flour sauce as gravy, and garnish with scallion rounds.

Iso Age Jinenjo SERVES 5

Oil for deep-frying
½ sheet of *nori*
1 cup grated *jinenjo,* approximately

Pour 3 inches of oil into a heavy skillet or deep-fryer and heat to 350°F. Cut the *nori* into 4 strips and cut each strip into 4 small rectangular pieces. Coat half of each piece with the grated *jinenjo* and drop into the hot oil. Deep-fry until crisp and golden. Drain on a wire rack or absorbent paper before serving.

Awayuki Jinenjo
SERVES 5

> 1½ cups stiff-beaten egg whites
> 1½ cups grated *jinenjo*
> ¼ teaspoon sea salt
> 5 pieces of aluminum foil, 3 inches square

Fold the stiff whites into the *jinenjo* and season with salt. Spoon 1 or 2 heaping tablespoons of the mixture onto the center of each piece of foil, gather the corners of the foil together, and twist closed. Steam for 15 to 20 minutes. Remove from foil and serve with lemon *shoyu* (p. 163) for dipping.

Sweet Potato with Sesame
SERVES 6

> 3 small sweet potatoes, peeled, cut
>   crosswise into halves
> Dash of salt
> 1 heaping tablespoon *tahini* (sesame butter)
> 1 teaspoon *shoyu*

Bring the sweet potatoes to a boil in water to cover and add a dash of salt. Cook for 20 to 30 minutes, or until sweet potatoes are tender and the water has been absorbed or evaporated. Blend the *tahini* and *shoyu* and add. Coat the potatoes thoroughly and serve.

Satsumaimo Yokan
SERVES 5 OR MORE

(Sweet Potato Mold)

> 3 cups sweet potato purée
> ½ teaspoon sea salt
> Few tablespoons of *kokoh*

Season the purée with salt to accentuate its sweetness, then press firmly into a lightly rinsed shallow mold. If the purée is too moist blend in a little *kokoh* to thicken it. Cool and allow to harden, then cut into little pieces and serve.

Sweet Potato and Scallion Nitsuke
SERVES 5

> 2 tablespoons sesame oil
> 3 or 4 scallions, sliced into 1-inch lengths
> 15 thick rounds of sweet potato (1 inch
>   thick)
> 4 cups *kombu dashi* (p. 136), approximately
> ¼ teaspoon sea salt
> *Shoyu*

Heat a heavy skillet and coat with the oil. Sauté the scallions over medium heat, stirring constantly, for 2 or 3 minutes. Add the sweet potato and sauté together for several minutes more. Add enough of the *dashi* to cover, bring to a boil, and cover pan. Cook for 20 minutes, or until sweet potato is tender. Season with salt and with *shoyu* to taste, and simmer until dry.

Panfried Sweet Potato
SERVES 5

> 15 diagonal slices of sweet potato (1 inch
>   thick)
> Oil for frying
> 1 cup *goma miso* (p. 164)

Steam the sweet potato for 15 to 20 minutes, or until tender. Transfer to a lightly oiled frypan and brown both sides. Coat each piece lightly with *goma miso* and serve.

Satsumaimo Dengaku
SERVES 5

(Grilled Sweet Potato)

> 5 small sweet potatoes, washed thoroughly
>   but not peeled
> Dash of sea salt
> 1 cup *goma miso* (p. 164)

Bring the unpeeled sweet potatoes to a boil in water to cover and add a dash of salt. Cook for 20 to 30 minutes, or until tender. Skewer each potato on 1 bamboo skewer and grill lightly. Coat with *goma miso* and grill for 1 minute more.

DAILY DISHES

Acorn Squash à la Mode   SERVES 4 OR 5

4 *shiitake* (dried Japanese mushroom)
1 ounce *biifun* (transparent noodles) or cooked vermicelli noodles
2 acorn squash or 1 Hokkaido pumpkin
3 tablespoons sesame oil
1 medium-size onion, cut into thin half-moons
1 small carrot, sliced fine on the diagonal
¼ pound *seitan*, chopped
1¼ teaspoons sea salt
3 tablespoons unbleached white flour
1½ cups water

Soak the *shiitake* in lightly salted water for 20 minutes, or until refreshed. Trim away tough portions of the stems and slice the caps fine. Drop the *biifun* into a pan of boiling water and cook for 2 or 3 minutes. Drain *biifun* thoroughly, cut into 1-inch lengths, and set aside.

Cut off a slice from the stem end of each squash, then hollow the center by scooping out the seeds and filaments.

Heat a heavy skillet and coat with 1 tablespoon oil. Sauté the onion over medium heat, stirring gently, for 5 minutes, or until lightly browned. Add mushrooms, carrot, and *seitan*, in that order, sautéing each lightly as you add it. Now stir in the *biifun*, mix the ingredients together, and season with ¼ teaspoon salt. Remove from heat and set aside.

Heat another skillet and coat with remaining 2 tablespoons oil. Add the flour and cook for 2 or 3 minutes, or until all lumps have been smoothed out. Remove from heat and cool, then return to stove and add 1½ cups water, stirring until smooth. Bring to a boil, stir in vegetable and *biifun* mixture, and season with remaining 1 teaspoon salt. Simmer for 1 or 2 minutes.

Heat oven to 350°F. Use the sauce and vegetable mixture to fill the hollowed squash; replace the slice and tie it to the squash with a piece of string. Put squash on a lightly oiled baking sheet and oil the squash. Bake for 30 to 40 minutes, or until squash is no longer resistant to the insertion of a food pick or skewer. Bring to the table to serve.

VARIATION: Cut squash crosswise into halves, then scoop out seeds and filaments. Substitute *harusame* for *biifun* and use whatever vegetables you have on hand to prepare a filling. Proceed as above.

Kabocha Miso Ni *(Pumpkin with Miso)*   SERVES 5

1 tablespoon corn or sesame oil
1 medium-size onion, sliced into thin half-moons
½ pound pumpkin, cubed
5 level tablespoons *miso*
½ cup water

Heat the oil in a skillet. Sauté onion over medium heat, stirring gently, for 5 minutes, or until lightly browned. Add pumpkin and sauté for 2 or 3 minutes more. Add water to cover, bring to a boil, and cover pan. Reduce heat and simmer for 30 minutes, or until tender. Add water during cooking if necessary to prevent burning. Thin the *miso* with ½ cup water and add, then simmer until dry.

Baked Pumpkin   SERVES 6

1 Hokkaido pumpkin or 2 acorn squash
Corn or sesame oil
Sea salt

Preheat oven to 400°F. Cut the pumpkin into 10 crescents and place on a lightly oiled baking sheet. Rub crescents with oil, then sprinkle lightly with salt. Cover pan with aluminum foil and bake for 20 minutes. Remove foil and bake until tops of crescents brown. Serve with *goma miso* sauce (p.164) and garnish with sprigs of parsley.

Deep-Fried Pumpkin and Peanut

SERVES 5

Oil for deep-frying
2 cups pumpkin purée
½ cup peanut butter
Dash of sea salt
1 cup brown rice flour
Whole peanuts

Pour 3 inches of oil into a heavy skillet or deep-fryer and heat to 350°F. Combine pumpkin, peanut butter and salt, blending until smooth. Add enough of the flour to hold the mixture together and form into balls approximately 1 inch in diameter. Embed 1 peanut in each ball. Drop balls into the hot oil and deep-fry for 2 or 3 minutes, or until crisp. Drain on absorbent paper before serving.

VARIATION: Dissolve 2 tablespoons *kuzu* in 1½ cups water and bring to a boil. Season with a dash of salt and 1 tablespoon *shoyu,* or to taste. Simmer, stirring constantly, for several minutes, until thick. Drop in the deep-fried pumpkin-peanut balls and remove when they rise to the surface. Serve sprinkled with lightly toasted sesame seeds.

Kuzu Kabocha Mold

SERVES 5

(Pumpkin Kuzu Mold)

1 cup white sesame seeds, washed
2 cups pumpkin or squash purée
½ cup *kuzu*
2 cups water

Dry-roast the seeds in a heavy skillet over moderately high heat for 5 minutes, or until lightly toasted and fragrant. Empty seeds into a *suribachi,* grind to a paste, and blend into the pumpkin purée.

Dissolve the *kuzu* in the water and bring to a boil. Add the pumpkin and sesame mixture and cook, stirring constantly, for 15 minutes. Transfer to a rinsed mold and chill.

Kabocha Isomaki *(Pumpkin Nori Rolls)*   SERVES 5

1 medium-size carrot
1 medium-size lotus root
1 tablespoon sesame oil
Dash of sea salt
1 teaspoon *shoyu*
3 sheets of *nori*
3 cups pumpkin or acorn squash purée
1 or 2 tablespoons *kokoh*

Quarter the carrot and lotus root lengthwise, then cut 1 quarter of each vegetable into thin sticks approximately $\frac{1}{3}$ inch thick. Heat a heavy skillet and coat with $\frac{1}{2}$ tablespoon oil. Sauté carrot sticks over medium heat for 1 or 2 minutes, stirring gently to coat them evenly with oil and prevent scorching. Add 2 or 3 tablespoons water, reduce heat, and simmer for 15 minutes. Season with a dash of salt. If any liquid remains, simmer uncovered until evaporated. Remove from heat and set aside.

Heat another skillet and coat with remaining $\frac{1}{2}$ tablespoon oil. Reduce heat to low and sauté lotus sticks for 2 or 3 minutes, stirring gently. Add water to half-cover sticks, cover pan, and simmer for 10 minutes. Season with *shoyu* and simmer until all liquid has been absorbed or evaporated. Remove from heat.

Wave the sheets of *nori* over low heat on one side only for several seconds. Place 1 sheet on a *sudare* or bamboo mat. Divide the purée into 3 portions and spread 1 portion over each *nori* sheet. If purée is too moist, add 1 or 2 tablespoons *kokoh* to thicken. Place a double row of carrot and lotus sticks across the center of the purée. Roll the mixture up in the mat, lightly pressing the ingredients together into a cylinder. Remove mat and repeat with remaining ingredients until all are used.

Use a sharp heavy knife to slice each *isomaki* into 1-inch rounds. Wipe the knife after each cut for neat slices. A wonderful snack for teatime.

Kabocha Fukume Ni   SERVES 4 OR 5
(Boiled Pumpkin with Shoyu)

1 Hokkaido pumpkin or 2 acorn squashes
$\frac{1}{2}$ to 1 cup *shoyu*, approximately

Cut the pumpkin into 8 or 10 crescents and trim away 1 inch of the peel at the center of each piece. Cover with water, bring to a boil, and cook for 15 minutes. Season with 2 to 4 tablespoons *shoyu* for each cup of water used and cook for 15 minutes more.

Kikuhana   SERVES 5
(Hokkaido Pumpkin with Chrysanthemum Leaves)

3 cups pumpkin purée
1 cup sweet potato purée
Sea salt
Chrysanthemum leaves

Combine the pumpkin and sweet potato and season with salt to taste. Set aside 1 cup of the mixture and form the remainder into 10 disks approximately 2 inches in diameter and $\frac{2}{3}$ inch thick. Divide the chrysanthemum leaves among 5 serving dishes and place 2 disks on each dish. Using a chopstick, draw a floral design on each disk. Form remaining cup of the mixture into 10 "teardrops" and place 1 teardrop at the center of each disk.

Horenso Goma-Ae *(Spinach with Sesame)*   SERVES 5

1 teaspoon sea salt
$\frac{3}{4}$ pound spinach
4 tablespoons white sesame seeds, washed
2 to 4 tablespoons *shoyu*
4 tablespoons water

Bring a large pan of water to a boil and add the salt. Drop in the spinach, return to the boil, and cook for 1 to 3 minutes, or until the stems are tender. Dip leaves into a basin of cold water to stop the cooking and set the color; drain thoroughly and chop.

Dry-roast the seeds in a heavy skillet over moderately high heat for 5 minutes, or until lightly toasted and fragrant, stirring constantly. Empty seeds into a *suribachi* and grind to a paste, adding *shoyu* and water. Add the spinach and toss the ingredients together.

Kabu no Maru Ni *(Boiled Turnips)* SERVES 5

5 medium-size turnips
4 cups *kombu dashi* (p. 136), approximately
$\frac{1}{4}$ to $\frac{1}{2}$ cup *shoyu*
2 to 4 teaspoons *kuzu* powder

Quarter the turnips through half their depth. Bring to a boil in enough *dashi* to cover and cook for 20 to 30 minutes, or until tender. Season the *dashi* with *shoyu* and simmer for 5 minutes more. Lift out the turnips and drain. Dissolve the *kuzu* in a little water to make a thin paste and add to the remaining *dashi*. Simmer, stirring constantly, for several minutes, until thick. Pour over the turnips and serve.

Kabu Miso-Ae *(Turnips with Goma Miso)* SERVES 5

5 turnips, cut lengthwise into halves
4 cups *kombu dashi* (p. 136), approximately
1 teaspoon sea salt
Leaves from 5 turnips
2 tablespoons *miso*
1 tablespoon *tahini* (sesame butter)
1 teaspoon minced lemon peel

Bring the turnips to a boil in enough *kombu dashi* to cover and cook for 30 minutes, or until tender. Bring a large pan of water (more than enough to cover the leaves) to a boil and add the salt. Drop in the leaves, return to the boil, and cook for 2 or 3 minutes, or until leaves are bright green and the stems are tender. Drain leaves in a colander, squeeze to remove excess liquid, and chop into $\frac{2}{3}$-inch sections.

Blend the *miso* and *tahini* in a *suribachi*. Thin the mixture with $\frac{1}{2}$ cup of the *dashi* used to cook the turnips.

Divide the leaves among 5 serving bowls and put 2 turnip halves into each bowl. Top with sesame *miso* sauce and serve garnished with minced lemon peel.

Kabu Gratin *(Turnip Gratin)* SERVES 5

5 *shiitake* (dried Japanese mushrooms)
2 small onions
5 small turnips
1 small carrot
3 tablespoons corn or sesame oil
2 ounces of *kofu* (wheat gluten), deep-fried until crisp and cut into thin strips, or substitute 2 ounces chopped *seitan*
1 or 2 tablespoons *shoyu*
2 heaping tablespoons unbleached white flour
$1\frac{1}{2}$ cups *kombu dashi* (p. 136)
$\frac{1}{2}$ teaspoon sea salt

Soak the *shiitake* in lightly salted water for 20 minutes, or until refreshed. Remove tough portions of stem and set aside. Slice remaining vegetables into half-moons.

Heat a heavy skillet and coat with 2 tablespoons oil. Sauté onions over medium heat, stirring gently, for 5 minutes, or until lightly browned. Add turnips, carrot, mushrooms and *kofu* (or *seitan*), in that order, sautéing each lightly as you add it. Mix ingredients together, season with *shoyu*, and remove from heat.

Heat remaining 1 tablespoon oil in another skillet. Add the flour and cook for 3 or 4 minutes, stirring constantly to heat evenly. Remove from heat and cool, then return to stove and add $\frac{1}{2}$ cup *dashi*, stirring until smooth. Bring just to a boil while adding remaining 1 cup *dashi* and season with $\frac{1}{2}$ teaspoon salt, or to taste.

Preheat oven to 400°F. Place the vegetables into a lightly oiled gratin dish and cover with the sauce. Sprinkle the top with 2 or 3 drops of oil. Bake for 20 to 30 minutes, or until nicely browned.

SPECIAL DISHES

The dishes that follow, several of which are traditionally served on the Japanese New Year, can be used as holiday dishes or for special occasions.

Gyoza
MAKES 10 GYOZA

    2 cups unbleached white flour
    ¼ teaspoon and a dash of sea salt
    4 tablespoons sesame oil
    ½ cup boiling water, approximately
    2 small onions, minced
    1 small carrot, slivered
    3 tablespoons minced *seitan*
    Oil for frying

Combine the flour and ¼ teaspoon salt. Add 2 tablespoons oil, rubbing mixture between your palms to blend evenly. Add boiling water while stirring vigorously with 4 long chopsticks held in the fist of one hand or with a long fork with 4 tines. When mixed well and cool enough to touch, knead for 8 to 10 minutes until dough is smooth and elastic. Divide into 10 parts and roll out on a floured board into thin rounds, 3 inches in diameter. Set aside.

Heat a heavy skillet and coat with 2 tablespoons oil. Sauté the onions over medium heat for 5 minutes, or until lightly browned. Add carrot slivers, then *seitan*; mix ingredients together. Taste before seasoning with a dash of salt (the *seitan* is salty). Turn off heat.

Place 1 or 2 tablespoons of the sautéed vegetables and *seitan* at the center of each dough round. Bring up sides of dought to form half-moon shapes. Seal edges by pinching dough with fingers. Prick sides once or twice with a fork to allow steam to escape.

Heat a heavy skillet and brush lightly with oil. Stand *gyoza* up in pan, cover, and cook over medium heat. When bottom of *gyoza* is lightly browned, sprinkle several drops of water on surface of skillet, re-cover, and steam-cook for 5 more minutes.

VARIATIONS: A. Drop *gyoza* into a large pan of boiling water and cook until they rise to the surface. Drain thoroughly.

B. Deep-fry precooked *gyoza* in hot oil until crisp. Drain before serving.

Onion Tsumemono *(Stuffed Onions)*
SERVES 10

    10 medium-size onions
    1 tablespoon sesame oil
    ½ small carrot, diced
    10 green beans, rinsed, trimmed, sliced
      fine on the diagonal
    5 tablespoons minced *seitan*
    Dash of sea salt
    1 heaping tablespoon unbleached white
      flour
    Oil
    2 cups mock Béchamel sauce (p. 162)

Cut 1 slice from the top of the onions, then scoop out and chop the centers.

Heat the oil in a skillet. Add the chopped onion and sauté, stirring gently, until lightly browned. Add carrot, then green beans, sautéing each lightly as you add it. Add *seitan* and mix the ingredients together. Season with a dash of salt, add the flour, and remove from heat.

Use the sautéed vegetables and *seitan* to fill the onions. Arrange onions on a lightly oiled baking pan and bake in a preheated 425°F. oven for 20 to 30 minutes, or until tender; or steam over *kombu dashi* (p. 136). Serve topped with mock Béchamel sauce.

Harumaki

(Chinese Spring Rolls)

1 cup and 1 tablespoon unbleached white flour
1 cup and 1 tablespoon water
1½ teaspoons sea salt
2 tablespoons corn or sesame oil
1 egg, beaten (optional)
3 ounces *biifun* (transparent noodles), or substitute 3 ounces cooked vermicelli
1 small onion, minced
1 small carrot, slivered
1 cup small cauliflowerets
Oil for deep-frying

To prepare *harumaki* crêpes* combine 1 cup flour, 1 cup water, 1 teaspoon salt, 1 tablespoon oil, and (if used) the beaten egg to form a batter. Preheat a heavy 7-inch skillet and reduce heat to low. Ladle in just enough of the batter to cover the surface of the skillet, turning the skillet as you add the batter to spread it as thin as possible. Heat until batter has set (not browned), then turn over and heat second side for a few seconds more. Remove and set aside. Repeat with remaining batter until all is used.

Drop the *biifun* into a pan of boiling water and cook for 2 or 3 mintues. Drain biifun and cut into 1-inch lengths.

Heat remaining 1 tablespoon oil in a skillet. Add onion and sauté over medium heat for 5 minutes. or until lightly browned. Add carrot, then cauliflowerets, sautéing each lightly as you add it. Add *biifun* and mix ingredients together. Season with ½ teaspoon salt and remove from heat.

Combine remaining 1 tablespoon flour and 1 tablespoon water to form a thin paste. Place 3 or 4 tablespoons of the vegetable and noodle mixture at one edge of a *harumaki* skin, and roll the *harumaki* twice to cover the filling. Tuck in edges of *harumaki,* roll again, and seal the seam with flour paste. Repeat with remaining ingredients until all are used.

Pour 3 inches of oil into a heavy skillet or deep-fryer and heat to 350°F. Drop the filled *harumaki* into the hot oil and deep-fry for 1 or 2 minutes, or until golden and crisp. Drain on a wire rack or absorbent paper before serving.

*available at Oriental food shops

Lima's Pizza

1½ cups unbleached white flour
1 teaspoon sea salt
3 tablespoons and a few drops of corn or sesame oil
½ cup water, approximately
2 or 3 small onions, cut into half-moons
Flowerets from ¼ small cauliflower, sliced fine
1 small carrot, diced
1 egg, white and yolk beaten separately
Grated cheese (optional)

Combine the flour and ½ teaspoon salt, mixing well. Add 2 tablespoons oil, rubbing mixture between palms to blend evenly. Add water gradually to form an elastic dough, and knead lightly for 3 or 4 minutes until smooth. Roll out on a floured board into a circular sheet. Place dough on a lightly oiled cookie sheet and set aside.

Heat remaining 1 tablespoon oil in a heavy skillet. Sauté the onions, stirring gently, until lightly browned. Add cauliflowerets, then carrot, sautéing each lightly as you add it. Season with remaining ½ teaspoon salt and remove from heat. Beat the egg yolk and add to vegetables when they have cooled to room temperature.

Spread vegetable mixture over top of dough and sprinkle with remaining few drops of oil. If used, top with grated cheese. Bake in a preheated 400°F. oven for 20 minutes. Pour on well-beaten egg white and bake for 10 minutes more, or until white is browned.

Zwiebelkuchen

SERVES 6 TO 8

1½ cups unbleached white flour
1 teaspoon sea salt
3 tablespoons sesame or corn oil
½ cup water, approximately
2 small onions, cut into thin half-moons
2 to 3 cups shredded cabbage
½ small carrot, slivered
1 egg, well beaten

Combine flour and ½ teaspoon salt, mixing well. Add 2 tablespoons oil, rubbing mixture between palms to blend evenly. Add water gradually to form an elastic dough, and knead for 8 to 10 minutes until smooth. Set aside ½ cup of dough. Roll out remaining dough on a floured board and use to line a 9-inch pie plate. Roll reserved dough into a thin round sheet and set aside.

Heat remaining 1 tablespoon oil in a heavy skillet. Sauté onions over medium heat, stirring gently, for 5 minutes, or until lightly browned. Add cabbage, then carrot, sautéing each as you add it. Mix ingredients together and season with remaining ½ teaspoon salt. Remove from heat and allow to cool, then stir in the beaten egg.

Preheat oven to 450°F. Fill dough-lined pan with vegetable and egg mixture and top with reserved round of dough. Prick a few holes in the dough to allow moisture to escape during baking, and seal edges with fork. Bake for 30 minutes, or until nicely browned.

Chou Farci

SERVES 5

1 cup buckwheat flour
½ teaspoon sea salt
3 cups water
Leaves of 1 small cabbage, rinsed
2 eggs, well beaten

Combine flour, salt and water. Arrange several cabbage leaves in the bottom of a casserole. Pour on some of the buckwheat mixture, then a little of the beaten egg. Top with a layer of cabbage and repeat with the remaining ingredients until all are used. Top the pile with cabbage leaves and cover casserole with a tight-fitting lid. Bake in a preheated 275°F. oven for 40 minutes to 1 hour. Serve hot and steaming.

VARIATION: Substitute 2 to 3 cups cooked buckwheat groats for the flour and proceed as above.

Turnip Chawanmushi

SERVES 5

5 pieces of *maki-yuba* (optional)
2 tablespoons *shoyu*
2 teaspoons sea salt
10 thin slices of flowered carrot
2 scallions, sliced into ¾-inch lengths
3 cups grated turnip
1 egg white, beaten to a foam
10 pieces of *zenibu*, deep-fried until crisp (optional)
5 thin strips of orange peel

Bring the *maki-yuba* to a boil in 1 cup water (or enough to cover) and season with *shoyu*. Cook for 15 to 20 minutes and drain. Set *maki-yuba* aside. Bring a small pan of water to a boil and add ½ teaspoon salt. Drop in the carrot slices and cook for 2 or 3 minutes, or until bright orange; drain and set aside. Bring another small pan of water to a boil and add ½ teaspoon salt. Drop in the scallions, return to the boil, and cook for 1 or 2 minutes, or until bright green. Dip scallions into a basin of cold water and drain in a colander.

Combine the turnip, egg white and remaining 1 teaspoon salt. Divide the mixture among 5 custard cups with tops. Arrange 1 piece of *maki-yuba*, 2 carrot slices, several pieces of scallion, 2 pieces of *zenibu* (if used) and 1 strip of orange peel in each cup. Cover and steam for 15 to 20 minutes.

Chestnut Kinton SERVES 5

1 cup pumpkin purée
½ cup sweet potato purée
Sea salt
1½ cups chestnut meats
4½ cups water

Combine the pumpkin and sweet potato purées. Season the mixture with salt to taste, and set aside.

Cook the chestnuts in the water for 1 to 1½ hours, or until pasty. Season with salt, then stir in the pumpkin and sweet-potato mixture. Bring just to a boil. A traditional New Year's specialty in Japan.

Renkon Fukumeni (*Lotus Root Surprise*) SERVES 5

2 tablespoons sesame oil
1 small lotus root
1 cup water, approximately
3 tablespoons *shoyu*

Heat a small skillet and coat with the oil. Put the whole lotus root in the pan and sauté for 2 or 3 minutes, turning the lotus root to coat it evenly with oil. Add water (enough to half-cover) and bring to a boil. Cover pan, reduce heat, and simmer for 20 to 30 minutes, or until lotus root is tender and no longer resistant to the insertion of a chopstick. Add *shoyu* and simmer until dry.

To serve, cut lotus root lengthwise into halves, then into thin half-moons. A pretty New Year's dish.

VARIATION: Grate the lotus root, then combine with ½ cup minced onion, 1 tablespoon salt and enough unbleached white flour to hold the mixture together. Form into balls approximately 1 inch in diameter. Drop into moderately hot (300° to 330°F.) *tempura* oil and deep-fry slowly until cooked through, pale golden and crisp. Drain on absorbent paper.

113

Daikon Age Rolls SERVES 4

4 or 5 cups *kombu dashi* (p. 136)
4 tablespoons *shoyu*
5 inches *daikon* of uniform width, quartered
  lengthwise
4 pieces of *aburage* (fried bean curd)
1 tablespoon unbleached white flour
1 tablespoon water
Oil for deep-frying

Bring the *dashi* (just enough to cover the *daikon* pieces) to a boil and season with *shoyu*. Drop in the *daikon* and simmer for 20 minutes, or until tender.

Open the *aburage* with scissors by cutting into 1 long and 2 short sides, and place the pieces on a flat surface. Combine flour and water to make a thin paste.

Drain *daikon* when tender. Place 1 stick at near edge of each piece of *aburage*. Roll each into a tight cylinder, and seal the seam with flour paste.

Pour 3 inches of oil into a heavy skillet or deep-fryer and heat to 350°F. Drop rolls into the hot oil. Remove rolls as soon as they return to the surface, and drain on absorbent paper. Cut each roll into 5 slices. Serve with *goma joyu* sauce (p. 163).

Kikusui Maki *(Orange Chrysanthemums)* SERVES 6

1½ inches *daikon* of uniform width
3 mandarin oranges, peeled and separated
  into halves

Pare the *daikon* into a sheet approximately 2 feet long. Soak the sheet in cold water for 15 to 20 minutes, then cut into 6 rectangular pieces 1½ by 4 inches. Place each orange half at the short edge of 1 *daikon* sheet, and wrap the sheet several times around the orange. Press sheet with palm to assure that it adheres to orange's surface. Let stand for 1 or 2 minutes. Slice crosswise into sections.

Vegetable Skewers with Koya-Dofu SERVES 5

4 small pieces of *koya-dofu* (dried *tofu*)
Shoyu
Oil for deep-frying
1 cake of *tofu*, drained (p. 173), cut into 5
  pieces
2 tablespoons sesame oil
5 irregular pieces of lotus root
5 irregular pieces of carrot
Dash of sea salt

Drop the *koya-dofu* into a small pan of boiling water and cook for 2 or 3 minutes. Drain, cool *koya-dofu* under running cold water, and press between palms while continuing to rinse until a white foam is no longer released. Cut pieces into thin strips, then cover with a mixture of one part water and one-quarter part *shoyu* and bring to a boil. Cook until the liquid has been absorbed or evaporated and the *koya-dofu* is puffed up and well flavored. Set aside.

Pour 3 inches of oil into a heavy skillet or deep-fryer and heat to 350°F. Drop in the *tofu* and deep-fry until browned and crisp. Transfer to a small pan and cover with a mixture of one part water and one-half part *shoyu*. Bring to a boil and cook until dry; set aside.

Heat a heavy skillet and coat with 1 tablespoon oil. Sauté the lotus root over low heat for 2 or 3 minutes. Add equal parts water and *shoyu* to cover and bring to a boil. Cover pan, and simmer for 20 minutes, or until lotus root is tender; uncover and simmer until dry.

Heat remaining 1 tablespoon oil in another skillet. Add carrot and sauté over medium heat for 2 or 3 minutes. Add water to cover and simmer until carrot is tender. Season with a dash of salt, and simmer until dry.

To serve, skewer 1 piece each of *tempura tofu*, lotus root and carrot, in that order, on a bamboo skewer. Accompany skewers with *koya-dofu* strips and citron *miso* for dipping (p. 164).

VARIATION: Another delicious combination of vegetables to serve on skewers is pumpkin, sweet potato and *konnyaku*. Serve coated with walnut *miso* (p. 163).

Takara Zutsumi (*The Treasure Chest*)   SERVES 5

> 5 pieces of *aburage* (fried bean curd)
> 1 ounce *harusame* or *biifun,* or substitute 1 ounce lightly cooked vermicelli
> Sea salt
> 10 green beans, rinsed and trimmed
> 10 strips (3 inches long) of *kampyo* (gourd) or *kombu*
> 1 small carrot, slivered
> 1 piece of *kombu*, 3 inches square, wiped clean
> *Shoyu*

Douse the *aburage* with boiling water to rid it of excess oil, and drain. Cut each piece into halves, open the center to form a pouch, and turn pouches inside-out. Set aside. Drop the *harusame* or *biifun* into a pan of boiling water and cook for 2 or 3 minutes; drain. Drop the green beans into a small pan of lightly salted boiling water (just enough to cover beans). Return to the boil and cook for 5 minutes, or until beans are bright green and just tender. Dip beans into a basin of cold water to stop the cooking. Drain beans and slice them fine on the diagonal. Rinse the *kampyo* in lightly salted water and squeeze the strips dry. Sprinkle the carrot slivers with salt.

Combine *harusame*, carrot and green beans, and use the mixture to fill the *aburage* pouches. Draw pouch edges together and tie with a gourd or *kombu* strip to form a sack.

Put the *kombu* in the bottom of a pan and place the *aburage* sacks on top of the *kombu*. Add just enough water to cover. Season with 2 teaspoons salt and 1 tablespoon *shoyu* for each cup of water added, and bring to a boil. Cover with a tight-fitting lid, or one that fits inside the pan and rests directly on top of the *aburage* sacks to keep them in place. Cook until half of the liquid has been absorbed or evaporated and the *aburage* are well flavored.

Place 2 *aburage* sacks into each of 5 individual serving bowls and ladle in a little of the remaining broth. Serve hot and steaming.

Pumpkin Roll   SERVES 6 TO 8

> ½ pound pumpkin purée
> ½ pound sweet potato purée
> ½ teaspoon and a dash of sea salt
> 2 cups whole-wheat flour
> ¼ teaspoon ground cinnamon
> 2 tablespoons sesame or corn oil
> ¾ to 1 cup water, approximately
> 1 egg yolk, well beaten
> Oil

Blend the pumpkin and sweet potato purées, and season with a dash of salt to bring out the sweetness of the vegetables.

Combine flour, remaining ½ teaspoon salt and the cinnamon in a large bowl, mixing well. Add oil, rubbing mixture between your palms to blend evenly. Add water gradually to form an elastic dough, and knead for 8 to 10 minutes, until smooth. Form dough into a ball, wrap in a damp cloth, and set aside in a cold place for 30 minutes.

Divide dough into 2 parts and roll each part on a floured board into a thin rectangular sheet. Spread the vegetable purée over the surface of both sheets and roll into cylinders. Seal edges of cylinders with a few drops of water. Brush tops of rolls with beaten egg yolk and place rolls on a lightly oiled baking pan. Bake in a preheated 350°F. oven for 30 minutes, or until nicely browned.

VARIATION: Substitute 2 cups *adzuki* jam (p. 168) for the purée and proceed as above.

                   SPECIAL DISHES

The seaweeds are rich in iodine and other minerals, and are an integral part of the macrobiotic diet. Develop a taste for their unique flavor and make them a part of your daily meals. Used in soups, cooked together with other vegetables or served as condiments they can be enjoyed regardless of season or locale.

Hijiki with Sesame Seeds
SERVES 5

1 ounce dried *hijiki*
1½ tablespoons sesame oil
3 tablespoons *shoyu*
1 or 2 tablespoons white sesame seeds

Wash the *hijiki* under cold running water, then soak in water to cover for 10 to 15 minutes; save the soaking water. Drain *hijiki* and cut into 1-inch lengths. Heat a heavy skillet and coat with the oil. Sauté the *hijiki* over medium heat for 10 minutes, or until it no longer releases its strong aroma. Add the saved soaking water and enough fresh water (if necessary) to cover and bring to a boil. Cover pan and cook for 30 to 40 minutes, or until *hijiki* is swollen and tender. Season with *shoyu* and simmer until dry.

Just before serving, toast the sesame seeds in a heavy skillet over moderately high heat for 4 or 5 minutes. Stir constantly and shake the pan to heat evenly. When the seeds turn light brown and release their distinctive fragrance, remove from heat and chop with a heavy knife. Sprinkle the chopped seeds over individual portions of *hijiki*, and serve.

Momi Wakame

Deep-fry *wakame* or grill directly over an open fire until crisp. Crumble and serve as a garnish with rice.

Hijiki with Lotus Root

SERVES 5

⅔ ounce dried *hijiki*
3 tablespoons sesame oil
3 ounces lotus root, cut into thin gingko
   leaves
Shoyu

Wash the *hijiki* under cold running water, then soak in water to cover for 10 to 15 minutes; save the soaking water. Drain *hijiki* and cut into 1-inch lengths. Heat a heavy skillet and coat with the oil. Sauté the lotus root over low heat for 1 or 2 minutes, stirring very gently. Try not to let the lotus root get sticky. Add the *hijiki* and sauté together for 5 to 10 minutes more, or until *hijiki* no longer releases its strong aroma. Add soaking water and enough fresh water (if necessary) to cover, and bring to a boil. Simmer for 30 to 40 minutes. Season with *shoyu* to taste and simmer until dry.

VARIATION: When using dried lotus root, soak the lotus root overnight, then proceed as above.

Kombu with Shoyu

1 strip of *kombu,* 10 inches long, wiped clean
Shoyu

Cut the *kombu* into 1-inch squares. Place in a deep skillet or heavy saucepan and add more than enough water to cover. Bring to a boil and cook for 30 to 40 minutes, adding water, if necessary, to keep the *kombu* covered. Add 1 part *shoyu* to the cooking liquid remaining and simmer until dry. Now re-cover with equal parts water and *shoyu* and simmer until dry again. Repeat this procedure once more. Serve only 1 or 2 pieces of this salty garnish per person. Store in an airtight container.

Kombu Root Nitsuke

¼ pound *kombu* root, wiped clean
Shoyu

Put the *kombu* root in a pressure cooker and add enough water to twice cover. Bring to full pressure over high heat, reduce heat to low, and simmer for 30 to 40 minutes. Remove from heat and allow pressure to return to normal. Transfer *kombu* root to a saucepan and cover with equal parts *shoyu* and water. Bring to a boil and simmer, covered, until root is tender, adding more *shoyu* and water if necessary. When root is tender, uncover and simmer until dry. Serve only 1 piece per person; *kombu* root is very *yang*.

Momi Nori

Toast 1 side of a sheet of *nori* by waving it over low heat until crisp. Crumble and use as a garnish with rice, vegetables, soups, etc.; or cut into strips and use to wrap *musubi* (p. 50).

Musubi Kombu

Oil for deep-frying
1 strip of *kombu*, 6 inches long, wiped clean
Sea salt

Pour 3 inches of oil into a heavy skillet or deep-fryer and heat to 350°F. Cut the *kombu* into strips ⅓ by 3 inches. Tie each strip into a loose knot; or cut a short slit in the middle of each strip and thread one end of strip through slit. Drop into the hot oil and deep-fry until swollen and crisp. Drain on absorbent paper and sprinkle with salt. A delicious relish with beer or sake.

TEMPURA

Vegetables and fish are often at their sweetest when coated with batter and deep-fried. Making good *tempura* is not difficult, but it does require concentration. If it is to be part of a meal, prepare the other dishes first so you can give this preparation your full attention. *Tempura* should be served hot; if you are making large amounts, keep already cooked morsels crisp in a warm oven.

Oil. Any good-quality vegetable oil will do but it is best to add some sesame oil to the pan for its nutlike taste and fragrance. Fill a 10- or 12-inch skillet, wok or deep-fryer with oil to a depth of 3 inches or more, and heat slowly to a temperature of 350°F. To test if the oil is hot enough, drop in a morsel of batter. If it falls to the bottom and rises to the surface at almost the same speed, the oil is ready for use. If the batter remains on the bottom of the pan, the oil is too cool and *tempura* fried in it will be oily; if the batter rises faster than it descends, the oil is too hot. During frying the temperature of the oil must be kept just right by raising and lowering the heat beneath the pan. Remember that each time you add vegetables or fish to the oil, the temperature will fall. At the start, therefore, oil can register 375°F.

Don't crowd the skillet: *tempura* should fall to the bottom of the pan, quickly rise to the surface, and have enough room to swim and bob on top of the oil. When one side has browned, turn and brown the second side then remove with a pair of chopsticks, a wire mesh strainer or a slotted spoon. Drain on a wire rack or place on absorbent paper. After removing the *tempura*, skim the oil with a strainer to remove any debris. If the oil clouds, drop in an *umeboshi* and let it char. In the process it will attract unnecessary particles of matter. Remove the charred plum and continue to deep-fry.

If leftover oil is stored in a glass jar with an *umeboshi* plum to keep it fresh, it can be used repeatedly for up to 1 to 2 months.

Batter. The flour or combination of flours used in the batter is a matter of personal preference and leaves room for good-tasting experimentation. Workable combinations include whole-wheat with buckwheat, rye or corn; whole-wheat pastry flour with unbleached flour; and buckwheat with rice flour. As a general rule, add $\frac{3}{4}$ cup water and $\frac{1}{4}$ to $\frac{1}{2}$ teaspoon sea salt to each cup of flour. Naturally, a thick batter requires less water, while a thin one calls for the addition of a little more. Add a well-beaten egg and/or 1 teaspoon of *kuzu* powder if desired. Mix the batter lightly; it is all right to have a few lumps remaining. Most important, the batter should be freshly made just before using. Keep an extra cup of flour at hand in case the batter runs out.

Ingredients. Almost any vegetable in season will make delicious *tempura*: carrot, burdock, lotus root, pumpkin or squash, *jinenjo* (mountain potato), sweet potato, onion, mushroom *(shiitake)*, greenbeans, green pepper, celery, asparagus, broccoli, cauliflower, parsley, carrot tops, celery leaves and *nori*. Slice the roots and bulbs into thin slivers or $\frac{1}{4}$-inch-thick diagonals or rounds. Cut the stalks into 1 to 3 inch lengths. Separate the broccoli and cauliflower into their flowerets. Green leaves turn out beautifully with only one of their surfaces coated with batter, while 2 or 3 sprigs of parsley drawn into a miniature bouquet and dipped stem down into batter to cover half the leaf cluster pleases the eye as well as the palate. Moist vegetables (pumpkin, broccoli, cauliflower, green leaves) can be coated with dry flour first to assure that the batter will adhere and then dipped into batter.

Shrimps are delicious when served as *tempura,* and are "yangized" in the process. To prepare, remove most of the shell, leaving the tail segment intact. With the fine point of a knife, remove the intestinal string running down the back. Cut 2 or 3 short incisions across the inner side of each shrimp and press flat with the side of a broad knife. For butterfly shrimps make an incision from the top end to the base of the tail and then flatten. Hold a shrimp by the tail, dip into batter, and fry. A $\frac{1}{4}$-inch-thick fillet of any white-fleshed fish can be dipped into batter, and then dropped into hot *tempura* oil.

Dipping Sauce. To 1 cup *kombu dashi* (p. 136) add $\frac{1}{4}$ cup *shoyu* and bring to a boil. Remove from the heat immediately and allow to cool slightly. Fill individual serving bowls with this sauce. Each person should add to the sauce grated *daikon* (which aids in the digestion of oil) or gingerroot to taste. When served without this sauce, *tempura* should be accompanied by a small mound of grated *daikon* seasoned lightly with *shoyu* for dipping. Children may be served a combination of equal parts grated *daikon* and carrot.

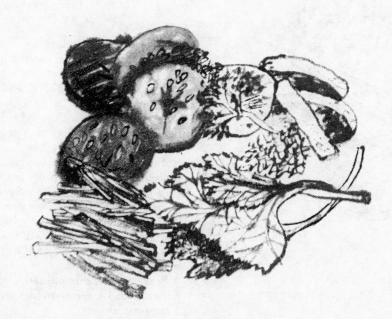

Vegetable Tempura

Oil for deep-frying
1 thick burdock root, 10 inches long, cut
   into 5 logs
8 slices (¼ inch thick) lotus root, cut into
   halves
1 small carrot, slivered
10 green beans, rinsed, trimmed, and cut
   diagonally, into halves
15 parsley sprigs, drawn together into 5
   miniature bouquets
1 sheet of *nori*, cut into halves, each half
   cut into 5 short strips
For the Batter:
2 cups unbleached white flour
½ teaspoon sea salt
1½ cups water, approximately
1 egg, beaten

Stand the burdock logs on end and score them grid-fashion through three fourths of their length. Separate the filaments at one end.

Heat *tempura* oil to 375°F. and combine the ingredients to form the batter. Using a pair of chopsticks, dip the vegetables one at a time into the batter. Coat only the filaments at one end of the burdock, leaving the knob at its other end dry. Coat 1 side of the *nori*, and half of the leafy tops of the parsley bouquets. Drop 1 serving (about 8 pieces) at a time into the hot oil. After 1 or 2 minutes turn the pieces over and fry for 1 minute longer, or until golden and crisp. Drain on absorbent paper. Arrange on serving dishes or in shallow bamboo baskets, and keep warm in a preheated 250°F. oven. Clear the oil of any debris, adjust the temperature, and fry the remaining ingredients.

Serve with a dipping sauce (p. 163), or provide each person with 1 tablespoon fine-grated *daikon* seasoned with 1 teaspoon *shoyu*.

Kabocha no Kawa Kaki Age
(Pumpkin Peel Tempura)

SERVES 5

> Peel from 1 organically grown pumpkin or
>   acorn squash
> Oil for deep-frying
> ½ cup whole-wheat flour
> ½ cup unbleached white flour
> ¾ cup water, approximately
> ½ teaspoon sea salt

Cut the peel into thin strips. Put the strips into a large bowl and add remaining ingredients to form a batter. Pour 3 inches of oil into a heavy skillet or deep-fryer and heat to 350°F. Spoon the batter-covered strips into the hot oil and deep-fry until golden and crisp. Drain on a wire rack or absorbent paper before serving.

A delicious way to prevent waste.

Satsumaimo no Tama Age
(Sweet Potato Ball Tempura)

SERVES 5

> 3 cups sweet potato purée
> 1 cup minced onion
> Oil for deep-frying
> 1 cup unbleached white flour
> 1 cup water
> ½ teaspoon sea salt
> 5 tablespoons grated *daikon*
> 5 teaspoons *shoyu*

Combine the sweet potato and onion, mixing thoroughly. Form into balls approximately 1 inch in diameter, and set aside.

Pour 3 inches of oil into a heavy skillet or deep-fryer and heat to 350°F. Combine flour, water and salt to form a batter. Dip the balls into the batter, coating thoroughly, and drop into the hot oil. Deep-fry until golden and crisp. Drain on absorbent paper and serve accompanied with small mounds of grated *daikon* seasoned lightly with *shoyu* for dipping.

Tempura Dumplings

SERVES 5

> Oil for deep-frying
> 1½ cups whole-wheat flour
> ¼ to ½ teaspoon sea salt
> 1 to 1½ cups water, approximately
> 1 cup slivered burdock root
> 1 cup slivered carrot
> 1 cup thin half-moons of lotus root

Fill a heavy skillet or deep-fryer with 3 inches of oil and heat to 370°F. Combine flour, salt and enough of the water to form a thick batter. Add the vegetables and mix thoroughly. Drop dumpling batter into the hot oil by the spoonful. After 1 or 2 minutes turn dumplings over and fry for 1 minute more, or until golden and crisp. Drain on absorbent paper, and keep individual servings warm in a preheated 250°F. oven. Serve the *tempura* with mounds of grated *daikon* seasoned lightly with *shoyu*. For special occasions add diced raw shrimps to the batter.

VARIATION: Substitute a mixture of precooked tender chestnuts and snow peas for the vegetables used above. Deep-fry by the spoonful. Or stir 2 cups tender (precooked) corn kernels into the batter, and serve *tempura* corn dumplings with deep-fried *harusame* (transparent noodles).

Konomi Tempura

Dip whole almonds, cashews or walnuts, olives or pitted *umeboshi* into *tempura* batter and deep-fry. Delicious as snacks with beer. Or, cook fava beans in water to cover. When tender, trim away outer skins and dip into *tempura* batter; deep-fry until crisp and golden.

Deep-Fried Vegetable Balls   SERVES 5

> Oil for deep-frying
> 1 small onion, minced
> 5 green beans, rinsed, trimmed, chopped
>   into small pieces
> ¼ pound pumpkin or squash, puréed
> 2 or 3 tablespoons *seitan*, minced
> 1 teaspoon sea salt
> 1 cup whole-wheat flour
> 2 cups bread crumbs or cornmeal

Fill a heavy skillet or deep-fryer with 3 inches of oil and heat to 360°F. Combine onion, beans, pumpkin or squash purée and *seitan*, and season with the salt. Add enough of the flour to hold the mixture together and form into balls approximately 1 inch in diameter. Coat balls with bread crumbs or cornmeal and drop into the hot oil. Fry both sides until golden and crisp. Drain on a wire rack or absorbent paper before serving.

Kabu Awayuki Age   SERVES 5
(Deep-Fried Turnip with Egg White)

> Oil for deep-frying
> 3 cups grated turnip
> 3 tablespoons unbleached white flour,
>   approximately
> 1 egg white, beaten until stiff
> 2½ tablespoons grated *daikon*
> 2½ tablespoons grated carrot
> 5 teaspoons *shoyu*

Pour 3 inches of oil into a heavy skillet or deep-fryer and heat to 350°F. Combine the turnip with enough of the flour to form a thick batter, then fold in the egg white. Drop into the hot oil by the spoonful and deep-fry for 2 or 3 minutes, or until browned and crisp. Drain on absorbent paper and serve with a mixture of grated *daikon* and carrot seasoned lightly with *shoyu* for dipping.

Kabocha Tempura *(Deep-Fried Pumpkin)*   SERVES 5

> 1 small pumpkin or acorn squash
> ½ teaspoon and a **dash** of sea salt
> Oil for deep-frying
> 1 cup unbleached white flour
> ¾ cup water, approximately
> 2 cups bread crumbs or cornmeal
> 5 tablespoons grated *daikon*
> 5 teaspoons *shoyu*

Peel pumpkin, then cut it into large chunks. Steam for 15 minutes, or until just tender. Season with a dash of salt to accentuate pumpkin's flavor.

Pour 3 inches of oil into a skillet or deep-fryer and heat to 350°F. Combine flour, water and remaining ½ teaspoon salt to form a batter. Dip pumpkin chunks into batter, then into bread crumbs, and drop into the hot oil. Deep-fry until golden and crisp. Drain on absorbent paper and serve accompanied with small mounds of *daikon* radish seasoned lightly with *shoyu* for dipping.

VARIATION: To deep-fry without first steaming, cut pumpkin into thin crescents. Dip immediately into batter and drop into hot oil.

Onion and Cauliflower Kaki Age   SERVES 5
(Onion with Cauliflower Tempura)

> Oil for deep-frying
> 1½ cups unbleached white flour
> ½ teaspoon sea salt
> 1 cup water, approximately
> 2 medium-size onions, sliced into half-
>   moons
> ½ medium-size cauliflower, spearated into
>   flowerets
> 5 tablespoons fine-grated *daikon*
> 5 teaspoons *shoyu*

Pour 3 inches of oil into a heavy skillet or deep-fryer and heat to 350°F. Combine the flour, salt and water to form a *tempura* batter. Stir the onions and cauliflowerets into the batter, then drop by the spoonful into the hot oil. Deep-fry until golden and crisp. Drain on a wire rack or absorbent paper. Serve accompanied by small mounds of grated *daikon* seasoned lightly with *shoyu*.

VARIATION: Drop thick half-moons of onions (uncoated with batter) into hot oil and deep-fry until cooked through, browned and crisp. Drain and serve with walnut *miso* (p. 163).

Renkon Miso Inro   SERVES 5

(Lotus Root Tempura with Miso)

Oil for deep-frying
1 cup unbleached white flour
¾ cup water, approximately
½ teaspoon sea salt
2 tablespoons *miso*, approximately
15 rounds (⅓ inch thick) of lotus root
5 tablespoons fine grated *daikon*
5 teaspoons *shoyu*

Pour 3 inches of oil into a heavy skillet or deep-fryer and heat to 350°F. Combine the flour, water and salt to form a batter. Use the *miso* to fill the holes in each lotus root round, then dip the rounds into the batter to coat thoroughly. Drop into the hot oil and deep-fry until golden and crisp. Drain on absorbent paper and serve with *daikon* lightly seasoned with *shoyu* for dipping.

VARIATION: Dip the lotus rounds into bread crumbs before dropping them into the oil or immediately after deep-frying. Crisp and delicious.

Kuri Igaguri *(Mock Chestnut Tempura)*   SERVES 5

Oil for deep-frying
1 cup unbleached white flour
1 to 2 tablespoons *yannoh* (grain coffee)
½ to ¾ cup water
¼ teaspoon sea salt
20 medium-size chestnuts, cooked in water
    to cover until tender
1 or 2 ounces *somen* noodles, broken into
    ⅓-inch lengths

Fill a heavy skillet or deep-fryer with 3 inches of oil and heat to 350°F. Combine flour, *yannoh*, water and salt to form a thick batter. Dip each chestnut into the batter to coat thoroughly, then cover with pieces of *somen*. Drop into the hot oil and deep-fry both sides until rich brown and crisp. Drain on absorbent paper before serving.

Pumpkin Croquettes   SERVES 5

3 cups pumpkin or acorn squash purée
½ cup minced onion
¼ cup grated carrot
1 heaping tablespoon whole-wheat flour
¾ teaspoon sea salt
Oil for deep-frying
1 cup unbleached white flour
1 cup water
2 cups bread crumbs or cornmeal

Combine the first four ingredients and add ½ teaspoon salt. Form into 10 croquettes and set aside.

Pour 3 inches of oil into a heavy skillet or deep-fryer and heat to 350°F. Combine the unbleached white flour, water and remaining ¼ teaspoon salt to form a batter. Dip the croquettes into the batter, then roll in bread crumbs. Drop into the hot oil and deep-fry until golden and crisp. Drain on absorbent paper before serving.

VARIATION: Brown the croquettes in a well-oiled skillet. Serve with gravy (p. 162).

WILD VEGETABLES

For well over a thousand years it has been a custom in Japan to eat *nanakusa-gayu,* rice gruel of seven greens, on the 7th day of January. This delicious gruel was thought to be the best insurance against colds and the flu even in the midst of influenza season. I remember as a child searching through the hills and valleys surrounding our village to gather *seri* (wild parsley), *nazuna* (shepherd's purse), *hakobera* (chickweed), *hotokenoza* (the Buddha's throne, similar to dandelion), *suzuna* (turnip leaves), *suzushiro* (*daikon* leaves) and *gogyo* (Gnaphalium Multiceps). They were prepared on the chopping board to the rhythm of an old folk song:

Sutonton ton ton	Chop-chop and chop
nanakusa nazuna	the seven greens and shepherd's purse
todo no tori ga	before the Chinese bird*
wataranu saki ni	flies o'er
pata kusa pata kusa	pound the greens, pound the greens

The greens used in this dish emerge from the earth in early spring and can often be seen peeking out over a heavy blanket of snow. More than just surviving the bitter cold, they are strengthened by it. Rich in minerals and slightly bitter in taste, they aid in the removal of excess salts, oil and protein stored throughout they body. Untended by human hands these *yang* and hardy plants grow free of the contamination of chemical fertilizers and insecticides. They are half-buried treasures well worth an exploratory outing to find. Here are some simple ways to prepare them; serve them in small portions or use them as a garnish.

*A euphemism for the diseases believed brought to Japan from the mainland by early Chinese and Korean immigrants.

Bracken

SERVES 5

Use the young shoots or fiddleheads found in early spring.

¼ pound bracken
1 teaspoon sea salt
1 tablespoon sesame oil
2 to 3 tablespoons *shoyu*

Wash the bracken thoroughly and trim off discolored (brownish) areas. Bring a small pan of water (just enough to cover the bracken) to a boil and add the salt. Drop in the bracken, return to the boil, and cook for 10 minutes. Drain bracken in a colander and cut into 1-inch lengths.

Heat a heavy skillet and coat with the oil. Add the bracken and sauté over medium heat for 5 minutes, stirring gently. Season with *shoyu*, reduce heat to very low, and simmer dry. Serve small portions.

VARIATIONS: A. Cut a sheet of lightly toasted *nori* into halves, and place on a *sudare* or bamboo mat. Divide the sautéed bracken between the 2 *nori* halves, arranging the bracken along one edge of each piece of *nori*. Sprinkle the opposite edge of each *nori* sheet with a few drops of water. Roll into a tight cylinder. Remove mat and slice rolls crosswise into rounds.

B. Douse 1 piece of *aburage* (fried bean curd) with boiling water, and drain. Using scissors, open the piece by cutting into 1 long and 2 short sides. Lay the piece out flat and cut it into halves, then place on a *sudare* or bamboo mat. Divide the sautéed bracken between the two *aburage* halves, arranging the bracken along one edge of each piece. Roll into a cylinder and tie each cylinder at 4 equidistant points with strips of *kampyo* (gourd) rinsed in lightly salted water. Bring 2 cups *kombu dashi* (p. 136) to a boil and season with ¼ cup *shoyu*. Drop in the rolls and cook for 15 minutes, or until all liquid has been absorbed or evaporated and the *aburage* is well flavored. Drain rolls and allow to cool, then slice each roll crosswise into 5 pieces.

WILD VEGETABLES

Coltsfoot Leaves Nitsuke

SERVES 5

Use the leaves while they are young and tender.

½ pound coltsfoot
1 tablespoon sesame oil
3 tablespoons *shoyu*

Wash and peel the coltsfoot, and cut into 1⅓-inch lengths. Heat a heavy skillet and coat with the oil. Sauté the coltsfoot over medium heat for 5 minutes, stirring constantly. Add a little water, and simmer until tender. Season with *shoyu*, then continue to simmer until dry.

Coltsfoot stores very well; the longer it is to be stored, the longer you must cook it initially.

VARIATIONS: A. Cook the coltsfoot in a pan of salted boiling water until tender. Drain and chop fine before sautéing as above.

B. Prepare coltsfoot *nori*-roll as in variation A on p.125.

Coltsfoot Bud Tempura

SERVES 5

Oil for deep-frying
10 coltsfoot buds
1 teaspoon *tahini* (sesame butter)
½ cup and 2 tablespoons water
½ cup whole-wheat flour
5 tablespoons grated *daikon*
5 teaspoons *shoyu*

Fill a heavy skillet or deep-fryer with 3 inches of oil and heat to 350°F. Rinse the buds in warm, lightly salted water; drain and pat dry. Blend the *tahini* with 2 tablespoons water. Combine the flour and remaining water to form a batter. Dip the buds one at a time into the *tahini*, then into the batter, and deep-fry until golden and crisp. Drain on absorbent paper and accompany each serving with a mound of grated *daikon* seasoned lightly with *shoyu*.

Coltsfoot Buds with Miso

SERVES 5

1 cup coltsfoot buds
1 tablespoon sesame oil
¼ cup *miso*, thinned with water to a cream

Put the coltsfoot buds in a colander and douse them with boiling water. Drain, then slice the buds fine. Heat the oil in a heavy skillet, add the coltsfoot buds, and sauté over medium heat for 5 minutes, stirring lightly. Add the thinned *miso* and simmer for 5 to 10 minutes more. Delicious as a garnish with rice.

Dandelion Nitsuke

SERVES 5

Pick dandelions while the leaves are still tender and before the flower blooms.

½ pound dandelion greens
1 tablespoon sesame oil
3 tablespoons *shoyu*, or 1 tablespoon *miso* thinned with 2 tablespoons water
1 tablespoon white sesame seeds, toasted and chopped

Wash the greens well and chop them fine. Heat the oil in a heavy skillet, add the chopped greens, and sauté over medium heat for 2 or 3 minutes. Season with *shoyu* or thinned *miso* and simmer until dry. Serve sprinkled with chopped sesame seeds.

VARIATION: To prepare dandelion roots, scrub them well, then mince. Sauté in a little sesame oil over medium heat for 3 or 4 minutes. Season with *shoyu* or thinned *miso*, and simmer dry. Use sparingly as a garnish with rice. A traditional remedy for arthritis.

Mustard Ohitashi

SERVES 5

½ pound mustard, washed thoroughly
1 teaspoon sea salt
3 tablespoons white sesame seeds, toasted
   and ground to a paste
2 or 3 teaspoons *shoyu*

Use the blossoms, leaves and tender portions of the stem. Bring a pan of water to a boil (more than enough to cover the mustard) and add the salt. Drop in the mustard, return to the boil, and cook for 5 minutes, or until the leaves are bright green and the stems are fully tender. Remove mustard before the blossoms have turned yellow. Drain mustard in a colander and quickly fan to room temperature. Blend the sesame paste and *shoyu*, and serve individual portions of the mustard topped with the sesame mixture.

Wild Parsley

SERVES 5

¼ pound parsley
1 tablespoon sesame oil
2 or 3 tablespoons *shoyu*
3 tablespoons black sesame seeds, toasted
   and ground to a paste in a *suribachi*
2 tablespoons water

Trim away the parsley roots and rinse the leaves thoroughly. Place leaves in a colander and douse with boiling water. Drain, then chop fine. Sauté in the oil over medium heat, stirring gently, for 2 or 3 minutes. Season with *shoyu* and simmer until dry.

Blend the sesame paste and water; add to the sautéed parsley and toss.

VARIATIONS: A. Roll the tossed parsley in lightly toasted *nori* (see variation A on p. 125)

B. Coat the leaves with *tempura* batter and deep-fry until pale golden and crisp. Serve as a canapé or hors d'oeuvre, or as an accompaniment with wine.

Wild Spinach

SERVES 5

½ pound wild spinach
2 tablespoons sesame oil
2 tablespoons water
2 or 3 tablespoons *shoyu*
2 tablespoons *tahini* (sesame butter)

Wash spinach well, then dip into a pan of boiling water for an instant; cut spinach into ⅔-inch lengths. Heat a heavy skillet and coat with the oil. Sauté the spinach over medium heat, stirring constantly, for 5 minutes. Add water and *shoyu*, cover pan, and simmer, stirring occasionally, for 20 minutes. Remove from heat and allow to cool. Serve individual portions topped with *tahini*.

Wild Spinach Ohitashi Goma-Ae

SERVES 5

1 teaspoon sea salt
¼ pound wild spinach
2 tablespoons white sesame seeds, washed
2 tablespoons water
2 tablespoons *shoyu*

Bring a large pan of water to a rolling boil and add the salt. Drop in the spinach, return to the boil, and cook for 5 minutes, or until leaves are bright green. Remove spinach and drain thoroughly in a colander.

Put the sesame seeds in a heavy skillet and roast over moderately high heat, stirring constantly, until brown and fragrant. Empty seeds into a *suribachi* and grind to a paste. Thin the paste with 2 tablespoons water and season with *shoyu*. Add drained spinach to the *suribachi* and toss ingredients together. Serve small portions.

WILD VEGETABLES

Wild Scallions

SERVES 5

> ¼ pound wild scallions
> 1 tablespoon sesame oil
> 2 or 3 tablespoons *shoyu*

Wash the scallions and cut them into 1-inch lengths. Sauté in the oil over medium heat for 3 or 4 minutes. Season with the *shoyu*, and simmer until dry. Or add the scallions to a *miso* soup about 5 minutes before adding the *miso*. Or dip the pieces into *tempura* batter and deep-fry.

Thistle Leaves Ohitashi

SERVES 5

> Gather thistle leaves in early spring while the stems are still tender.

> 1 teaspoon sea salt
> ½ pound thistle leaves, rinsed well
> *Shoyu*
> Sesame, peanut or cashew butter

Bring a pan of water to a boil and add the salt. Drop in the leaves, return to the boil, and cook for 3 to 5 minutes, or until leaves are bright green. Drain. Serve seasoned with *shoyu* alone, or tossed with sesame, peanut or cashew butter.

VARIATION: For delicious *tempura*, coat 1 side of the leaves with batter and deep-fry until crisp. Serve with grated *daikon* lightly seasoned with *shoyu*.

Thistle Roots Nitsuke

> ½ pound thistle roots
> 2 tablespoons sesame oil
> 2 tablespoons *shoyu*

Wash and scrub the roots very well; slice fine on the diagonal. Heat the oil in a heavy skillet, add the thistle roots, and sauté over medium heat, stirring gently, for 2 or 3 minutes. Add water to cover, bring to a boil, and cover pan. Reduce heat to low and simmer for 30 minutes, or until tender. Season with *shoyu* and simmer until dry. Use sparingly as a garnish with rice. Thistle roots are a traditional remedy for rheumatism.

Trefoil

To prepare as *ohitashi*, drop the rinsed leaves into a pan of boiling salted water and cook until leaves are bright green. Drain and serve with *shoyu* or tossed with *tahini* (sesame butter); or add the leaves to *miso* soup several minutes before adding the *miso*.

To prepare the roots, scrub, then mince. Sauté in sesame oil over medium heat, stirring lightly, for 3 or 4 minutes. Season with *shoyu* and simmer until dry. Serve as a garnish with rice; or drop the roots, without batter, into hot *tempura* oil and deep-fry until crisp. Drain and then chop.

SALADS

Salads made with raw, pressed or lightly boiled vegetables are relatively *yin*. Serve them to balance *yang* ingredients in your meals or to keep in tune with the climate.

Pressed Salad

Salting, then pressing raw vegetables removes excess liquid, making the vegetables more *yang*. Pressed salads are therefore ideal in *yin,* wintry climates. The longer the vegetables are pressed, the more they come to resemble pickles. Cabbage, lettuce, cucumber, carrot, onion, and most other vegetables are delicious prepared in this way.

Cut roots into thin slices or slivers, chop green leaves fine, and cut heads into 1-inch-wide pieces. Place the vegetables in a large bowl, sprinkle with salt, and cover with a dish that sits directly on top of the ingredients. Put a stone or other heavy object on top of the plate for added pressure; or combine the vegetables and salt in a salad press, and press from 30 minutes to 3 days, pouring off water as it is expressed. Serve small portions—1 to 2 tablespoons—to each person.

Endive Salad

SERVES 5

3 small endives
1 medium-size cucumber
5 small flowered red radishes
2 tablespoons olive or corn oil
½ tablespoon sea salt, or 1 tablespoon *umeboshi* juice (p. 207)
2 or 3 drops of lemon juice

Cut the endives into ½-inch pieces; cut the cucumber into diagonal slices. Soak the red radishes in cold water until they open. Combine olive oil, salt and lemon juice in a large bowl. Add the vegetables and toss the ingredients together lightly.

Biifun Salad

SERVES 5

1⅓ tablespoons sea salt
6 ounces *biifun* (rice flour noodles)
1 small cauliflower, separated into flowerets
½ bunch watercress
1 small carrot, slivered
3 tablespoons corn or olive oil
1 teaspoon fresh orange juice, approximately
1 hard-cooked egg, yolk and white separated
Parsley sprigs

Bring 1 quart water to a rolling boil and add 1 teaspoon salt. Drop in the *biifun* noodles, return to the boil, and cook for 3 or 4 minutes. Drain through a strainer and set noodles aside.

Bring a second pan of water to a boil and add 1 teaspoon salt. Drop in the cauliflowerets, return to the boil, and cook for 5 minutes, or until flowerets are just tender but still crisp. Lift the flowerets out with a strainer or slotted spoon and set them aside to drain. Drop the watercress into the pan and cook for 2 or 3 minutes, or until the leaves are bright green. Dip leaves into a basin of cold water and set aside in a colander. Now drop the carrot slivers into the water and cook for 2 or 3 minutes, or until bright orange. Lift out, drain, and set aside.

Combine oil, remaining 1 tablespoon salt and the orange juice in a large bowl. Add noodles and vegetables, toss ingredients together, and place salad on a large platter. Garnish with egg white and yolk, grated separately, and parsley sprigs.

Cauliflower Salad

SERVES 5

3 pieces of *koya-dofu* (dried *tofu*), fine-grated
2 tablespoons corn or sesame oil
1½ teaspoons and a dash of sea salt
1 or 2 tablespoons *shoyu*
3 small carrots, grated
1 small cauliflower, separated into
  flowerets
½ pound watercress
2 or 3 flowered red radishes

Place *koya-dofu* at the center of 3 layers of cheesecloth or a piece of unbleached muslin approximately 1 foot square, and gather corners to form a sack. Hold sack in a pan of boiling water for 2 or 3 minutes, then cool under running cold water. Press sack between palms while continuing to rinse until white foam is no longer released, then squeeze out excess liquid.

Heat a heavy skillet and coat with the oil. Sauté the *koyu-dofu* over medium heat for 2 or 3 minutes, stirrring constantly. Add water to cover and cook until dry. Season with ½ teaspoon salt and the *shoyu,* trying to keep the *koya-dofu's* color light. Remove from heat and cool to room temperature. Blend in grated carrots and set mixture aside.

Bring a large pan of water to a boil and add 1 teaspoon salt. Drop in flowerets, return to the boil, and cook for 5 minutes, or until tender but still crisp. Drain flowerets in a colander. Now drop in the watercress and cook until leaves are bright green and stems are tender. Dip leaves into a basin of cold water to stop the cooking, and drain in a colander. Squeeze leaves to rid them of excess liquid, chop, and sprinkle lightly with remaining salt.

Arrange cauliflowerets at the center of a large platter. Ring flowerets with the *tofu*-carrot mixture, then with the green watercress leaves. Garnish with a few red radishes.

Boiled Salad

Another way to "yangize" raw vegetables for use in salads is to steam them or boil them in lightly salted water. Cook until just tender but still crisp. Cut ingredients fine to cook them quickly. Use the cooking water for baking, or as a weak *dashi* for cooking other vegetables.

Chick-Pea Salad

SERVES 5

2 ounces *harusame* (transparent noodles), or
  substitute 2 ounces cooked vermicelli
1½ teaspoons sea salt
½ small carrot, cut into thin half-moons
1 teaspoon minced onion
2 tablespoons corn or olive oil
Few drops of fresh orange juice
1 medium-size cucumber, sliced fine on the
  diagonal
2 cups cooked chick-peas (p. 169)

Bring 4 to 6 cups water to a boil, drop in the *harusame,* and cook for 3 or 4 minutes. Drain *harusame* and rinse under cold running water until thoroughly cooled; cut into 1-inch lengths.

Bring a small pan of water to a boil and add ½ teaspoon salt. Drop in the carrot slices, return to the boil, and cook for several minutes, or until bright orange and just tender. Drain carrot and set aside.

Put minced onion in a large bowl. Add oil, remaining 1 teaspoon salt and the orange juice, and let stand for 10 minutes. Now add noodles, carrot, cucumber and chick-peas, and toss ingredients together.

Mixed Vegetable Salad

SERVES 5

        1 medium-size cucumber
        1 *daikon* stem
        1 teaspoon sea salt
        10 thin rounds of lotus root
        2 ounces watercress
        1 coltsfoot
        1 small carrot, slivered
        2 tablespoons white sesame seeds, washed
        1 level tablespoon *miso*
        3 tablespoons olive oil
        Few drops of fresh lemon juice

Trim away cucumber tips, then rub tips against exposed ends of cucumber until a white foam is no longer released. Discard tips and rinse away foam. Slice the cucumber on the diagonal and set aside. Trim *daikon* leaves away from the stem; cut the stem into 5 pieces, and score each piece to half its depth. Soak the pieces in cold water for 20 minutes.

Bring 4 to 6 cups of water to a rolling boil and add the salt. Drop in the lotus root, return to the boil, and cook for 1 or 2 minutes, or until just tender; set lotus root aside to drain. Drop watercress into the same pan and cook for 1 or 2 minutes, or until the leaves are bright green. Dip leaves into a basin of cold water to stop the cooking, and drain in a colander. Now drop in the coltsfoot, return to the boil, and cook for 2 or 3 minutes, or until just tender. Drain coltsfoot, then peel and slice on the diagonal. Drop the carrot slivers into the pan and cook for several minutes, or until bright orange and just tender. Lift out and set aside.

Toast the sesame seeds in a heavy skillet over moderately high heat, stirring constantly, until brown and fragrant. Empty seeds into a *suribachi* and grind to a paste. Blend *miso* into the paste, then add olive oil and lemon juice. Add the vegetables and toss ingredients together.

Wakame and Cucumber Salad

SERVES 5

        1½ ounces *wakame*
        Dash of sea salt
        1 medium-size cucumber, sliced very fine on
            the diagonal
        Pulp of 1 orange
        ¼ cup *umeboshi* juice (p. 207)

Wash *wakame* and soak for 10 to 15 minutes. Strain *wakame*, press between palms to remove excess liquid, and cut into ⅔-inch squares. Rub the salt into the cucumber slices, let stand for 10 minutes, then squeeze out liquid.

Combine *wakame*, cucumber, and orange in a large bowl. Pour in *umeboshi* juice, and toss. Delicious on a hot summer day.

Fruit Salad

SERVES 5

        1⅓ tablespoons sea salt
        1 small carrot, cut into thin half-moons
        1½ cups gingko leaves of lotus root
        1 teaspoon minced onion
        4 tablespoons corn or olive oil
        2 medium-size apples, chopped
        2 small cucumbers, cut into thin half-
            moons, sprinkled with salt
        20 strawberries, rinsed in salted water
        5 flowered red radishes
        1 hard-boiled egg, yolk and white separated

Bring a small pan of water to a boil and add 1 teaspoon salt. Drop in the carrot slices, return to the boil, and cook for several minutes, until carrot is bright orange and just tender. Drain and set aside. Now drop in the lotus root and cook for 2 or 3 minutes, or until just tender; drain.

Put onion in a large bowl. Add oil and remaining 1 tablespoon salt, and allow to stand for 10 minutes. Add carrot slices, lotus root and apples, and toss ingredients together. Arrange on a large platter and surround with cucumber slices, strawberries and radishes. Top with egg white and yolk, grated separately.

III. SOUPS, STEWS and *NABE RYORI*

SOUPS AND STEWS

Life originated in the sea. Re-creating ourselves at each meal, we include a small replica of life's original womb in the form of a salty soup, or we cook our vegetables in a diluted form of seawater. Soups are an excellent way to drink liquid. A bowl of delicious *miso* soup made with your favorite vegetables and served at breakfast, lunch or dinner will provide you with protein and stamina to meet the day's needs.

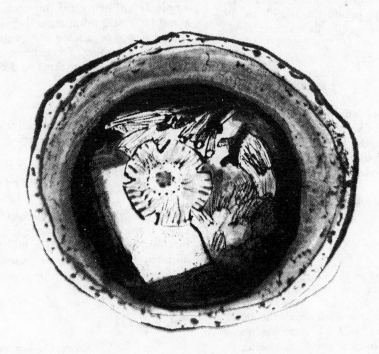

Ichiban Dashi

MAKES 2½ QUARTS

1 strip of *kombu*, 7 by 3 inches
10 cups cold water
1 cup *katsuobushi* (dried bonito flakes)

Wipe the *kombu* clean with a dry cloth. Combine with the water and bring to a boil over high heat. Boil *kombu* for 2 to 4 minutes, then remove and reserve, or allow it to remain in the pan while you stir in the dried bonito flakes. Return to the boil and turn off heat. Let stand for 2 or 3 minutes, or until the bonito flakes sink to the bottom. Strain, reserving the bonito flakes (and *kombu* if still in the pan).

Niban Dashi

MAKES 2½ QUARTS

To the leftover *kombu* and bonito flakes reserved from the *ichiban dashi* now add 10 cups water and any vegetable trimmings that may be on hand. Over high heat bring to a boil and cook with the lid slightly ajar for 5 minutes. Turn off heat and allow to stand until the bonito flakes again sink to the bottom of the pan. Strain, discarding flakes and trimmings. Use as a weaker stock for cooking vegetables.

Kombu Dashi

MAKES 1 QUART

1 strip of *kombu*, 7 by 3 inches
4 cups cold water

Wipe the *kombu* clean with a dry cloth. Soak the *kombu* in the water for 2 to 3 hours, or boil for 1 hour. Strain and use the *kombu* water in place of clear water in cooking.

Vegetable Stock

MAKES 2 QUARTS

10 cups water
1 piece of *kombu*, 3 inches square
3 cups vegetable trimmings (onion, carrot, celery, etc.)
2 or 3 eggshells

Bring the water to a boil and add *kombu*, trimmings and eggshells. Return to the boil and cook for 30 to 40 minutes, leaving the lid slightly ajar to prevent boiling over. The eggshells will help clear the stock. Turn off heat, allow to stand for 2 or 3 minutes, and strain, reserving the liquid.

Try never to discard any vegetable parts when preparing other dishes. You can make a delicious stock using carrot crowns, onion skins and other trimmings.

Fish Stock

MAKES 2 QUARTS

3 cups chopped trimmings of any white-fleshed or red-fleshed fish (heads, tails, etc.)
1 small onion, minced
1 teaspoon fine slices of gingerroot
10 cups water

Do not use white- and red-fleshed fish trimmings together. Place trimmings into a saucepan, adding onion, gingerroot and water. Bring to a boil and cook for 30 to 40 minutes, skimming off any scum rising to the surface. Turn off heat, let stand for several minutes, and strain, reserving the liquid.

Chicken Stock

MAKES 2 QUARTS

Leftover chicken bones (1 to 2 pounds)
½ cup chopped onion
1 cup shredded cabbage
1 small carrot
1 celery stalk
10 cups water
4 or 5 eggshells

Break or chop the bones into 2- to 3-inch lengths. Place in a saucepan with vegetables and water, bring to a boil, and cook for 30 to 40 minutes. Drop in the eggshells and return to a boil, while skimming off any surface debris. When clear, turn off heat, allow to stand for several minutes, and strain, reserving the liquid.

Wakame Miso Soup
SERVES 5

½ ounce dried *wakame*
5 cups *kombu dashi* (p. 136)
1 cake of *tofu*, cubed (optional)
5 level tablespoons *miso*

If the *wakame* comes in thin sheets, it need not be soaked; if in bunches, soak in water to cover for 10 minutes. Cut the *wakame* into small pieces. Bring the *dashi* to a boil and remove *kombu* if still in *dashi*. Add *wakame* and cook for 5 to 10 minutes. Add *tofu* cubes. Thin the *miso* with a few tablespoons of the cooking broth and add, stirring until smooth. Return just to a boil and turn off heat.

Mugi-miso Soup
SERVES 5

2 scallions or leeks
2 turnips
1 ounce *wakame*
1 tablespoon sesame oil
4 to 5 cups water
2 or 3 tablespoons *mugi-miso*

Slice the scallions or leeks diagonally into ½-inch lengths, separating greens parts, white parts and root fibrils. Slice the turnips into thin half-moons, and chop their greens fine. If the *wakame* is in bunches, rinse carefully, soak in water for 10 minutes, then cut into ⅓-inch lengths; if it is in sheets, cut into small squares.

Heat the oil in a heavy saucepan. Sauté the scallion greens over medium heat for 1 minute, stirring constantly. Add whites, then roots, and sauté together for 1 minute more. Add turnip leaves, then turnips, sautéing each

lightly as you add it. Now add water and bring to a boil over high heat. Reduce heat to medium, add *wakame*, and cover pan. Cook for 15 to 20 minutes, or until vegetables are tender. Thin the *miso* in ½ cup of the cooking broth and add, stirring to blend *miso* evenly. Bring just to a boil and turn off heat. Serve immediately.

VARIATIONS: A. If using *hatcho-miso*, reduce amount of *miso* per cup of soup.

B. When preparing *miso* soup for children or older adults, substitute *daikon* for the turnips and reduce amount of *miso* by ¼ to ½.

Sake-no-kasu Jiru
SERVES 5
(Miso Soup with Sake Lees)

1 tablespoon sesame oil
2 scallions or leeks, sliced diagonally into 1-inch lengths
2 cups rectangles of *daikon*
5 taro roots, sliced lengthwise into halves (optional)
5 slices of flowered carrot
5 cups and 3 or 4 tablespoons water
2 heaping tablespoons *miso*
½ to 1 cup *sake-no-kasu* (sake lees)*

Heat a heavy saucepan and coat with the oil. Sauté the scallions or leeks over medium heat for 1 or 2 minutes, stirring constantly. Add consecutively *daikon*, taro root (if used) and carrot. Mix the ingredients together and sauté for 1 minute more. Pour in 5 cups water and bring to a boil over high heat. Reduce heat to medium, cover, and cook for 30 minutes, or until the vegetables are tender. Thin the *miso* in 4 or 5 tablespoons of the cooking soup, and thin the sake lees in remaining tablespoons water. Blend the *miso* and then the lees into the soup, stirring until smooth. Bring just to a boil and turn off heat. Serve immediately.

*Sake lees can be found at Oriental food shops.

SOUPS AND STEWS

Corn Soup

2 tablespoons corn oil
1 small onion, minced
3 medium-size ears of corn, kernels cut
   from cobs
1 piece of *kombu*, 3 inches square, wiped
   clean
6 cups and 2 tablespoons water
½ teaspoon sea salt
½ small cauliflower, separated into
   flowerets
1 tablespoon *kuzu*
Sea salt
2 tablespoons croutons
2 tablespoons minced parsley

Heat a heavy saucepan and coat with the oil. Sauté the onion over medium heat for 2 or 3 minutes, stirring gently. Add the corn kernels and sauté together lightly for 1 minute more. Do not allow the kernels to brown. Place the *kombu* in the pan, pour in 6 cups water, and bring to a boil over high heat. Reduce heat to medium, cover, and cook for 20 to 30 minutes.

While the soup is cooking bring a small pan of water (enough to cover the flowerets) to a boil over high heat, and add ½ teaspoon sea salt. Drop in the cauliflowerets, return to the boil, and cook for 5 minutes, or until tender but still crisp. Lift out the flowerets with a slotted spoon, and drain in a colander.

Dissolve the *kuzu* in 2 tablespoons water. When the soup is done, season with salt to taste, then pour in the *kuzu*. Simmer for 1 or 2 minutes more, stirring while the soup thickens. Serve topped with cauliflowerets, croutons, and a sprinkling of minced parsley.

Corn Cream I

2 tablespoons corn oil
1 small onion, minced
1 cup corn flour
1 small carrot, cut into slivers
6 cups *kombu dashi* (p. 136)
1 tablespoon sesame oil
¼ cup unbleached white flour
¾ cup water
Sea salt
3 tablespoons croutons
2 tablespoons minced parsley

Heat a heavy saucepan and coat with the corn oil. Sauté the onion over medium heat, stirring gently, until lightly browned. Add the corn flour and sauté until golden. Add the carrot and *dashi*, and bring to a boil. Cover and simmer over an asbestos pad for 30 minutes, stirring occasionally.

While the cream is cooking, prepare a flour sauce. Heat a heavy skillet and coat with the sesame oil. Add the white flour and cook until lightly browned and fragrant, stirring constantly to heat evenly. Remove from stove and cool, then gradually add the water, stirring until smooth. Return pan to stove and cook, stirring constantly, for 2 to 3 minutes, or until edges of sauce bubble.

When the corn cream is ready, blend in the flour sauce. Season with salt to taste, and simmer for 5 minutes more. Serve topped with croutons and sprinkled with minced parsley.

Corn Cream II

SERVES 5

> 2 tablespoons corn oil
> 1 medium-size onion, minced
> 3 medium-size ears of corn, kernels cut
>   from cobs
> 6 cups *kombu dashi* (p. 136)
> Sea salt
> 1 heaping tablespoon *kuzu*
> 2 or 3 tablespoons water
> 1 egg, beaten
> 2 tablespoons chopped parsley
> 5 thin strips of lemon peel

Heat a heavy saucepan and coat with the oil. Add onion and sauté over medium heat, stirring gently, for 2 or 3 minutes. Add corn and sauté together lightly for 1 minute more. Do not allow the kernels to brown. Pour in the *kombu dashi* and bring to a boil over high heat. Reduce heat to medium, cover, and cook for 20 to 30 minutes. When done, season with salt to taste.

Dissolve *kuzu* in the water, then add the egg, stirring until smooth. Add to soup after seasoning with salt, and stir constantly while soup thickens. Serve sprinkled with parsley and garnished with lemon peel.

Gemmai Suiton

SERVES 5

(Clear Soup with Brown Rice Dumplings)

> Oil for deep-frying
> 20 green beans, rinsed and trimmed
> 2 tablespoons sesame oil
> 2 or 3 scallions or leeks, sliced diagonally
>   into 1-inch lengths
> 5 small turnips, quartered
> 5 cups *kombu dashi* (p. 136)
> ½ cup boiling water, approximately
> 1 cup brown rice flour
> 1 teaspoon sea salt
> 1½ tablespoons *shoyu*
> 1 sheet of *nori*

Fill a heavy skillet or deep-fryer with 2 to 3 inches of oil and heat to 350° F. Drop in the beans and deep-fry until crisp. Drain beans on absorbent paper and slice on the diagonal into thirds. Set aside in a warm oven until ready to use.

Heat a heavy saucepan and coat with sesame oil. Sauté the scallions or leeks over medium heat for 4 or 5 minutes, or until lightly browned. Add the turnips and sauté together for 1 minute more. Cover with the *dashi* and bring to a boil over high heat. Reduce heat to medium, cover, and cook for 20 to 30 minutes, or until tender.

While the soup is cooking, and boiling water to the rice flour while stirring vigorously with 4 long wooden chopsticks held in your fist, or with a long fork with 4 tines. Knead for 3 or 4 minutes, until the dough is smooth and somewhat stiff. Pinch off 10 portions of the dough and roll each into a small dumpling.

When the vegetables are tender, season the soup with salt and *shoyu*. Now drop in the 10 dumplings. They will sink to the bottom of the pan; when they return to the surface they are ready. Turn off heat.

Just before serving, toast 1 side of the *nori* by waving it over low heat for 30 seconds, or until crisp. Using scissors, cut the *nori* into halves, the crosswise into thin strips. Ladle the soup into individual serving bowls, and garnish each bowl with some of the green beans and toasted *nori*.

Borscht SERVES 5

3 tablespoons sesame oil
3 small onions, quartered
5 small cabbage leaves, cut into 2-inch
   squares
1 tomato, quartered (optional)
1 beet, cubed
2 small carrots, cubed
½ tablespoon sea salt
5 to 6 cups water
2 bay leaves
2 celery stalks, cubed
Sea salt

Heat a heavy saucepan and coat with the oil. Sauté the onions over medium heat for 5 minutes, or until lightly browned. Add consecutively cabbage, tomato (if used), beet and carrots, mixing the ingredients together. Season with salt (early, to keep the vegetables firm and to help hold their color). Add the water (enough to cover), and drop in the bay leaves. Bring to the boil over high heat, reduce heat to medium and cook, covered, for 20 to 30 minutes, or until the vegetables are tender. Add the celery and cook for 5 minutes more. Season with salt to taste, and serve.

Soup of Wild Mountain Potato

Prepare a soup using your favorite vegetables. When done, add 1 tablespoon finely grated *jinenjo* per cup of soup. Simmer for 1 or 2 minutes more, then season with *shoyu* to taste.

Jinenjo, or mountain potato, grows wild in the mountains of Japan. When grated it clings together in a very viscous paste, telling us that it is very *yang.* It is available at macrobiotic outlets and Oriental food shops. Try it; it's delicious and invigorating.

Kokoh Soup SERVES 5

1½ teaspoons sea salt
½ small cauliflower, separated into
   flowerets
1 tablespoon sesame or sunflower oil
2 small onions, cut into thick crescents
2 cups cubed pumpkin or squash
1 small carrot, diced
3 tablespoons *seitan,* minced
5¾ cups water
5 tablespoons *kokoh*
Sea salt
2 tablespoons minced parsley
1 teaspoon minced orange peel

Bring a small pan of water to a boil over high heat and add ½ teaspoon salt. Drop in the cauliflower, return to the boil, and cook for 3 minutes, or until flowerets are tender but still crisp. Set flowerets aside in a colander to drain.

Heat a heavy saucepan and coat with the oil. Sauté the onions over medium heat, stirring gently, for 5 minutes, or until well browned. Add pumpkin or squash, carrot and *seitan.* Pour in 5 cups water (enough to cover), season with remaining 1 teaspoon salt, and bring to a boil over high heat. Reduce heat to medium, cover pan, and cook for 25 minutes, or until tender.

Thin the *kokoh* in ¾ cup water. When soup is ready, blend in *kokoh.* Cook for 5 minutes more, stirring constantly, and season with salt to taste. Serve topped with cauliflowerets, minced parsley and a sprinkling of orange peel.

Go Jiru (Soybean Potage)   SERVES 5

1 cup soybeans, soaked in water overnight
2 pieces of *aburage*
1 tablespoon sesame or corn oil
2 scallions or leeks, sliced diagonally into
  1-inch lengths
1 small carrot, diced
1½ teaspoons sea salt
5 green beans, rinsed and trimmed
Shoyu

Grind the soybeans to a smooth paste in a *suribachi* or electric mixer. Douse the *aburage* with boiling water, and drain. Cut the pieces into ½-inch squares.

Heat a heavy saucepan and coat with the oil. Sauté the scallions or leeks over medium heat for 2 or 3 minutes, stirring constantly. Add soybean paste, carrot and *aburage* squares. Add enough water to twice cover the ingredients, season with 1 teaspoon salt, and bring to a boil over high heat. Reduce heat to medium, cover, and cook for 30 minutes, stirring occasionally.

While the soup is cooking bring a small pan of water to a boil over high heat and add remaining ½ teaspoon salt. Drop in the green beans, return to the boil, and cook for 4 or 5 minutes, until beans are bright green and just tender. Dip beans into a basin of cold water to stop the cooking and set the color, then drain in a colander. Slice beans diagonally into thirds.

When soup is done, season with *shoyu* to taste. Serve garnished with green beans.

Iwashi no Tsumi-ire   SERVES 5
(Fish Dumpling Soup)

3 medium-size sardines, cleaned and filleted
1 tablespoon fine-grated gingerroot
3 small scallions, rinsed and chopped fine
½ cup unbleached white flour
12 cups water
1 tablespoon corn or sesame oil
1½ cups thin gingko leaves of *daikon*
4 leaves of Chinese cabbage, chopped into
  1-inch-wide strips
5 taro roots, quartered (if available)
1 small carrot, sliced thin on the diagonal
1 piece of *kombu*, 3 inches square, wiped
  clean
Dash of sea salt
Shoyu

Place the sardines in a *suribachi* and grind them to a smooth paste. Blend in the gingerroot and chopped scallions, then add enough of the flour to enable you to shape the mixture into 10 small dumplings that hold together. Bring 6 cups of water to a boil in a 2-quart saucepan and drop in the dumplings. When they rise to the surface, remove them, drain, and set aside.

Heat a heavy saucepan and coat with the oil. Sauté the *daikon* over medium heat for 2 or 3 minutes, stirring gently. Add cabbage, taro roots (if used) and carrot, and drop in the *kombu*. Cover with remaining water and bring to a boil over high heat. Reduce heat to medium, cover, and cook for 20 to 30 minutes, or until tender. Drop in the dumplings and simmer for 3 or 4 minutes more, or until dumplings are heated through. When done, season with a dash of salt and with *shoyu* to taste.

New Year Ozoni SERVES 5

3½ teaspoons sea salt, approximately
1 or 2 scallions or leeks, sliced diagonally
    into 1-inch lengths
10 thin slices of flowered carrot
½ pound spinach or 1 bunch of watercress,
    washed and trimmed
Oil for deep-frying
5 *maki-yuba* (optional)
5 tablespoons sesame oil
1 shallot, minced
1 piece of *kombu*, 3 inches square, wiped
    clean
½ cup unbleached white flour
10 pieces of *omochi* rice cake (p. 61)
2 tablespoons minced parsley

Bring 6 cups water to a boil in a 2-quart saucepan over high heat, and add 1 teaspoon sea salt. Drop in the scallions or leeks, return to the boil, and cook for 5 minutes, or until vegetables are tender. Remove, drain, and set aside. Now drop in the flowered carrot slices and cook for 2 or 3 minutes, or until just tender. Remove the slices, drain them, and set aside. Finally, drop in the spinach or watercress. Cook for 1 to 3 minutes, or until stems are tender. Remove greens and dip into a basin of cold water to stop the cooking and set the color. Squeeze lightly to remove excess water. Arrange in a bundle and slice into 1-inch-long mounds. Set aside, reserving the cooking liquid.

Heat a heavy saucepan and coat with 1 teaspoon sesame oil. Sauté the shallot over medium heat for 1 or 2 minutes, or until its strong aroma is no longer released. Add 5 cups of the reserved cooking liquid, bring to a boil over high heat, and drop in the *kombu*. Reduce heat to medium, cover, and cook for 20 minutes. Remove *kombu* and season the broth with 1 to 2 teaspoons salt, or to taste.

Fill a heavy skillet or deep-fryer with 2 or 3 inches of oil and heat to 350° F. Drop in the *maki-yuba* and deep-fry for 2 or 3 minutes, or until crisp and golden. Drain on absorbent paper, and set aside in a warm oven until ready to use.

Heat a heavy skillet and coat with 3 tablespoons sesame oil. Add the flour and cook over medium heat, stirring constantly, until browned and fragrant. Remove from heat and cool, or dip bottom of pan into cold water. Stir in 2 cups water, blending smooth. Return to the heat, bring to a boil, and simmer for 10 to 15 minutes, stirring constantly. Season with salt to taste, and continue to simmer the sauce until ready to use.

Heat remaining sesame oil in a heavy skillet and brown the *omochi* rice cakes over medium heat. When nicely browned, remove from pan and set aside.

To assemble, place 2 rice cakes in each of 5 serving bowls. Arrange the scallions or leeks, carrot slices and spinach or watercress mounds around the cakes. Pour in the hot broth and spoon some of the thickened sauce on top of each serving. Crown the sauce with a piece of *maki-yuba*, sprinkle with minced parsley, and serve.

Kenchin Jiru *(Vegetable Stew)* SERVES 5

1 tablespoon corn or sesame oil
2 or 3 scallions or leeks, sliced diagonally
    into 1-inch lengths
1 cup shaved burdock
1½ cups thick gingko leaves of *daikon*
1 small carrot, sliced into thick half-moons
1 block of *konnyaku*, cut into 5 pieces
    (optional)
1 piece of *kombu*, 3 inches square, wiped
    clean
Dash of sea salt
6 tablespoons *shoyu*

Heat a heavy pot and coat with the oil. Sauté the scallions or leeks over medium heat for 5 minutes, or until lightly browned. Add consecutively burdock, *daikon*, carrot and *konnyaku* (if used). Mix the ingredients together and sauté for 1 or 2 minutes more. Drop in the *kombu*, add slightly more than enough water to cover, and bring to a boil over high heat. Reduce heat to medium, cover with lid slightly ajar, and cook for 40 minutes or more. Season with salt and *shoyu* to taste, simmer for 1 or 2 minutes more, and serve.

Um-Pen *(Seasonal Stew)*   SERVES 5

> 5 small *shiitake* (dried Japanese mushrooms), soaked in cold water for 20 to 30 minutes, or substitute 10 fresh mushrooms rinsed in lightly salted water
> 2 tablespoons sesame oil
> 1 celery stalk, sliced diagonally into ¾-inch lengths
> 2 cups rectangles of lotus root
> 1 cup rectangles of carrot
> ½ teaspoon and a dash of sea salt
> 10 green beans, rinsed and trimmed
> *Shoyu*
> 2 tablespoons *kuzu*
> 3 tablespoons water
> 5 thin strips of lemon peel

After soaking the *shiitake,* remove their hard stems and slice their broad caps fine. Use fresh mushrooms whole.

Heat a heavy pot and coat with the oil. Sauté the *shiitake* over medium heat for 2 or 3 minutes, stirring gently. Add celery, lotus root and carrot, mixing the ingredients together. Sauté for 1 or 2 minutes more, then add enough water to cover and bring to a boil over high heat. Reduce heat to medium, cover with lid slightly ajar, and cook for 40 minutes or more.

While the stew is cooking bring a small pan of water (enough to cover the green beans) to a boil over high heat, and add ½ teaspoon salt. Drop in the beans, return to the boil, and cook for 5 minutes, or until beans are bright green and tender but still crisp. Drain the beans and dip them into a basin of cold water to stop the

cooking and set the color. Slice beans fine on the diagonal, then set them aside in a colander.

When the stew is ready, season it with *shoyu* to taste. Dissolve the *kuzu* in 3 tablespoons water, and add. Simmer for 2 or 3 minutes more, stirring while the broth thickens. Serve individual portions garnished with some beans and a strip of lemon peel.

Bouillabaisse of Fish   SERVES 5

> 1 tablespoon corn or sesame oil
> 5 small onions, cut vertically into halves
> 6 cups water
> ½ pound red snapper, cut into 5 pieces
> 10 medium-size shrimps, shelled and deveined (p. 119)
> 5 medium-size clams, washed carefully
> 5 bay leaves
> 1 teaspoon sea salt
> 2 celery stalks, sliced diagonally into 1-inch lengths
> ½ teaspoon ground saffron
> Sea salt

Heat a heavy pot and coat with the oil. Sauté the onions over medium heat for 2 or 3 minutes, or until their strong aroma is no longer released. Add 1 cup water and bring to a boil, then drop in the red snapper, shrimps and clams. Now add the bay leaves, season with salt, and pour in remaining 5 cups water. Bring to a boil over high heat, reduce heat to medium, and cover with the lid left slightly ajar. Cook for 40 minutes. Add celery and saffron, and cook for 5 minutes more. Season with salt to taste, and serve.

Sampei Jiru *(Salmon Stew)* SERVES 5

2 pieces of *aburage*
2 tablespoons sesame oil
3 scallions or leeks, sliced diagonally into
⅔-inch lengths
2 cups diced *daikon*
2 potatoes, cubed
1 small carrot, cubed
5 cups water, approximately
½ pound salted salmon, cubed
Dash of sea salt
Shoyu
½ to 1 cup *sake-no-kasu* (sake lees)

Pour boiling water over the *aburage* to rid it of excess oil. Drain, and cut the pieces into small squares.

Heat a heavy pot and coat with the oil. Sauté the scallions or leeks over medium heat for 2 or 3 minutes, stirring constantly. Add consecutively *daikon,* potatoes, carrot and *aburage,* mixing the ingredients together. Add enough of the water to cover, drop in the salmon cubes, and bring to a boil over high heat. Reduce heat to medium, cover with lid ajar, and cook for 30 to 40 minutes. Season with a dash of salt and *shoyu* to taste if the salty salmon has not already flavored the stew. Just before turning off heat, add *sake-no-kasu* thinned with an equal amount of water. Stir until smooth. Perfect for a cold day.

Happosai *(Chinese Stew)* SERVES 5

2 tablespoons corn or sesame oil
3 small onions, quartered
2 cups ¼-inch-thick rounds of lotus root
1 small carrot, cut into 5 irregular chunks
¼ pound *kofu*-loaf (p. 85), cubed, deep-
fried for 2 or 3 minutes, or until crisp,
and drained on absorbent paper
2 teaspoons sea salt
½ small cauliflower, separated into flowerets
20 green beans, rinsed and trimmed
Shoyu
2 tablespoons *kuzu*
3 tablespoons water

Heat a heavy pot (cast iron if available) and coat with the oil. Sauté the onions over medium heat for 5 minutes, or until lightly browned. Add lotus root, carrot and *kofu* cubes. Half-cover the vegetables and *kofu* with water, add 1 teaspoon sea salt, and bring to a boil over high heat. Reduce heat to medium, cover with lid slightly ajar, and cook for 40 minutes or more.

While the stew is cooking, bring a pan of water (enough to cover the cauliflowerets) to a boil over high heat and add 1 teaspoon salt. Drop in the flowerets, return to the boil, and cook for 5 minutes, or until flowerets, are tender but still crisp. Drain in a colander and set aside. Now drop the beans into the same pan of water and cook for 5 minutes, or until bright green and just tender. Dip beans into a basin of cold water to stop the cooking and set the color, and drain in a colander. Cut the beans diagonally into halves.

When the stew is ready, season it with *shoyu* to taste. Dissolve the *kuzu* in 3 tablespoons water, and add. Simmer for 2 or 3 minutes more, stirring while the broth thickens. Serve individual portions garnished with cauliflowerets and beans.

Noppei Jiru (*White Fish Stew*)   SERVES 5

1 tablespoon corn or sesame oil
2 cups thick gingko leaves of *daikon*
5 taro roots, quartered
2 small carrots, sliced into thick rounds
2 *gammodoki* (p. 175), each cut into 5 pieces
   (optional)
½ pound white-fleshed fish, cut into 5
   pieces
1 strip of *kombu*, 3 inches square, wiped
   clean
5 cups and 3 tablespoons water,
   approximately
1 teaspoon sea salt
Shoyu
1 tablespoon *kuzu*

Heat a heavy pot and coat with the oil. Sauté the *daikon* over medium heat for 2 or 3 minutes, stirring constantly. Add consecutively taro, carrots and *gammodoki*, mixing the ingredients together. Drop in the fish and *kombu*, and add enough of the water to slightly more than cover. Season with the salt and bring to a boil over high heat. Reduce heat to medium, cover with lid ajar, and cook for 40 to 50 minutes. Season with *shoyu* to taste, then add the *kuzu* thinned in 3 tablespoons water. Simmer for several minutes more, stirring while the broth thickens.

Vegetable Bouillabaisse   SERVES 10

10 large *shiitake* (dried Japanese mushrooms)
20 strips (2 inches long) of *kampyo* (gourd)
5 pieces of *aburage*
1 medium-size burdock root, cut into slivers
2 tablespoons sesame oil
10 small onions, quartered
2 small carrots, cut into thick diagonal slices
4 bay leaves
6 cups *kombu dashi* (p. 136), approximately
1 teaspoon sea salt
2 celery stalks, sliced diagonally into 1-inch
   lengths
1 cake of *tofu*, grilled (p. 174), and cut into
   10 blocks
½ teaspoon ground saffron
Sea salt

Soak the *shiitake* in cold water for 20 to 30 minutes, and trim away the hard stems. Rinse the gourd strips in lightly salted water, squeeze them dry, and set aside.

Pour boiling water over the *aburage* to rid it of excess oil; drain. Using scissors, open the *aburage* by cutting into 1 long and 2 short sides. Spread the pieces open lengthwise with outer surfaces facing up. Arrange a row of burdock slivers along 1 edge of each piece of *aburage*. Roll into a cylinder and tie with gourd strips at 4 equidistant points. Slice the roll at points midway between the gourd strips and you should have 4 *age* rolls, each held closed at its center by a strip of gourd. Set aside.

Heat a heavy pot and coat with the oil. Sauté the onions over medium heat until their strong aroma is no longer released. Add *shiitake* and then carrots, sautéing each lightly. Now add the *age* rolls, bay leaves and enough of the *dashi* to cover. Season with 1 teaspoon salt, and bring to a boil over high heat. Reduce heat to medium, cover with lid ajar, and cook for 40 minutes. Add celery, *tofu* and saffron, and simmer for 5 minutes more. Season with salt to taste.

SOUPS AND STEWS

Oden with Ninjin and Gobo Kombu Maki

1 pound *shirataki* (bean thread) noodles
12 pieces of *kombu*, each 3 by 1½ inches, wiped clean
20 strips (3 inches long) of *kampyo* (gourd)
5½ small carrots
1 burdock root (1 inch thick)
10 pieces of *aburage*
1½ tablespoons sea salt
10 cabbage leaves
1 tablespoon sesame oil
3 small onions, cut into thin crescents
Oil for deep-frying
1 lotus root (6 inches), grated fine
1 cup unbleached white flour
10 Brussels sprouts
2 cakes of *konnyaku*, cut into wedges
10 thick rounds of *daikon*
10 small turnips
1 or 2 strips of lemon peel
Shoyu

Soak the *shirataki* in water overnight. Soak the *kombu* pieces in cold water for 20 to 30 minutes, or until soft and pliable; save the soaking water. Rinse the gourd strips in salted water, squeeze the strips dry, and set aside.

Cut 2 carrots into slivers; quarter 3 carrots lengthwise, then cut each quarter into 1½-inch lengths; fine-grate remaining ½ carrot. Set each aside separately. Cut the burdock into logs 1½ inchs long, quarter each log lengthwise, and set aside.

Pour boiling water over the *aburage* to rid it of excess oil. Drain, then cut the pieces into halves. Pull open the center of the pieces to make pouches, and set them aside.

Bring 6 cups of water to a boil and add 1 teaspoon salt. Using long chopsticks, hold the stems of the cabbage leaves in the water and cook until they are just tender. Submerge the upper portion of the leaf for an instant, then dip the leaves into a basin of cold water. Drain the leaves, trim the cores smooth, and set aside.

Heat a heavy skillet and coat with the oil. Sauté the onions over medium heat for 2 or 3 minutes, or until they no longer release the strong aroma. Add carrot slivers and sauté together for 1 minute more. Mix ingredients together, sprinkle with a dash of salt, and remove from heat. Allow the mixture to cool, then divide it into 2 parts. Use 1 part to fill all of the *aburage* pouches. Fold over the lip of each pouch to form a flap, and tie with gourd strips. Divide the remaining sautéed vegetables among the cabbage leaves, and roll up the leaves, tucking in the edges. Tie each cabbage roll with a strip of gourd.

Roll 1 piece of *kombu* into a tight cylinder and slice crosswise into thin strips to be used as threads. To prepare *kombu maki,* arrange 2 pieces of carrot and 2 pieces of burdock along the short edge of each of 10 remaining pieces of *kombu.* Roll into a tight cylinder and tie each with *kombu* threads. Set aside.

Fill a heavy skillet or deep-fryer with 3 inches of oil and heat to 350° F. Combine the lotus root and grated carrot, adding enough of the flour to hold the mixture together. Form into 20 balls 1 inch in diameter, and drop into the hot oil. Deep-fry until golden and crisp, then drain on absorbent paper. Skewer 2 lotus balls and 1 Brussels sprout on each of 10 bamboo skewers, and set aside.

Place the remaining piece of *kombu* in the bottom of a shallow, cast-iron pot. Put the ingredients that require long cooking (*kombu*-rolls, *konnyaku, daikon* and turnips) in the center of the pot. Arrange the ingredients that have already been partially cooked or are done quickly near the sides. Now add the water in which the *kombu* soaked and enough fresh water (if necessary) to cover. Bring to a boil over high heat and add 1 tablespoon salt. Reduce heat to low, cover with lid ajar, and drop in the lemon peel. Simmer for 2 to 4 hours. Remove the ingredients arranged near the sides of the pot as soon as they are done. To reheat, replace them when the other ingredients are ready. Do not stir while cooking. Season with *shoyu* to taste and serve steaming hot.

In *nabe ryori* most of the actual cooking is done right at the table. Prepare the ingredients in advance, then arrange them attractively on a large platter placed within everyone's reach. Use a portable gas ring or alcohol burner as a heat source and over it place a heavy pot, skillet or casserole filled with the stock you wish to use. Adjust the heat so that the stock simmers throughout the entire time you will be using it. Provide each person with a dish, a small bowl for dipping and a pair of chopsticks, then let everyone choose the desired ingredients and cook them to taste.

Nabe ryori is most appropriate during winter when the cold *(yin)* draws people together *(yang)* and feeds the fires of community.

Chinese Cabbage Nabe

SERVES 5

16 ounces *udon* (whole-wheat noodles)
1 teaspoon and a dash of sea salt
9 leaves of Chinese cabbage
½ pound spinach or 1 bunch of watercress
1 cake of grilled *tofu* (p. 174)
3 pieces of *aburage*, doused with boiling water and drained
15 strips (3 inches long) of *kampyo* (gourd), rinsed in lightly salted water and squeezed dry
5 *maki-yuba*, soaked in cold water for 5 minutes, or until soft
5 scallions or leeks, sliced diagonally into 1½-inch lengths
1 piece of *kombu*, 3 inches square, wiped clean
Shoyu

Bring 2 quarts unsalted water to a rolling boil and drop in the noodles. Return to the boil and add 1 cup cold water. Cook for 10 minutes, or until noodles are tender and crisp. Remove, rinse in a colander under running cold water, and set aside to drain.

Bring 6 cups of water to a boil in another pan and add 1 teaspoon salt. Using long chopsticks, hold the stems of the Chinese cabbage leaves in the water and cook until they are just tender. Submerge the upper portion of the leaf for an instant, then dip the leaves into a basin of cold water. Drain the leaves, then trim the cores smooth. Into the same pan now drop the spinach or watercress and return to the boil for 1 or 2 minutes, or until the stems are tender. Remove, dip into cold water, and drain. Place 3 cabbage leaves, their edges overlapping, on a *sudare* or bamboo table mat. Arrange the cabbage leaves with stems and leaves overlapping alternately. Lay the spinach or watercress leaves in a neat double row, alternating stem and leaf, horizontally across the center. Roll from the wide edge of the mat into a tight cylinder. Remove *sudare*, slice the vegetable roll into 1-inch-thick sections, and set aside.

Slice the *tofu* into 6 long blocks. Using scissors, open the *aburage* by cutting into 1 long and 2 short sides. Spread the pieces open lengthwise and arrange 2 *tofu* blocks along 1 edge of each piece of *aburage*. Roll into a cylinder and tie with gourd strips at 5 equidistant points. Slice the roll at points midway between the gourd strips and you should have 5 *age-tofu* rolls, each held closed at its center by a strip of gourd.

Center the boiled noodles on a large platter and arrange the cabbage and *age-tofu* rolls, the *maki-yuba* and scallions or leeks attractively around them. Place a piece of *kombu* into a shallow cast-iron pot and cover with 6 cups water. Bring to a boil (in the kitchen) and season with salt and *shoyu*. Transfer the pot to the table, serve the platter of ingredients, and provide each guest with a dish, a small bowl for dipping and a pair of chopsticks. Serve with rice and *kimpira* (p. 90). When all the ingredients have been eaten, serve the remaining broth as a soup.

VARIATIONS: A. Substitute ¼ pound *harusame* (transparent noodles, dropped into boiling water for 3 or 4 minutes and rinsed under cold water) for the *udon*. *Gammodoki* (p. 175) and *kurumabu* (deep-fried) may be used in addition to or in place of the *age-tofu* rolls. Use whatever seasonal vegetables are at hand.

B. One third of your ingredients may consist of shellfish, cod, or other favorite seafood.

C. *Miso Nabe:* Arrange your ingredients on a large platter. Fill the cooking pot halfway with water, and coat the upper half of the pot with a thick layer of *miso*. As the water simmers, the miso will slowly dissolve into the broth. If too thin at first, add a little *miso* directly to the cooking water.

D. For an even more tempting soup add 1 cup mock Béchamel sauce (p. 162) add some sake or white wine to the remaining broth.

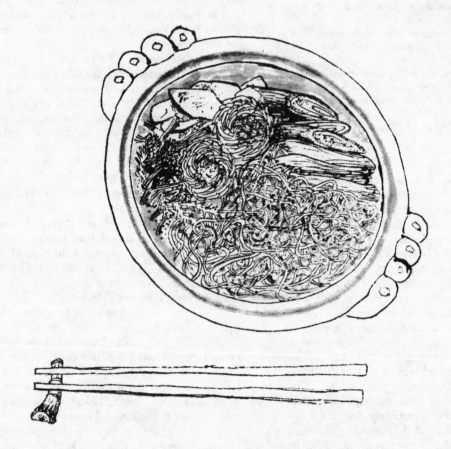

NABE RYORI

IV. CONDIMENTS and PICKLES

CONDIMENTS and PICKLES

Condiments and pickles should be part of our daily menu, adding flavor and balance to our dishes. Pickles, especially *takuwan,* are wonderful aids to digestion and should be enjoyed at the end of a meal.

Takuwan was the name of a Zen monk renowned throughout Japan as a master cook. A famous tale is told about a prominent samurai who wrangled an invitation to one of Takuwan's meals. The warrior arrived at the appointed hour and waited stoically for the monk to bring him his food. An hour passed and then another, but still neither monk nor food appeared. As he grew hungrier, the samurai passed the empty hours congering up the extravagant, hence time-consuming, feast the monk must have been preparing. To the warrior's relief, Takuwan finally arrived, placing before his dinner guest the long awaited feast: a bowl of brown rice garnished with the pickled *daikon* that was his specialty. The samurai ate very slowly, savoring every morsel, then gratefully assured Takuwan that his fame was well earned. Taking his leave, the samurai thanked the bowing monk for the most delicious meal he had ever eaten.

Gomashio *(Sesame-Salt)* 1 WEEK'S SUPPLY FOR 5

1 cup sesame seeds (white or black)
1 level tablespoon and a dash of sea salt

Wash the sesame seeds in a fine-mesh strainer; drain. Dab the strainer with a dry sponge to draw off any excess water, and set the seeds aside.

Roast the salt in a heavy skillet over medium heat, stirring constantly to heat evenly. When the salt no longer releases a strong chlorine odor, transfer to a *suribachi* and crush with a wooden pestle until fine grained.

Put the sesame seeds in the skillet and toast them over moderately high heat for 3 to 5 minutes, stirring constantly and shaking the pan to warm the seeds evenly. When seeds turn a light brown and release their distinctive fragrance, remove from heat and add to the *suribachi* containing the salt.

Place the *suribachi* in your lap, grasp the lower third of the pestle with one hand and gently lay the palm of your other hand on the pestle's top. Lightly grind the mixture together using a steady, circular motion. Crush 70 to 80 percent of the seeds, making sure that you do not express their oil. Store the *gomashio* in an airtight container.

Gomashio is a very versatile condiment used in place of ordinary table salt. Sea salt alone is very *yang;* the *yin* oil of the sesame seed helps balance it in our body. The combination makes for a delicious harmony, perfect for use with grain or vegetable dishes.

Since it will keep long only when it is made very well, begin by making just enough to last a week. I have made *gomashio* that stood the test of a six-month voyage, but only after years of practice. It is in the preparation of simple foods like rice and *gomashio* that a cook's real skill is tried. It is far easier to assemble a rich gourmet feast than to produce consistently delicious, well-balanced sesame-salt. Mastery of this simple condiment means mastery of the center of your life.

Most people, children and adults alike, develop a special affection for *gomashio* and often overindulge. As a result they grow thirsty and find themselves drinking excessively. The proportion of 15 parts sesame seeds to 1 part salt that I have recommended, therefore, is moderate. Modify it to suit your needs and taste.

Tekka Miso MAKES 2 CUPS
(Sautéed Vegetables with Miso)

3 ounces burdock root
2 ounces lotus root
1½ ounces carrot
⅔ cup sesame oil
10 ounces *miso*
1 tablespoon grated gingerroot

Mince vegetables very fine. Heat the oil in a heavy skillet, add burdock, and sauté over medium heat until it no longer releases its strong earthy aroma. Add lotus root, then carrot, sautéing each as you add it. Add the *miso*, mix the ingredients together, and reduce heat to low. Continue to sauté for 1 to 2 hours, stirring constantly. Stir in gingerroot, reduce heat to very low, and sauté for 2 more hours, stirring constantly, until dry and crumbly. Serve with rice or other grains.

Making *tekka* at home requires great patience. It is available prepackaged at macrobiotic outlets.

Shigure Miso *(Moist Tekka)* MAKES 2 TO 3 CUPS

½ pound onions
2 ounces burdock root
2 ounces lotus root
1½ ounces carrot
½ cup sesame oil
10 ounces *miso*
1½ cups water
1 tablespoon fine-grated gingerroot
1 teaspoon fine-grated orange peel

Mince vegetables very fine. Heat oil in a heavy skillet, add onions and sauté over medium heat, stirring gently, for 5 minutes, or until lightly browned. Add consecutively burdock root, lotus, and carrot, sautéing each lightly as you add it. Thin the *miso* in the water and add, then stir in gingerroot and orange peel. Reduce heat to low and cover pan. Simmer, stirring occasionally, for 1 hour or more.

Miso Sauté   MAKES ⅓ CUP

> 1 or 2 tablespoons sesame oil
> 3 tablespoons *miso*

Heat the oil in a heavy skillet. Add the *miso* and sauté over medium heat for 3 to 5 minutes, or until deeply aromatic. Serve as a garnish with rice.

Soybeans with Miso and Burdock   MAKES 2 TO 3 CUPS

> 1 cup soybeans
> 3 to 4 cups water, approximately
> 2 cups fine-shaved burdock root
> 1 heaping tablespoon *miso*

Wash the soybeans and soak them overnight in water to cover. Combine beans with 2 cups water in a heavy saucepan and cook for 40 to 50 minutes, adding a little water occasionally to prevent burning. Add burdock root and enough water to cover, and cook for 30 minutes more, or until burdock is tender. Thin *miso* in 2 or 3 tablespoons of the cooking liquid and add, blending smooth. Simmer for 10 more minutes and turn off heat. Serve as a garnish with grains.

Soybeans with Miso   MAKES 1½ CUPS

> 2 tablespoons sesame oil
> 1 cup soybeans, washed
> 1¼ cups water
> ¼ cup *miso*

Heat a heavy skillet and coat with the oil. Sauté the beans over medium heat until no longer completely resistant to the bite. Stir constantly to heat evenly and prevent scorching. Add 1 cup water, reduce heat, and simmer until dry. Thin *miso* in remaining ¼ cup water and add. Simmer until dry, then serve as a garnish with rice.

Miso Pickles *(Fall and Winter)*

Bury the vegetables you want to pickle in a keg or crock of *miso*.

*Carrot or Burdock: Use whole vegetables or cut them into lengths that will fit the container. Drop pieces into boiling water for 30 seconds, remove, and allow to cool. Embed in *miso* and wait for at least 10 days.

*Daikon: Dry whole *daikon* for 1 day, then cut lengthwise into halves (and crosswise, if necessary, to fit the container). Embed and wait for 1 month.

*Cucumber: Use whole or cut into lengths that will fit the container. Sprinkle with sea salt and press in a bowl under a heavy weight for 1 day. Discard excess liquid and bury in *miso* for 1 month.

*Gingerroot: Sprinkle with sea salt and press in a bowl under a heavy weight for 1 day. Discard excess liquid and embed in *miso*. Wait for 1 month. Delicious served with pickled *daikon* and cucumber.

The longer the pickles remain in the miso, the stronger (and more *yang*) they become. Try *yin* vegetables like green peppers or tiny eggplants.

To serve, rinse off the *miso* under cold running water, and cut pickles into small pieces.

Takuwan (Pickled Daikon)   MAKES 1 TO 2 POUNDS

>   5 pounds *daikon*
>   5 pounds *nuka* (fresh rice bran) or brown
>   rice flour
>   2 to 2½ pounds sea salt

Hang whole *daikon*, leaves intact, in a cool dry place for 2 weeks, or until each *daikon* softens and bends; then trim away the leaves, but keep them. To clean, brush or scrape but do not wash the *daikon*. Combine the rice bran or rice flour and salt, mixing thoroughly. Spread a thick layer of the mixture on the bottom of a keg or crock. Tightly pack the *daikon*, cut into pieces that fit the container, into a layer above the *nuka*. Follow with another layer of the bran-salt mixture, and again of radish, until all the ingredients are used. Place the dried *daikon* leaves around the sides and over the top of the pile. Cover with a lid the size of the bottom of the keg or crock so that it fits inside the top of the container and rests directly on the pile. Place 2 heavy rocks, each equal to the weight of the *daikon*, on top of the lid. When the salt has drawn enough liquid out of the *daikon* to fill the container, remove one of the rocks. Keep in a cool dark place for at least 8 months before using.

For faster pickling, reverse the porportion of *nuka* and salt. For pickles ready in 3 months use 1 part salt to 3 parts *nuka*.

To serve, rinse off the *nuka* under cold running water, and drain *daikon* thoroughly. Soak the *daikon* if too salty, changing the water occasionally. Squeeze out excess water, and chop or slice.

Nuka Pickles (Spring and Summer)

>   10 cups *nuka* (fresh rice bran)
>   1½ cups sea salt
>   3 cups water, approximately
>   Seasonal vegetables (cabbage, carrots,
>   cucumber, etc.)

Toast the *nuka* in a heavy skillet over low heat, stirring constantly, for 10 minutes, or until fragrant. Remove from heat and allow to cool. Combine salt and water, bring to a boil for 1 or 2 minutes, then set aside to cool. Now combine salted water and *nuka* into a thick paste. Fill a crock with the paste, pressing the paste firm. Insert chopped cabbage leaves, whole or sliced cucumbers, pieces of *kombu* or melon rind, or any other seasonal vegetable. When inserting vegetable slivers, tie them in a small cloth bag. Keep *nuka* paste in a cool place, pressed firm and well covered. Turn and mix the *nuka* every day. If it gets too watery, press out excess water through a strainer or add bread crumbs or more rice bran.

Yin vegetables like cucumber can be pickled in 1 day. Turnips and cabbage require 2 days. Whenever you add fresh vegetables always add more salt. The older the *nuka* paste, the better; use it for years.

To serve, rinse off the *nuka* under cold running water and drain vegetables thoroughly. Chop or slice.

Chinese Cabbage Pickles

  10 pounds Chinese cabbage
  1 pound sea salt
  1 lemon peel, cut into slivers

Quarter the Chinese cabbage heads through the core but do not separate the leaves. Wash under cold running water. Dry cabbage in a cool, dark place for 1 day. Spread a layer of salt on the bottom of a keg or crock and add a few slivers of lemon peel. Tightly pack the cabbage into a layer above the salt. Sprinkle cabbage with salt and a few strips of lemon peel, then add another criss-cross layer of cabbage. Repeat until all the ingredients are used. Cover with a lid the size of the bottom of the keg or crock so that it fits inside the top of the container and rests directly on the pile. Place a heavy rock on top of the lid. Wait at least 10 days (the longer the better).

To serve, remove cabbage and wash under cold running water. Squeeze to remove excess water and chop into small pieces.

Asa-zuke (*24-Hour Pickles*)   MAKES 2 TO 3 CUPS

  2 turnips, or ½ small daikon, leaves intact
  2 or 3 carrot slivers
  1 or 2 strips of lemon peel
  2 tablespoons sea salt

Wash the turnip or *daikon* leaves and chop them fine. Sprinkle leaves with a little salt and squeeze out excess liquid. Cut the turnip into thin half-moons, or the *daikon* into thin gingko leaves. Mix all the ingredients together and place in a salad press. Press from 2 to 24 hours.

Achara-zuke (*Mixed Pickles*)   MAKES 2 TO 3 CUPS

  2 turnips, leaves intact
  1 heaping tablespoon sea salt
  1 beet, quartered
  2 cabbage leaves, cut into 1-inch squares
  ½ small carrot, cubed

Dice the turnips and chop the leaves. Sprinkle the leaves with a little salt and squeeze out excess liquid. Place all ingredients in a bowl and sprinkle with remaining salt. Cover with a plate that fits inside the top of the bowl and rests directly on the pile, and put a stone or heavy weight on top of the plate. Press for 1 to 3 days. These pickles are rather *yin;* enjoy only a few at a time.

VARIATION: Separate the leaves from a head of cabbage and rinse them well. Using a pair of long chopsticks, submerge the stems in a pan of boiling water until they are just tender. Drop in the upper portions of the leaves for an instant, then remove leaves and dip them into a basin of cold water to stop the cooking. Trim the stems smooth. Fill each leaf with carrot and cucumber slivers and roll, tucking in the edges. Place the cabbage rolls in a bowl and sprinkle with salt. Cover with a plate that rests directly on the cabbage, and put a heavy weight on top of the plate. Wait for 2 or 3 days. To serve, cut each roll crosswise into 4 or 5 slices.

V. SAUCES, SPREADS and SALAD DRESSINGS

SAUCES SPREADS and SALAD DRESSINGS

Sauces add color and flavor to your dishes. They can be served with grains, vegetables or animal foods to accentuate the natural flavors already present. Serve flour sauces with *yang* preparations, and *kuzu* sauces with *yin*.

Mock Béchamel Sauce (White)   MAKES 1½ CUPS

¼ cup sesame oil
½ cup unbleached white flour
3 cups *kombu dashi* (p. 136) or water
½ teaspoon sea salt

Heat the oil in a heavy skillet, add the flour, and cook over medium heat, stirring constantly. When the lumps have been smoothed out and the flour is still pale, remove from heat and allow to cool, or dip the bottom of pan into cold water. Return pan to stove and gradually add liquid, stirring until smooth. Bring to a boil over medium heat, slip an asbestos pad under pan, and reduce heat to low. Simmer for 10 to 12 minutes. Season with salt to taste, and simmer for 1 or 2 minutes more. To keep the sauce from stiffening, continue to warm over very low heat or in a double boiler until ready to serve.

For brown sauce use whole-wheat flour and cook until flour is rich brown and nutlike in fragrance. For light sauce use whole-wheat pastry flour and cook until the flour is lightly browned.

VARIATIONS: A. Add a pinch of grated nutmeg, ground coriander, ground ginger, or curry powder to the simmering sauce for extra tang.

B. Add ½ cup sautéed or puréed vegetables for added color and flavor.

C. Gravy: After panfrying any food add 1 to 3 parts flour to 1 part oil remaining in the pan and proceed as for the basic sauce.

Lyonnaise Sauce   MAKES 1½ CUPS

1 cup mock Béchamel sauce
1 teaspoon sesame oil
1 cup minced onion
½ teaspoon sea salt
¼ cup white wine

Prepare the mock Béchamel sauce according to the directions given above. While allowing the cooked flour to cool, heat 1 teaspoon oil in a heavy skillet. Add the onion and sauté for 4 or 5 minutes, or until lightly browned, stirring constantly. Return flour to stove, add water, and bring to a boil. Stir the sautéed onion into the sauce and simmer together for 10 minutes. Season with salt, pour in the white wine, and turn off heat. Serve with fish.

Pumpkin-Peanut Sauce   MAKES 1½ CUPS

1 cup puréed pumpkin or squash
2 tablespoons peanut butter
½ cup water
¼ teaspoon sea salt

Blend the ingredients together. Serve at room temperature with vegetable dishes.

Sesame Sauce   MAKES 1 CUP

1 tablespoon sesame oil
1 small onion, minced
2 tablespoons *tahini* (sesame butter)
2 tablespoons water
2 tablespoons *shoyu*
1 tablespoon white wine (optional)

Heat a small skillet and coat with the oil. Sauté the onion over medium heat for 5 minutes, or until lightly browned. Add water to cover, place lid on pan, and bring to a boil. Simmer for 10 to 15 minutes, or until tender. Thin the sesame butter with 2 tablespoons water, and add to onion. Stir in *shoyu* and bring just to a boil. Add wine (if used) and immediately turn off heat.

This sauce is delicious with rice or boiled vegetables. When serving with fish add 5 or 6 drops of gingerroot juice.

Lemon Shoyu

Into 1 tablespoon *shoyu* squeeze 1 or 2 drops of fresh lemon juice. Serve with fish, *tempura*, and *wakame* and cucumber salad (p. 131).

Ginger Shoyu

To each tablespoon of *shoyu* and 1 or 2 drops of juice of grated gingerroot. Delicious with fish.

Orange Shoyu

To 1 tablespoon *shoyu* add up to 1 teaspoon freshly squeezed orange juice. Good with fish and summer salads.

Tsuke-jiru Dipping Sauce — MAKES 4 CUPS

4 cups *kombu dashi* (p. 136)
½ teaspoon sea salt
5 tablespoons *shoyu*
1 tablespoon sake (optional)
2 tablespoons sliced scallion rounds

Bring the *dashi* to a boil, add salt and *shoyu,* and bring just to the boil again. Pour in sake (if used), then quickly turn off heat so the alcohol does not evaporate. Serve in individual bowls, topped with scallion rounds, for dipping.

Goma Joyu Sauce — MAKES ½ CUP

1 heaping tablespoon *tahini* (sesame butter)
1 tablespoon *shoyu*
4 tablespoons water

Combine all ingredients in a small saucepan and bring to a boil. Simmer for several minutes, stirring constantly while the sauce thickens.

Scallion Miso — MAKES 1 CUP

1 tablespoon sesame oil
1 bunch of scallions, minced
3 tablespoons water
2 tablespoons *miso*

Separate scallion root fibrils, and white and green portions. Heat a small skillet and coat with the oil. Sauté the scallion roots over medium heat for 1 minute. Add the greens and then the whites, sautéing each portion lightly as you add it. Add 2 tablespoons water, cover pan, and simmer for 5 minutes. Thin *miso* in remaining water, add to vegetables, and simmer for 2 or 3 minutes more. Remove from heat and serve as spread or garnish.

Kuzu Sauce

When simmering vegetables have become tender, remove them from their cooking liquid and arrange on serving dishes. Thin *kuzu* in a little water and add to remaining liquid. For a thick sauce add 1 tablespoon *kuzu* for every 1½ cups liquid; for a thin sauce add 1 teaspoon *kuzu* for every 1½ cups liquid. Simmer for several minutes, stirring while the sauce thickens. If serving with *yang* foods you need not season the sauce itself. If serving with *yin* foods season sauce with salt and/or *shoyu* to taste. Delicious with *fu, tofu,* and vegetable dishes.

Walnut Miso — MAKES 1½ CUPS

1 cup walnut meats
¼ cup *miso*
¼ cup water

Roast the nut meats in a heavy skillet over medium heat until lightly toasted. Remove from heat and sliver. Place slivers in a *suribachi* and grind to a paste. Add *miso* and water, and blend to a smooth cream.

Citron Miso
MAKES 1 CUP

5 tablespoons *tahini* (sesame butter)
1 tablespoon *miso*
3 teaspoons *yuzu* (Japanese citron) or lemon juice

Blend ingredients together until smooth and creamy. Delicious with *chapati* (p. 80).

Goma Miso
MAKES 1 CUP

5 tablespoons *tahini* (sesame butter)
1 tablespoon *miso*
1 tablespoon water

Mix all ingredients together until creamy. Makes a delicious spread. If desired, add 1 or 2 teaspoons grated orange rind.

Party Spreads

For accompaniments or hors d'oeuvres at parties, cut bread into canapé-size pieces and spread with any of the following:
*peanut, sesame, or apple butter
*adzuki-chestnut paste (p. 197)
*pumpkin or sweet potato purée
*tekka or scallion miso (p. 163)

Arrange attractively on a large platter, garnish with sprigs of parsley, and serve.

VARIATIONS: A. Pour 3 inches of oil into a heavy skillet or deep-fryer and heat to 360° F. Season 1 cup fine-grated carrot or *daikon* with ¼ teaspoon salt, and add 1 tablespoon unbleached white flour to make a paste. Spread on 20 canapé-size pieces of bread and drop into the hot oil. Deep-fry until crisp, then drain on absorbent paper.

B. *Zakuska:* Heat oven to 350° F. Divide ½ cup salmon roe among 5 whole pieces of leavened bread, and set aside. Spread another 5 pieces of bread with puréed sweet potato, and 5 more with *tahini* (sesame butter). Put latter two into the oven and bake for 10 minutes. Arrange on a platter with the salmon roe slices. Serves 5.

Salad Dressing
MAKES ½ CUP

4 tablespoons corn or olive oil
1 teaspoon salt, or 1 *umeboshi*, shredded
1 tablespoon orange juice, or 1 teaspoon lemon juice
1 teaspoon minced onion, approximately

Pour the oil into a large bowl. Add salt and juice and mix thoroughly. Gently add minced onion, and let stand for 10 minutes. Add to salad vegetables and toss.

Mayonnaise
MAKES 1 CUP

1 egg yolk
1 cup corn or olive oil, brought to the boil and cooled
1 teaspoon lemon juice
1 or 2 teaspoons sea salt, or 1 tablespoon *umeboshi* juice (p. 207)

Place the egg yolk in a bowl and beat with a wire whisk. Add oil drop by drop, until you have added 1½ to 2 tablespoons. Beat constantly as you slowly add the remainder of the oil; increase the amount you add each time. When the new consistency has been reached, add lemon juice and salt, and beat until thoroughly blended.

VARIATION: For a delicious tartar sauce, mix 2 tablespoons pickled cucumber, 1 tablespoon parsley, and 1 hard-cooked egg, all minced, into the mayonnaise. Superb with fish.

VI. BEANS

BEANS (*Adzuki*, etc.)

    All beans can be prepared following the same general methods: they can be simmered with 4 parts water in a regular saucepan over low heat for several hours, or they can be pressure-cooked in 3 parts water for about 1 hour. *Adzuki* beans should not be cooked under pressure or they may become very bitter. Chick-peas, black beans and soybeans should be soaked for at least several hours, or ideally overnight, before use. Cooking the beans with a small strip of *kombu* helps soften them; season with salt and/or *shoyu* only after the beans have already become tender.

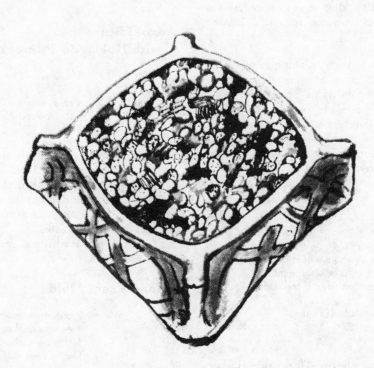

Adzuki Beans

SERVES 5 TO 8

> 1 piece of *kombu*, 5 by 3 inches, wiped clean
> 1 cup *adzuki* beans, washed
> 4 cups water
> Dash of sea salt and/or *shoyu*

Place the *kombu* in the bottom of a heavy saucepan. Add the *adzuki* beans and water and bring rapidly to a boil. Reduce heat to low and cover with a tight-fitting lid. Simmer for 1 hour, or until the beans are swollen and tender. Do not stir while beans simmer. When done, uncover and season with salt and/or *shoyu* to taste. Add a little water if none remains from cooking, and simmer until dry before serving.

VARIATION: *Adzuki An* (Jam): When making *adzuki* jam, do not season the beans when done. Mash beans in the pot until half have been turned to a paste. Season the paste with salt, then mix into the whole beans. Now mash remaining beans. Transfer jam to a large bowl and allow to cool. The *an* will dry and harden. It can be used as a spread on bread, as a coating for *manju* (p. 198), etc., or cut into blocks and eaten cold.

Adzuki Bean Potage

SERVES 5

> Oil for deep-frying
> 2 ounces *udon* (whole-wheat noodles)
> 1 tablespoon corn or sesame oil
> 1 medium-size onion, cut into thin crescents
> 3 cups cooked *adzuki* beans
> Dash of sea salt
> 4 to 5 cups water

Pour 2 to 3 inches of oil into a heavy skillet or deep-fryer and heat to 350° F. Break the *udon* into 1-inch lengths and drop them into the hot oil. Deep-fry for 2 or 3 minutes, or until brown and crisp. Remove and drain on absorbent paper, then set aside in a warm oven until ready to use.

Heat a heavy saucepan and coat with 1 tablespoon oil. Sauté the onion over medium heat, stirring gently, for 5 minutes, or until lightly browned. Add the beans, mix the ingredients together, and sauté for 1 minute more. Now season lightly with salt, remove from heat, and crush through a strainer or purée in an electric blender. Return the *adzuki* and onion mixture to the stove and bring to a boil over low heat; add 4 to 5 cups water and stir smooth. Serve topped with a sprinkling of the fried *udon*.

Adzuki Beans
with Hokkaido Pumpkin

SERVES 5

> 1 cup *adzuki* beans, washed
> 1 strip of *kombu*, 5 by 3 inches, wiped clean
> 4 cups water
> $\frac{1}{4}$ to $\frac{1}{2}$ pound Hokkaido pumpkin, cubed
> Sea salt

Combine beans, *kombu,* and water in a heavy saucepan and bring rapidly to a boil. Reduce heat to low, cover, and simmer for 1 hour, or until the beans are swollen. Add pumpkin cubes and water to cover, and simmer for 20 to 30 minutes longer, or until the pumpkin is tender. Season with salt to taste.

This dish is a traditional remedy for kidney ailments.

Udon-Adzuki Mold

SERVES 5

> 2 tablespoons sesame oil
> 4 ounces cooked *udon* (whole-wheat noodles)
> 1 cup cooked *adzuki* beans
> Dash of sea salt

Heat a heavy skillet and coat with the oil. Sauté the noodles over medium heat for 2 or 3 minutes, then add the *adzuki* beans and sauté together for 1 minute more. Add just enough water to cover the bottom of the pan, season with sea salt, and simmer until dry. Transfer the mixture to a rinsed mold and allow to cool and become firm (refrigerate in summer). Free the edges, invert the mold, and turn out on a serving plate. Serve with sesame sauce (p. 162).

Black Bean Ni   SERVES 5

> 1 cup black beans, soaked in 3 cups water
>   for several hours or overnight
> 4 cups cold water, approximately
> Dash of sea salt
> *Shoyu*

Drain the beans through a strainer placed over a bowl, reserving any soaking water. Combine beans and soaking water in a heavy saucepan, adding enough fresh water to equal 4 cups, and bring to a boil over high heat. Reduce heat to low, cover, and simmer for 1 to 2 hours, or until tender. Add water during cooking if liquid completely evaporates. Toss pan gently to stir. When done, season with salt and/or *shoyu* to taste and simmer until dry.

Always prepare black beans in a saucepan, for their skins fall away easily and may clog the valve of your pressure cooker. In Japan this exquisitely sweet dish is a must on New Year's Day. It gets even sweeter after standing for a day or two. This dish is deceptively simple to make but really requires a delicate hand.

Chick-Pea Fukume Ni   SERVES 5

> 1 cup chick-peas, soaked in 3 cups water
>   overnight
> 4 cups water, approximately
> 1 tablespoon sesame oil
> 1 teaspoon sea salt

Drain the chick-peas through a strainer placed over a bowl, reserving any soaking water. Combine chick-peas and soaking water in a heavy saucepan, adding enough fresh water to equal 4 cups, and bring rapidly to a boil. Reduce heat, cover, and simmer for 2 hours, or until swollen and tender. To cook under pressure, combine the chick-peas with 3 cups water and bring to full pressure over high heat. Slip an asbestos pad under the pot, reduce heat to low, and simmer for 45 minutes. Turn off heat and allow pressure to return to normal.

Drain beans through a colander placed over a large bowl, reserving cooking liquid. Heat a heavy skillet and coat with the oil. Add the beans and sauté over medium heat for 2 or 3 minutes. Season the beans with salt, and add enough of the cooking liquid to cover the bottom of the pan. Simmer until dry before serving. (Use remaining cooking water in baking.)

The chick-pea, grown in many parts of the world, has a unique *yang* quality. In his many travels, Georges Ohsawa became very fond of it. It is an extremely versatile bean that can be used in over a hundred different ways.

Beignets de Pois Chiche   SERVES 4 TO 5

> Oil for deep-frying
> 1 cup unbleached white flour
> 1 cup water, approximately
> 1 teaspoon sea salt
> 2 cups cooked chick-peas
> 1 cup minced onion

Fill a heavy skillet or deep-fryer with 3 inches of oil and heat to 360°F. Combine the flour with enough water to form a rather thick batter. Add salt and stir in the chick-peas and minced onion. Drop into the hot oil by the spoonful and deep-fry until golden and crisp. Drain on absorbent paper before serving. Delicious.

VARIATION: Substitute 2 cups cooked kidney beans for the chick-peas, and proceed as above.

Chick-Peas with Vegetables

SERVES 5

3 large *shiitake* (dried Japanese mushrooms)
1 piece of *koya-dofu* (dried tofu)
2 tablespoons corn or sesame oil
2 small onions, minced
1 small carrot, cubed
3 cups cooked chick-peas
Dash of sea salt
Shoyu

Soak the *shiitake* in cold water for 20 to 30 minutes; remove their hard stems and slice their caps fine. Drop the *koya-dofu* into a small pan of boiling water, cook for 2 or 3 minutes, and drain. Press the *koya-dofu* lightly between the palms while rinsing it under running cold water. When white foam is no longer released, press out excess water, and cut into cubes.

Heat a heavy skillet and coat with the oil. Sauté the onions over medium heat for 5 minutes, or until lightly browned. Add *shiitake*, then carrot, then *koya-dofu*, sautéing each lightly as you add it. Now add the chick-peas and enough water to cover. Bring to a boil, season with a dash of salt, and cook for 30 minutes, or until all ingredients are tender. Season with *shoyu* to taste, simmer for 1 or 2 minutes longer, and serve.

Spanish Chick-Peas

SERVES 6

1 cup shelled clams
1 tablespoon sesame oil
3 cups brown rice, washed
3 cups cooked chick-peas
1 small carrot, cut into thick rounds
12 small raw shrimps, shelled and deveined
$4\frac{1}{2}$ cups water
1 tablespoon sea salt

Rub the clams with salt, then rinse them thoroughly under running cold water.

Heat the oil in a pressure cooker. Add the rice and sauté over medium heat, stirring constantly, until rich brown. Add the chick-peas and sauté together for 1 or 2 minutes more. Add the carrot rounds, cover, and bring to full pressure over high heat. Slip an asbestos pad under the pot, reduce heat to low, and simmer for 40 minutes. Turn off heat and remove pressure regulator to permit steam to escape. Leaving the pot on the stove, uncover and mix lightly. Gently stir in the shrimps and clams, then replace both lid and pressure regulator. Allow to stand for 10 minutes to absorb the heat retained in the metal burner and asbestos pad. Delicious served with a clear soup of watercress and *tofu*.

Chick-Pea Croquettes

SERVES 5

2 tablespoons corn or sesame oil
1 small onion, minced
$\frac{1}{2}$ small carrot, diced
3 cups cooked chick-peas, mashed
1 teaspoon sea salt
3 tablespoons unbleached white flour
Oil for deep-frying
1 egg, beaten
2 to 3 cups bread crumbs or cornmeal

Heat a heavy skillet and coat with 2 tablespoons oil. Sauté the onion over medium heat, stirring gently, for 5 minutes, or until lightly browned. Add the carrot, then the chick-peas, mixing the ingredients together, and season with the salt. Transfer to a large bowl and add enough of the flour to hold the mixture together. Form into 10 croquettes.

Fill a heavy skillet or deep-fryer with 3 inches of oil and heat to 350°F. Coat the croquettes with the remaining flour, dip into beaten egg, then roll in bread crumbs, coating thoroughly. Drop into the hot oil and deep-fry until golden and crisp. Drain on absorbent paper, and serve on a bed of lightly sautéed cabbage.

Chick-Pea Stew

SERVES 5

3 tablespoons corn or sesame oil
2 heaping tablespoons unbleached white
   flour
2 small onions, cut into thin crescents
1 small carrot, diced
4 cups cooked chick-peas
4 cups water, approximately
1½ teaspoons sea salt
10 green beans, rinsed and trimmed
2 or 3 tablespoons minced parsley or
   watercress

Heat a heavy skillet and coat with 1 tablespoon oil. Cook the flour over medium heat until browned and fragrant, stirring constantly to heat evenly. Remove from heat and set aside to cool.

Heat a heavy saucepan and coat with remaining 2 tablespoons oil. Sauté the onions over medium heat, stirring gently, for 4 or 5 minutes, or until lightly browned. Add the carrot, then the chick-peas, sautéing each lightly as you add it. Mix the ingredients together, add enough of the water to cover, and bring to the boil over high heat. Reduce heat to medium and gradually stir in the sautéed flour, blending smooth. Cover pan and cook for 40 minutes, or until vegetables are tender and chick-peas have fallen apart.

While the stew is cooking, bring a small pan of water to a boil over high heat and add ½ teaspoon salt. Drop in the beans, return to the boil, and cook for 5 minutes, or until beans are bright green and just tender. Drain beans and dip them into a basin of cold water to stop the cooking and set the color. Slice beans fine on the diagonal and set them aside in a colander.

When the stew is ready, season with salt to taste. Serve individual portions garnished with some of the beans and topped with a sprinkling of minced watercress or parsley.

Deep-Fried Fava Beans

Peel away the bean's outer skin, then score its surface once or twice. Drop into hot oil and deep-fry until crisp. Drain on absorbent paper and sprinkle lightly with salt. Makes a delicious snack with beer.

Kidney Bean Cream

SERVES 5

3 tablespoons sesame oil
3 tablespoons whole-wheat flour
1 cup water, approximately
½ cup cooked kidney beans
½ teaspoon sea salt

Heat a heavy skillet and coat with the oil. Cook the flour over medium heat until lightly browned and fragrant, stirring constantly. Remove from heat and cool, or dip bottom of pan into cold water. Return pan to stove and add the water, stirring until smooth. Bring the mixture to a boil and simmer for 10 minutes. Stir in the beans and simmer for 5 minutes more. Season with salt to taste.

Kidney Bean Kinton

SERVES 5

2 cups kidney beans, washed
5 cups water, approximately
1 teaspoon sea salt

Combine beans and water in a heavy saucapan and bring to a boil over high heat. Reduce heat to medium, cover, and cook for 1 to 2 hours, until beans are tender, adding more water it necessary. Transfer half of the cooked beans to a separate bowl; mash them and season with salt. Mix whole and mashed beans together and serve.

Soldier Bean Potage

SERVES 5

1 tablespoon corn or sesame oil
2 small onions, minced
1 cup soldier beans, washed
8 cups and 3 tablespoons water
Sea salt
1 heaping tablespoon *kuzu*
2 or 3 tablespoons croutons
2 or 3 tablespoons minced parsley

Heat the oil in a pressure cooker. Sauté the onions over medium heat for 5 minutes, or until lightly browned. Add beans and 3 cups water, cover, and bring rapidly to full pressure over high heat. Reduce heat to low and simmer for 50 minutes to 1 hour. Remove from heat and allow pressure to return to normal.

Drain bean and onion mixture, then crush through a strainer or purée in an electric blender. Season with salt to taste. Return to the stove and bring to a boil over low heat; add 4 to 5 cups water and stir smooth. Now stir in *kuzu* thinned in 3 tablespoons water and simmer for several minutes more, stirring while the broth thickens. Serve topped with croutons and sprinkled with minced parsley.

We thicken this potage with *kuzu (yang)* because the soldier bean is *yin*. We use a mock Béchamel sauce to thicken the soups of beans that are more *yang*.

Gomoku-mame *(Soybean Nitsuke)*

SERVES 5

1 piece of *koya-dofu* (dried tofu)
1 tablespoon sesame oil
2 cups diced burdock
½ cup diced lotus root
1 cup diced carrot
1 cup cooked soybeans
4½ to 5½ cups water
4 tablespoons sesame butter *(tahini)*
5 tablespoons *shoyu*

Drop the *koya-dofu* into a small pan of boiling water and cook for 2 or 3 minutes. Press the *koya-dofu* lightly between the palms while rinsing it under running cold water. When a white foam is no longer released, press out excess liquid, and dice.

Heat a heavy skillet and coat with the oil. Sauté the burdock for several minutes, or until its strong aroma is no longer released. Add, in this order, lotus root, carrot, *koya-dofu*, and soybeans, mixing the ingredients together. Add enough of the water to cover (4 to 5 cups), and bring to a boil over high heat. Reduce heat to low, cover pan, and simmer for 30 minutes, or until the vegetables are tender.

Combine sesame butter, *shoyu* and ½ cup water, stirring until smooth. Add to simmering vegetables when they are done, spreading the mixture evenly. Simmer until dry before serving.

TOFU RYORI (Soybeans)

Tofu or bean curd is rich in vegetable protein. Although it is rather *yin* in our classification of foods, the recipes I have included here balance its *yin* characteristics with *yang* so don't hesitate to use it occasionally. It's delicious in *miso* soup, stews and *nabe*, and as a dish by itself. It is available at Oriental food shops and can also be made at home.

When necessary to drain *tofu*, wrap it in a clean cloth and place between 2 chopping blocks set at an angle over the sink. Let drain for 30 minutes to 1 hour; or squeeze the *tofu* in the cloth to express excess liquid.

Homemade Tofu

    3 cups soybeans
    4½ teaspoons *nigari**, or substitute
    2 teaspoons fresh lemon juice

Soak beans in water overnight; drain, and grind in an electric blender.

Put in a large pot, add 2 parts water, and bring to a boil; reduce heat and simmer for 5 minutes. Pour liquid through 2 or 3 layers of cheesecloth or fine muslin. Gather up the corners of the cloth to form a sack and squeeze the pulp to remove excess liquid. Set pulp (*unohana*) aside for use in other cooking.

Sprinkle the *nigari* over the *tofu* liquid, and stir lightly. Within 20 minutes the *tofu* should begin to curdle. Line a bamboo strainer with a clean cotton cloth and spoon in the curdling *tofu*. Cover with another cloth and top with a wooden lid that rests directly on top of the upper cloth. Place a light weight on top of the lid for pressure. After 1 hour add another weight to increase the pressure. Let stand for 1 hour more, then carefully transfer *tofu* to a basin of cold water water for 30 minutes.

Refrigerate to store.

VARIATION: For grilled *tofu,* preheat the broiler to its highest point. Place 1 or 2 cakes of *tofu* in a baking dish with enough water to come halfway up the sides of the *tofu*. Slide the dish under the broiler, as close to the heat as possible. Sear the *tofu* for a few seconds until speckled, then turn the pieces with a spatula and sear the other side. Remove pan from broiler and drain the *tofu*.

*To make *nigari* dampen 5 pounds sea salt with cold water. Tie the dampened salt in a cloth sack and hang over a bowl in a cool dark place. The liquid that drips from the sack is *nigari* (sea brine).

Unohana Pouches

    6 pieces of *aburage*
    10 strips (3 inches long) of *kampyo* (gourd)
    2 tablespoons sesame oil
    2 small onions, minced
    1 small carrot, cut into slivers
    ½ cup thin gingko leaves of lotus root
    1 teaspoon sea salt
    3 cups *unohana**
    1 piece of *kombu*, 3 inches square, wiped clean
    5 tablespoons *shoyu*

Pour boiling water over the *aburage* to rid it of excess oil. Drain, then cut 5 pieces into halves and 1 piece into thin strips. Pull open the centers of the halves to form pouches and set them aside. Rinse the *kampyo* strips in lightly salted water, squeeze them dry and set aside.

Heat a heavy skillet and coat with the oil. Sauté the onions over medium heat, stirring gently, for 5 minutes, or until lightly browned, Add the carrot, then the *aburage* strips, mixing the ingredients together. Now add the lotus, season with salt, and add water to cover. Bring to a boil, cover pan, and cook for 20 minutes. Stir in the *unohana* and cook for 5 more minutes, stirring constantly.

Combine the *kombu* with 5 cups water (enough to cover the pouches) and bring to a boil. Fill the *aburage* pouches with the *unohana* mixture and tie each pouch closed with a strip of gourd. Season the *kombu dashi* with the *shoyu*. Put the pouches in the *dashi* and cook covered until all the liquid has been absorbed or evaporated and the pouches are well flavored.

*Unohana is the dry pulp left over from making *tofu*. It does not keep and should be used immediately.

Gammodoki

SERVES 5

2 cakes of *tofu*
Oil for deep-frying
½ cup minced onion
¼ cup minced *shiitake* (dried Japanese
    mushroom)
½ cup slivered carrot
⅓ teaspoon sea salt
5 tablespoons fine-grated *daikon*
5 teaspoons *shoyu*

Wrap the *tofu* in a clean cloth and place between 2 chopping blocks set an an angle over the sink. Let drain for 30 minutes to 1 hour; or squeeze the *tofu* in the cloth to express excess liquid. Transfer to a *suribachi* and mash.

Fill a heavy skillet or deep-fryer with 3 inches of oil and heat to 320° to 340°F. Mix onion, *shiitake* and carrot into the *tofu,* and season with the salt. Form the mixture into 5 or 10 flattened ovals and drop into the hot oil. Deep-fry for 3 to 5 minutes, or until cooked through and a crisp reddish brown. Drain on a wire rack or absorbent paper. Accompany each serving with 1 tablespoon of grated *daikon* seasoned lightly with *shoyu* for dipping.

Tofu with Kuzu Sauce

SERVES 5

1½ cakes of *tofu*
1 teaspoon sea salt
2 cups *kombu dashi* (p. 136)
2 tablespoons *shoyu*
1 tablespoon *kuzu* dissolved in 1 tablespoon
    water
1 teaspoon fine-grated gingerroot

Cut the *tofu* into 2-inch cubes. Bring a small pan of water to a boil and add 1 teaspoon salt. Drop the *tofu* cubes into the pan, return to the boil, and cook just long enough for the *tofu* to be warmed through. Lift out the cubes carefully with a slotted spoon and place on prewarmed serving dishes.

Bring the *dashi* to a boil and add the *shoyu*. Stir in the thinned *kuzu* and simmer for several minutes while the *kuzu* thickens, stirring constantly. Serve the *tofu* covered with the *kuzu* sauce and topped with a tiny mound of grated gingerroot.

Tofu Roll

SERVES 5

3 pieces of *aburage*
Shoyu
2 tablespoons sesame oil
1 medium-size onion, chopped
10 fresh mushrooms, rinsed in lightly salted
    water and cut into thin pieces
1 small carrot, cut into slivers
1 teaspoon sea salt
2 cakes of *tofu,* drained and mashed (p. 173)
1 heaping tablespoon powdered *kuzu*

Using scissors open the *aburage* by cutting into 1 long and 2 short sides. Put the pieces into a small saucepan with water to cover and bring to a boil, then season with 1 to 2 tablespoons *shoyu* for each cup of water added. Cook covered until all the water has been absorbed or evaporated and the *aburage* are well flavored. Drain the *aburage* and set aside.

Heat a heavy skillet and coat with the oil. Sauté the onion over medium heat, stirring gently, for 5 minutes, or until lightly browned. Add mushrooms, then carrot, sautéing each as you add it. Season with salt and add the *tofu,* sautéing the mixture for several minutes more. Remove from heat, stir in the *kuzu* powder, and allow to cool.

Open the *aburage* and spread the surface of each piece with the sautéed vegetables and *tofu*. Roll each piece of *aburage* into a cylinder and steam over high heat for 20 minutes. Allow to cool before slicing.

3 pieces of *koya-dofu* (dried tofu)
4 cups *kombu dashi* (p. 136)
¼ teaspoon sea salt
4 tablespoons *shoyu*
1 or 2 small carrots, cut lengthwise into
  sticks
Oil for deep-frying
1 tablespoon unbleached white flour
1 tablespoon water
3 sheets of *nori*

Drop the *koya-dofu* into a small pan of boiling water and cook for 2 or 3 minutes. Drain, then press the pieces lightly between the palms while rinsing under cold running water. When white foam is no longer released, squeeze to remove excess liquid.

Bring the *dashi* to a boil, adding salt and *shoyu*. Drop in the *koya-dofu* and carrot sticks, cover, and cook for 20 to 30 minutes. Drain, reserving remaining cooking broth for use in other cooking. Allow *koya-dofu* to cool.

Fill a heavy skillet or deep-fryer with 3 inches of oil and heat to 360°F. Combine the flour and water to form a thin paste. Cut each piece of *koya-dofu* first vertically then horizontally into halves. Trim the carrot sticks to the length of the *koya-dofu* and sandwich them between 2 layers. Cut the *nori* sheets into halves, then trim each half to the length of the *koya-dofu*. Use the *nori* to wrap each of the six sandwiches, and seal the edges of the *nori* and the exposed edges at the opposite ends of each sandwich with the flour paste. Now drop into the hot oil and deep-fry until crisp and golden. Drain on absorbent paper and cut each sandwich diagonally into halves before serving.

Tofu Nitsuke

2 tablespoons corn or sesame oil
2 small onions, minced
1 small carrot, cut into slivers
1 piece of *aburage*, cut into thin strips
½ teaspoon sea salt
3 tablespoons *shoyu*
1 cake of *tofu*, drained and mashed (p. 173)

Heat the oil in a heavy skillet. Add the onions and sauté over medium heat, stirring gently, for 3 or 4 minutes. Add the carrot slivers, then the *aburage* strips, mix the ingredients together, and sauté for 10 minutes more. Season with salt and *shoyu* (generously) and stir in the mashed *tofu*. Reduce heat to low and sauté for 10 to 15 minutes more, stirring constantly.

Chinese Dow-Foo Oroshi-Ae

Oil for deep-frying
2 cakes of Chinese *dow-foo*
1 tablespoon *shoyu*
½ cup fine-grated *daikon*
1 teaspoon minced *yuzu* or orange peel
1 or 2 tablespoons white wine

Fill a heavy skillet or deep-fryer with 3 inches of oil and heat to 360°F. Drop in the *dow-foo* and deep-fry until well browned and crisp. Drain on absorbent paper. Now combine the *dow-foo* with the *shoyu* in a small saucepan and bring to a boil, cooking until all the liquid has been absorbed or evaporated. Allow *dow-foo* to cool, then slice very fine.

Combine *daikon*, orange peel and wine. Add *dow-foo* and toss together.

Tofu Mold

1½ cakes of *tofu*, drained (p. 173)
Dash of sea salt
1 piece of *aburage*
2 large *shiitake* (dried Japanese mushroom)
2 tablespoons sesame oil
1 or 2 scallions, cut into thin rounds
1 small carrot, cut into slivers
4 tablespoons *shoyu*
¼ cup *kuzu*
½ cup water, approximately
Parsley sprigs

Mash the *tofu* in a *suribachi* and season with a dash of salt. Set aside. Pour boiling water over the *aburage* to rid it of excess oil. Drain, then cut the piece into thin strips. Soak the *shiitake* in cold water for 20 to 30 minutes. Trim away the hard stems and slice the broad caps fine.

Heat a heavy skillet and coat with the oil. Sauté the scallions over medium heat in this order: green part, white part, root fibrils. After 1 minute add, in this order, *shiitake,* carrot and *aburage* strips, sautéing each lightly as you add it. Add *tofu*, mix the ingredients together, and sauté for 5 minutes more, stirring constantly. Season with *shoyu*, then stir in the *kuzu* thinned in ½ cup water. Cook for 1 or 2 minutes, then remove from heat and transfer the mixture to a lightly moistened mold. Allow to cool and become firm. Invert the mold and tap out carefully. Serve individual portions garnished with sprigs of parsley.

Tofu Tempura

1½ cakes of *tofu*
Oil for deep-frying
1 cup whole-wheat flour
⅔ cup water
½ teaspoon sea salt
5 tablespoons fine-grated *daikon*
5 teaspoons *shoyu*

Wrap the *tofu* in a clean cloth and place between 2 chopping blocks set at an angle over the sink. Let drain for 30 minutes to 1 hour, then cut into 1½-inch cubes.

Fill a heavy skillet or deep-fryer with 3 inches of oil and heat to 350°F. Combine the flour, water and salt to form a batter. Dip the *tofu* cubes into the batter, coating thoroughly, then drop into the hot oil. Deep-fry for 3 to 5 minutes, or until golden brown and crisp. Drain on a wire rack or absorbent paper. Accompany each serving with a small mound of grated *daikon* seasoned lightly with *shoyu* for dipping.

Goma Dofu *(Sesame Tofu)*

1 cup sesame seeds, washed
1 cup *kuzu*
7 cups water

Toast the seeds in a heavy skillet over moderately high heat for 3 to 5 minutes, stirring constantly and shaking the pan to warm the seeds evenly. When the seeds turn a light brown and release their distinctive fragrance, remove from heat and grind to a paste in a *suribachi*.

Dissolve the *kuzu* in the water and stir in the sesame paste. Bring to a boil, then simmer over low heat for 40 to 50 minutes, or until the mixture is thick and stringy. Stir occasionally. Pour mixture into a lightly moistened mold and allow to cool and become firm. When firm, tap out carefully and cut into 2-inch cubes.

Serve the cubes in small bowls, and cover with a clear *shoyu* broth accented with a few drops of gingerroot juice and garnished with lemon peel.

VII. SEAFOOD and EGGS

SEAFOOD and EGGS

Seafood is the easiest from of animal food to balance healthfully and it lends itself to a wide variety of preparations: broiling, baking, panfrying or deep-frying. Some fish can be enjoyed almost raw or pickled in *miso*. Small fish can be cooked and eaten whole, while the trimmings of large fish make delicious soups.

Always keep balance in mind and accompany *yang* seafood or egg dishes with lightly sautéed vegetables, a fresh salad, or a favorite dessert.

Seafood Tempura
SERVES 4

1 pound red snapper, cut into small fillets
Sea salt
Oil for deep-frying
4 tablespoons unbleached white flour
2 eggs, beaten
1 cup bread crumbs or cornmeal

Sprinkle the fillets with salt and let stand for 30 minutes to 1 hour. Fill a heavy skillet or deep-fryer with 3 inches of oil and heat to 350°F. Coat fillets with flour, dip into beaten egg, then roll in the bread crumbs. Drop into hot oil and deep-fry slowly over medium heat until fish is cooked through, golden and crisp. Drain on absorbent paper. Serve with mounds of grated *daikon* seasoned lightly with *shoyu*, or with *tsuke-jiru* dipping sauce (p. 163) accented with a little grated gingerroot.

VARIATIONS: A. Use whole small red snappers. Scale and clean the fish, then sprinkle them with salt and allow to stand for 30 minutes to 1 hour. Sprinkle the fish with a few drops of water, coat with powdered *kuzu*, and drop into hot oil. Deep-fry slowly until cooked through, golden and crisp; drain. Serve two per person.

B. Fillet sardines, cutting away their heads. Dip fish into *tempura* batter (p. 118), then into bread crumbs. Deep-fry until golden and crisp.

C. Sprinkle small salmon fillets with salt and pepper, dip them immediately into *tempura* batter, then coat with bread crumbs. Deep-fry until golden, and drain. Serve with celery strips.

D. Clean but do not scale a 1- to 1½-pound carp. Rub fish with salt and coat thoroughly with powdered *kuzu*. Drop into hot oil and deep-fry slowly until cooked through and crisp. Place on a large platter and serve covered with a *kuzu* sauce of onion, carrot, *shiitake*, and green beans (p. 163).

Panfried Mackerel
SERVES 5

5 small mackerel, cleaned and filleted
2 teaspoons sea salt, or 1 cup equal parts *shoyu* and water
Oil for frying
1 cup mock Béchamel sauce (p. 162)
5 lemon slices
2 tablespoons minced parsley

Rub fish with salt, or marinate in equal parts *shoyu* and water, and let stand for 30 minutes. (If fish has been marinated, pat it dry before proceeding.) Now panfry in ¼ inch of oil until golden. Serve with mock Béchamel sauce, and garnish with lemon slices and minced parsley.

VARIATION: Place the mackerel in a lightly oiled baking pan and bake in a 350°F. oven for 15 minutes; or broil. Garnish as above and serve.

Salmon Croquettes
SERVES 5

1 pound salmon fillets
2 small onions, minced
1 tablespoon fine-grated gingerroot
1 cup whole-wheat flour
Oil for frying

Shred the salmon, and combine with minced onions and grated gingerroot. Now add enough of the flour, and a little water if necessary, to hold the mixture together. Shape into 5 croquettes, and panbrown in ¼ inch of oil until deep golden and crisp. Use oil remaining from frying and unused flour to prepare gravy (p. 162).

VARIATION: Add 1 cup bread crumbs or cornmeal to the ingredients listed above. Shape the mixture into croquettes, then roll in bread crumbs, coating thoroughly. Drop immediately into *tempura* oil heated to 350°F. and deep-fry for 2 to 4 minutes, until cooked through, golden and crisp. Drain on absorbent paper before serving.

Naruto Squid

SERVES 5

2 small squid, about ½ pound
6 parsley sprigs
Shoyu

Cut squid open, lay flat, and remove skin. Place 3 parsley sprigs at the center of each squid, then tie squid closed. Bring to a boil in equal parts water and *shoyu* to cover, and cook for 20 minutes, or until tender. Remove string and slice each squid crosswise into 5 pieces.

Squid and Scallion Miso-Ae

SERVES 5

2 small squid, about ½ pound
½ teaspoon sea salt
2 scallions, cut into 1-inch lengths
2 tablespoons *miso*
3 tablespoons water
2 or 3 drops of lemon juice

Cut squid open, lay flat, and remove skin. Now cut squid vertically into halves and score the surface. Slice into thin strips. Bring a small pan of water to a boil over high heat and drop in the squid. Return to the boil and cook for 1 minute. Remove squid, drain, and set aside.

Bring another small pan of water to a boil over high heat and add the salt. Drop in the scallions, return to the boil, and cook for 1 or 2 minutes, or until bright green. Dip scallions into a basin of cold water to stop the cooking and set the color, and drain in a colander.

Combine the *miso* and water in a large bowl, thinning the *miso* to a cream. Add squid and scallions, and toss. Just before serving, sprinkle with a few drops of lemon juice.

Seafood Dumplings

SERVES 5

½ pound flounder fillets
½ cup minced onion
¾ teaspoon sea salt
Few drops of fresh gingerroot juice
½ cup whole-wheat flour

Grind the fillets to a paste in a *suribachi*. Add minced onion, ¼ teaspoon salt, the gingerroot juice, and enough of the flour to hold the mixture together. Form into 10 dumplings.

Bring a large pan of water to a boil and add ½ teaspoon salt. Drop in the dumplings, return to the boil, and cook until dumplings rise to the surface. Drain. Add cooked dumplings to soups 5 minutes before the soups are done.

Salmon Head Soup

SERVES 5

1 cup soybeans, soaked in water overnight
4 cups water, approximately
1 salmon head
Shoyu

Combine the drained beans and 3 cups water and bring to a boil. Cook for 30 minutes. Wrap the salmon head in cheesecloth, and add; cook for 2 to 3 hours more, adding water occasionally to keep the ingredients covered. Remove the salmon head and season with *shoyu* to taste.

VARIATION: Whenever using only parts of a fish, reserve its trimmings (head, tail, bones) and bring them to a boil with a small strip of *kombu*. Cook for 30 minutes or more, then strain. Serve the broth garnished with scallion rounds.

Surimi Shinoda

2 pieces of *aburage* (fried bean curd)
1 cup water
2 teaspoons *shoyu*
¼ pound white-fleshed fish
½ cup minced onion
¼ teaspoon sea salt
2 or 3 drops of fresh gingerroot juice
1 egg
1 tablespoon unbleached white flour

Pour boiling water over the *aburage* to rid it of excess oil. Using scissors, open the pieces by cutting into 1 long and 2 short sides. Combine in a small saucepan with the water and *shoyu*, and bring to a boil. Cook until all liquid has been absorbed or evaporated and the *aburage* is well flavored. Drain and allow to cool.

Grind the fish to a paste in a *suribachi*; add onion, salt and gingerroot juice. Beat the egg and thicken it slightly with the flour, then add to fish paste. Spread the paste over the surface of each piece of *aburage*, roll into a cylinder, and tie with string. Steam over high heat for 20 minutes. Allow rolls to cool, remove strings, and slice each roll into 5 rounds.

Red Snapper in Miso

½ pound red snapper fillets
1 teaspoon grated gingerroot
Miso

Rub the raw fillets with the gingerroot, then bury in a keg or crock of *miso*. Wait for 1 week. Delicious.

Koi Koku *(Carp Soup)*

1 pound carp, whole
1 tablespoon sesame oil
3 pounds burdock root, shaved
1 cup used *bancha* tea leaves, tied in cheese-cloth
3 heaping tablespoons *miso*
1 teaspoon gingerroot juice

When purchasing the carp have only the green gall bladder removed by the fishmonger, leaving the remaining innards of the fish intact. Wash carp well but do not remove fins or scales. Chop into large pieces, and set aside.

Heat a pressure cooker and coat with the oil. Sauté the burdock until it no longer releases its strong aroma. Add just enough water to cover and bring to a boil. Now add the carp and used *bancha* leaves, cover, and bring rapidly to full pressure. Reduce heat to low and simmer for 40 minutes. Turn off heat and allow pressure to return slowly to normal. Remove cheesecloth bag of tea leaves* and add enough water to reach 2 inches above ingredients. Cover with an ordinary lid and bring to the boil over high heat.

Remove 3 or 4 tablespoons of the broth and use to thin the *miso* to a cream. Add *miso* to soup, reduce heat, and simmer for 20 minutes. Stir in gingerroot juice, turn off heat, and let stand for 3 or 4 minutes before serving.

Koi koku stimulates milk flow in nursing mothers and is very invigorating. Will keep for 1 week if refrigerated.

*The tea leaves, in combination with the pressure, soften the bones and make them edible.

Tazukuri *(Tiny Dried Fish)* MAKES 1 CUP

1 tablespoon corn or sesame oil
1 cup *tazukuri*
1 tablespoon *shoyu*

Heat the oil in a heavy skillet, add the *tazukuri* and sauté over medium heat for 2 or 3 minutes. Season with *shoyu* and simmer until dry. Serve as a condiment with rice.

Tazukuri, *chirimen iriko*, and *chuba iriko* can be used in place of *katsuobushi* for flavoring soup stocks. Or they can be ground raw and used as a condiment with rice. They are also delicious when deep-fried, then simmered in a little *shoyu* until dry.

Arai Carp *(Raw Fish)*

Cut fresh carp fillets on the diagonal into paper-thin slices. Place in a colander and douse with boiling water, then cool immediately under running cold water. Serve individual portions with citron *miso* (p. 164) and garnish with thin slices of cucumber that have been rubbed with salt and squeezed to remove excess liquid.

Shrimps and Eggs SERVES 5

4 tablespoons sesame oil
2 scallions or leeks, cut into 1-inch lengths
5 fresh mushrooms, rinsed in salted water and quartered
5 medium-size shrimps, dropped into boiling water for 1 or 2 minutes, shelled, deveined, chopped
¼ teaspoon sea salt
½ teaspoon juice of grated gingerroot
5 eggs, beaten
2 tablespoons snow peas, dropped into salted boiling water and cooked until bright green and tender

Sauté the scallions in 1 tablespoon oil for several minutes, stirring constantly. Add the mushrooms and shrimps, sautéing them lightly. Mix the ingredients together, season with salt, and sprinkle with ginger juice. Remove from heat and cool.

Beat eggs well, then add sautéed vegetables and shrimps. Heat 3 tablespoons oil in a wok and pour in the mixture. Cook over medium-low heat, stirring constantly. Add snow peas just before eggs set.

Serve with lightly boiled watercress.

VARIATION: Substitute ½ cup crab meat for the shrimps and proceed as above.

Egg Tofu SERVES 5

2 heaping tablespoons unbleached white flour
3 or 4 tablespoons water, approximately
5 eggs
½ to 1 teaspoon sea salt

Combine flour and water to form a milky liquid. Beat eggs well and add, then season with salt. Pour through a strainer to make perfectly smooth. Use mixture to fill a rinsed square mold. Put mold in a steamer, and cover mouth of steamer with a dry cloth before fitting on the lid. Steam over high heat for 20 minutes, then remove mold from heat and allow to cool. Tap out carefully onto a serving plate and cut *tofu* into 5 blocks. Serve with *tsuke-jiru* dipping sauce (p. 163) topped with toasted and chopped sesame seeds.

Chawanmushi (*Egg Custard*)   SERVES 5

10 small shrimps, cooked in boiling salted
    water for 1 or 2 minutes, then shelled
    and deveined
10 small pieces of red snapper, cooked in
    equal parts *shoyu* and water until tender
5 fresh mushrooms, cut into halves
2 eggs
½ teaspoon sea salt
4 cups *kombu dashi* (p. 136)
5 small spinach leaves, cooked in lightly
    salted boiling water for 3 or 4 minutes,
    then dipped into a basin of cold water
    and drained

Distribute the shrimps, red snapper and mushrooms among 5 custard cups with tops. Beat eggs well and add sea salt. Stir in the *kombu dashi* and use egg-*dashi* mixture to fill each cup four-fifths full. Place tops on cups and steam over high heat for 15 to 20 minutes. If steamer is not available, place cups on a rack in a pressure cooker over 1 inch of water. Bring rapidly to full pressure, reduce heat, and simmer for 5 minutes. Remove from heat and allow pressure to return to normal.

Uncover custard cups, place 1 spinach leaf on top of each, then quickly re-cover. Serve hot in place of soup or as a side dish, letting each person season the *chawanmushi* with *shoyu* to taste.

Datemaki (*Rolled Omelet*)   SERVES 5

6 eggs
½ teaspoon sea salt
2 tablespoons unbleached white flour
3 tablespoons minced watercress or parsley
1 tablespoon corn or sesame oil

Beat eggs well while adding salt and sifting in flour. When well beaten, add watercress.

Heat a small skillet and coat with the oil. Pour in eggs and cook covered over medium-low heat. When set, turn carefully and cook for 1 or 2 minutes more. Omelet should be ½ inch thick. Transfer to a plate and allow to cool slightly, then trim into a square or rectangle. Place trimmed omelet on a *sudare* or bamboo table mat, and roll into a cylinder, gently pressing firm. Tie *sudare* closed with a thin string. Allow omelet to cool thoroughly, then remove mat, slice omelet roll, and serve.

VARIATION: Set the trimmed omelet on the *sudare* or bamboo mat. Place a row of lightly boiled watercress along the near edge of the omelet and a row of lightly sautéed carrot slivers along the far edge. Now roll from both edges until they meet. Wrap in the mat and tie closed with string. Allow to cool thoroughly. Remove mat, slice roll, and serve.

SEAFOOD AND EGGS

VIII. PASTRIES and DESSERTS

PASTRIES and DESSERTS

Pastries and desserts add a happy finishing touch to a meal and help to balance *yang* dishes of animal food. To evoke the natural flavors from your ingredients learn to use just the right amount of salt.

Tarte aux Pommes

SERVES 6 TO 8

1 cup unbleached flour or whole-wheat
  pastry flour
¼ teaspoon sea salt
3 tablespoons sesame oil
¼ to ½ cup water, approximately
3 apples, peeled, sliced into thin half-moons,
  dipped into salted water
1 teaspoon ground cinnamon
2 heaping tablespoons *kuzu*
3 cups water

Combine flour and salt, mixing well. Add oil and rub the mixture gently between your palms to blend evenly. Add water gradually to form an elastic dough, and knead for 8 to 10 minutes, until smooth. Shape into a ball, cover with a damp cloth, and let stand in a cold place for 30 minutes. Roll out on a floured board, and use to line a 9-inch pie plate. Flute edges.

Preheat oven to 400°F. Fill pastry-lined pan with apple slices and sprinkle with cinnamon; cover with foil. Bake for 30 minutes. Remove foil and continue to bake until apples are nicely browned.

While the tart is baking, dissolve the *kuzu* in 3 cups water and bring to a boil. Simmer over an asbestos pad, stirring occasionally, for 30 minutes. After removing tart from oven, cover top with *kuzu* sauce and allow to stand. When tart has cooled and *kuzu* has thickened, slice and serve.

Chestnut-Apple Pie

SERVES 6 TO 8

1 cup chestnut meats
3 cups and 2 tablespoons water, approximately
½ teaspoon and a dash of sea salt
1½ cups and 2 tablespoons unbleached
  white flour
1 tablespoon ground cinnamon
2 medium-size apples, peeled, dipped into
  lightly salted water, chopped
3 tablespoons sesame oil
1 egg yolk, beaten

Pressure-cook the chestnuts in 2½ cups water for 40 to 45 minutes. Remove pressure regulator and allow steam to escape. Season chestnuts with a dash of salt, then grind through a food mill or purée in a *suribachi*. Set aside. Combine 2 tablespoons flour with 2 tablespoons water and ½ tablespoon cinnamon; add chopped apples, mix thoroughly, and set aside.

Combine remaining flour and salt, mixing well. Add oil and rub mixture gently between palms to blend evenly. Add remaining water (¼ to ½ cup) gradually to form an elastic dough. Knead for 8 to 10 minutes, until smooth; then shape into a ball, wrap in a damp cloth, and set aside in a cold place for 30 minutes.

Preheat oven to 450°F. Set aside ½ cup of dough. Roll out remaining dough on a floured board and use to line a 9-inch pie plate. Roll reserved dough into a thin sheet and set aside.

Fill dough-lined pan with chestnut purée and cover with the chopped apple-and-cinnamon mixture. Sprinkle with remaining cinnamon and top with reserved round of dough. Brush top of pastry with beaten egg yolk and bake for 30 to 40 minutes, or until nicely browned.

VARIATION: For a pie that is more *yang* use 2 or 3 cups cooked *kokoh* (p. 70) or *adzuki* jam (p. 168) for the filling.

Pumpkin-Apple Pastry SERVES 8 TO 10

½ pound pumpkin
1 medium-size sweet potato
1 teaspoon and 2 dashes of sea salt
2 medium-size apples
3 cups unbleached white flour
1 teaspoon ground cinnamon
6 tablespoons sesame oil
1 cup water, approximately
1 egg yolk, beaten

Peel the pumpkin and sweet potato, and steam them over high heat until tender. Purée together in a *suribachi* or grind through a food mill. Season with a dash of salt and set aside. Peel and chop the apples, then simmer in a small saucepan for 5 to 10 minutes, stirring occasionally. Season with a dash of salt, then blend the apples into the pumpkin purée.

Combine flour, cinnamon and remaining 1 teaspoon salt, mixing well. Add oil, and rub the mixture through your palms to blend evenly. Gradually add enough water to form an elastic dough, and knead for 8 to 10 minutes, until smooth. Form dough into a ball, wrap in a damp cloth, and set aside in a cold place for 30 minutes.

Separate the dough into 2 portions, one slightly larger than the other. Roll out the smaller piece on a floured board into a rectangular sheet approximately 2½ inches wide, and arrange the pumpkin purée down the center of the sheet. Roll out the larger piece on a floured board into a rectangular sheet a little larger than the first. Fold the larger sheet lengthwise into halves and score it crosswise at ½-inch intervals. Place second sheet of dough on top of first, over the filling, attaching the edges of the upper pastry to the edges of the lower pastry to form a cylinder. Seal the two edges by pinching the upper pastry to the lower. Place on a lightly oiled cookie sheet and bake in a preheated 350°F. oven for 30 to 40 minutes, or until well browned. Allow to cool before slicing.

Apple Dumplings

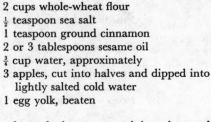

2 cups whole-wheat flour
½ teaspoon sea salt
1 teaspoon ground cinnamon
2 or 3 tablespoons sesame oil
¾ cup water, approximately
3 apples, cut into halves and dipped into
    lightly salted cold water
1 egg yolk, beaten

Combine flour, salt and cinnamon, mixing thoroughly. Add oil and rub mixture between palms to blend evenly. Add water gradually to form an elastic dough. Knead for 8 to 10 minutes, until smooth: shape into a ball and wrap in a damp cloth. Set aside in a cold place for 30 minutes. Divide dough into 5 or 6 parts and roll out each part on a floured board into a thin 5- or 6-inch round. Place 1 piece of apple at the center of each round, fold over pastry and pinch edges closed. Arrange pastry packages on a lightly oiled cookie sheet and brush with egg yolk. Bake in a preheated 400°F. oven for 20 to 30 minutes.

Apple Pie

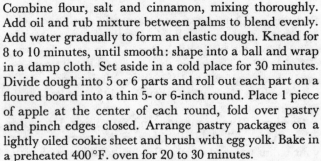

1½ cups unbleached white flour
½ teaspoon and a dash of sea salt
3 tablespoons sesame oil
¼ to ½ cup water, approximately
4 medium-size apples, chopped
1 tablespoon raisins
1 teaspoon ground cinnamon

Combine flour and ½ teaspoon salt, mixing well. Add oil and rub mixture gently between palms to blend evenly. Add water gradually to form an elastic dough. Knead for 8 to 10 minutes, until smooth; then shape into a ball, wrap in a damp cloth, and set aside in a cold place for 30 minutes.

Put the apples and raisins in a saucepan with enough water to prevent from burning. Bring to a boil and simmer for 15 to 20 minutes, or until turned to a sauce. Season with remaining dash of sea salt and remove from heat.

Preheat oven to 450°F. Set aside ½ cup of dough. Roll out remaining dough on a floured board and use to line a 9-inch pie plate. Roll reserved dough into a thin round sheet and set aside.

Fill dough-lined pan with apple-and-raisin mixture, sprinkle with cinnamon, and top with reserved round of dough. Prick a few holes in the dough to allow moisture to escape during baking, and seal edges with fork. Bake for 30 minutes, or until nicely browned.

Sandwich Cookies   MAKES 20 COOKIES

1 cup buckwheat flour
1 cup unbleached white flour
1 teaspoon sea salt
2 tablespoons corn or sesame oil
½ cup water, approximately
1 teaspoon ground cinnamon
½ cup crushed peanuts
2 tablespoons raisins
1 egg yolk, beaten

Preheat oven to 350°F. Combine flours and salt, mixing thoroughly. Add oil, rubbing mixture through your palms to blend it evenly. Add water gradually to form a dough. Knead lightly for 3 or 4 minutes, until smooth and elastic. Roll out on a floured board into a ¼-inch-thick sheet, and cut into halves. Place 1 piece on a lightly oiled cookie sheet, sprinkle with cinnamon, and cover with peanuts and raisins. Top with second sheet, press lightly together, and cut into squares with cookie cutter or heavy knife. Brush tops of cookies with beaten egg yolk. Bake for 20 to 25 minutes, or until nicely browned.

Pumpkin Cookies   MAKES 15 TO 20 COOKIES

1½ cups unbleached white flour
1 teaspoon sea salt
1 teaspoon ground cinnamon
1 cup pumpkin or squash purée
2 tablespoons peanut butter

Preheat oven to 350°F. Combine dry ingredients, mixing thoroughly. Blend in pumpkin and peanut butter, adding a little water if necessary, to form a dough. Knead lightly for 3 or 4 minutes, until smooth and elastic. Roll out on a floured board into a ⅓-inch-thick sheet, and cut into small rounds. Place rounds on a lightly oiled cookie sheet, and brush tops of cookies with beaten egg yolk. Bake for 25 minutes, or until nicely browned.

Camellia Mochi   SERVES 5

1½ cups sweet brown rice, washed
1½ cups water
½ teaspoon sea salt
½ cup pumpkin, *adzuki* or chestnut purée
5 camellia leaves

Pressure-cook the rice with the water and salt for 25 minutes. Remove from heat and allow pressure to return slowly to normal. Uncover, then transfer half of the rice to a *suribachi* and pound it to a paste with a moistened pestle. Mix paste with the whole rice, then divide the mixture into 10 parts. Flatten each part into a 2-inch round. Place 1 tablespoon of the purée at the center of each round and roll into dumplings. Arrange 2 dumplings on each camellia leaf, and serve.

PASTRIES AND DESSERTS

Kashiwa Mochi

(Omochi Wrapped in Fresh Leaves)

2 cups sweet brown rice flour
1 teaspoon sea salt
1½ cups boiling water, approximately
½ to ¾ cup *adzuki* jam or pumpkin purée
Beech or Oak leaves

Combine flour and salt, mixing well. Gradually add boiling water while stirring vigorously with 4 long chopsticks held in the fist of one hand, or with a wooden fork with four tines. When well mixed and cool enough to touch, knead dough for 10 minutes, until smooth, then steam on a damp cloth over high heat for 20 minutes. Transfer dough to a *suribachi* and pound with a moistened pestle for 5 to 10 minutes. Divide into 10 parts and press each part into a flat round on a floured board. Place 1 tablespoon of jam or purée at the center of each round, then fold over one side of the dough to form a half-moon shape. Seal edges by pinching dough with fingers. Wrap each *omochi* in a beech or oak leaf, with the leaf's shiny surface touching the dough. Replace on damp cloth and steam for 10 minutes more before serving.

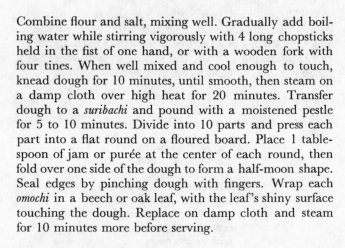

Awa Zenzai

(Sweet Millet with Adzuki)

1 cup glutinous millet, washed
1½ cups water
Dash of sea salt
1½ cups *adzuki* jam thinned with 1 cup
  water

Pressure-cook the millet with the water and salt for 20 minutes. Remove from heat and allow pressure to return slowly to normal. Before serving bring the thinned *adzuki* jam just to a boil. Serve the sweet millet topped with the *adzuki* sauce.

Adzuki-Chestnut Rolls

SERVES 6 TO 8

> ½ cup *adzuki* beans, washed
> ½ cup chestnut meats
> 3¾ cups water, approximately
> ½ teaspoon and a dash of sea salt
> 2 cups unbleached white flour
> 2 to 3 tablespoons sesame oil

Boil the *adzuki* beans in 1½ cups water for 20 to 30 minutes, or until wrinkled. In another pan, cook the chestnuts in 1½ cups water. Combine beans and chestnuts and simmer together for 40 minutes to 1 hour, or until pasty. Season with a dash of salt, then purée the mixture in a *suribachi* or an electric blender.

Combine the flour and remaining ½ teaspoon salt, mixing well. Add oil and rub the mixture between palms to blend evenly. Add remaining water gradually to form an elastic dough. Knead for 8 to 10 minutes, until smooth; shape into a ball and wrap in a damp cloth. Set aside in a cold place for 30 minutes.

Divide dough into 6 to 8 parts and roll out each part on a floured board into a thin rectangular sheet. Spread some *adzuki* jam and chestnuts over the surface of each sheet and roll into a cylinder; seal the edge of cylinder with a few drops of water. Steam on a damp cloth over high heat for 20 minutes.

Chestnut and Adzuki Paste

SERVES 5

> 1 cup fresh chestnut purée
> 1 cup fresh *adzuki* jam

Fill a rinsed shallow mold with the chestnut purée, and top with the *adzuki* jam. Press firm. Allow to cool and become firm before slicing.

Gozen Shiruko (*The Master's Favorite*)

SERVES 5

> 1 cup *adzuki* jam
> ½ cup chestnut purée
> 1 cup water, approximately
> Oil for frying
> 10 *omochi* rice cakes (p. 61)
> 1½ to 2 tablespoons fine-chopped *miso* pickles (p. 155)

Combine the *adzuki* jam and chestnut purée, and thin the mixture to a cream with the water. Bring just to a boil; keep warm over very low heat.

Heat a heavy skillet and coat it lightly with oil. Pan-brown the rice cakes over medium-low heat until they are puffed up and golden.

Divide the freshly toasted rice cakes among 5 serving bowls, pour in the hot cream, and garnish with chopped *miso* pickles.

An Balls with Kuzu Sauce

SERVES 5

> ½ pound pumpkin purée
> ½ pound *adzuki* jam
> 1 cup *kuzu*
> 2½ cups water
> Dash of sea salt

Form the pumpkin purée and *adzuki* jam separately into balls 1 inch in diameter, and arrange on a rinsed platter.

Dissolve the *kuzu* in 1 cup water and add a dash of salt. Pour through a strainer to make perfectly smooth, then add to the remaining 1½ cups water and bring to a boil. Simmer stirring constantly, for 20 to 30 minutes, until almost translucent. Pour *kuzu* sauce over the pumpkin and *adzuki* balls, and allow to cool and become firm; or refrigerate and serve chilled.

Dango *(Three-Colored Dumplings)*   MAKES 2 DOZEN

1 cup black sesame seeds, washed
½ teaspoon and a dash of sea salt
1 pound sweet brown rice flour
2 cups boiling water
1 cup pumpkin purée or *adzuki* jam
1 cup soybean flour

Roast the seeds in a heavy skillet over moderately high heat, stirring constantly, for 3 or 4 minutes, or until fragrant. Empty seeds into a *suribachi* and grind to a paste, seasoning with a dash of salt.

Combine rice flour and ½ teaspoon salt, mixing well. Add boiling water gradually while stirring vigorously with 4 long chopsticks held in the fist of one hand, or a wooden fork with four tines. When well mixed and cool enough to touch, knead for 10 to 20 minutes, until dough is smooth and elastic. Pinch off and roll into 24 small balls. Steam on a damp cloth, or boil in a large pan of water, for 20 minutes, then remove and allow to cool.

Coat 8 of the *dango* with pumpkin purée or *adzuki* jam, 8 with black sesame paste, and the remainder with soybean flour. Place 1 of each type on a skewer in this order: pumpkin, sesame, and soybean flour, and serve.

VARIATIONS: A. Use equal parts sweet brown rice and millet flour, and proceed as above.

B. Drop ¼ pound of mugwort (dandelion or watercress) into a small pan of salted boiling water and cook for 1 or 2 minutes, or until just tender. Drain, then squeeze the mugwort gently to rid it of excess water, and tear it into little pieces. Place the steamed or boiled *dango* in a *suribachi*, work the mugwort into the *dango* with your fingers, and re-roll. Coat *dango* with *shoyu* and grill until lightly browned. Skewer and serve.

C. After steaming or boiling the *dango* put them in a lightly oiled skillet and sauté over medium heat, stirring constantly and shaking the pan, for 10 minutes. Season with *shoyu* to taste. Or deep-fry the *dango* in *tempura* oil until pale golden and crisp; drain before serving.

D. Roll out the dough on a floured board into 3 rectangular sheets, then roll into long cylinders about 1 inch in diameter. Steam on a damp cloth for 20 minutes; allow to cool. Roll 2 threads together into a double-helix, wrap around the cylinder, and pull through to slice. Serve coated with *adzuki* jam.

Amazake Manju *(Sweet Sake Dumplings)*   MAKES 15

1 cup homemade *amazake* (p. 207)
3 cups unbleached white flour
Few tablespoons of cold water
2 cups *adzuki*, pumpkin or chestnut purée

Combine *amazake* and flour, and gradually add water if necessary, to form an elastic dough. Knead for 10 to 20 minutes, until dough is smooth. Form into a ball, cover with a damp cloth, and let stand in a warm place overnight. Knead again for 20 minutes, then pinch off into 15 parts. Roll each part into a ball. Press a finger into the ball, fill with a tablespoon of the purée, and seal the hole. Steam on a damp cloth over high heat for 20 minutes. Serve warm or cold.

VARIATIOS: A. For country-style *manju* use whole-wheat flour and a little warm water to form the dough, then proceed as above.

B. Roll out the dough on a floured board into a rectangular sheet. Spread the purée over the sheet, then roll into a cylinder. Steam on a damp cloth over high heat for 20 minutes, allow to cool, and slice; or place the cylinder on a lightly oiled cookie sheet, brush top of cylinder with beaten egg yolk, and bake in a preheated 425°F. oven for 20 minutes, or until nicely browned.

Winter Gelatin

SERVES 5

> 1 stick of *kanten* (agar)
> 2 cups water
> ¼ teaspoon sea salt
> 1 medium-size apple, cooked and puréed
> 1 egg, yolk and white beaten separately
> ¼ teaspoon grated lemon rind

Bring the *kanten* to a boil in the water and simmer, stirring occasionally, for 20 to 25 minutes, or until stringy. Season *kanten* with sea salt and divide between 2 small saucepans. Add the apple purée to 1 pan and quickly fold in beaten egg yolk. Bring just to a boil and pour immediately into a rinsed mold. Beat the egg white until stiff, then fold into the *kanten* in the other pan, adding grated lemon rind. Pour into the mold on top of the first layer and chill. When firm, tap out and serve both kinds to each person. A delicious winter landscape.

Sesame Halwah

SERVES 5

> 1½ sticks *kanten* (agar)
> 2 cups water
> 1 cup white sesame seeds, washed
> ¼ teaspoon sea salt
> Mint leaves

Dissolve the *kanten* in the water and bring to a boil. Simmer uncovered, stirring occasionally, for 20 to 25 minutes, or until stringy.

Roast the sesame seeds in a heavy skillet over medium heat, stirring constantly, for 4 or 5 minutes, or until lightly browned and fragrant. Empty seeds into a *suribachi* and grind to a paste, seasoning with salt. Blend the fresh sesame butter into simmering *kanten* and pour into a rinsed mold. Allow to cool and harden, then cut into 5 blocks. Serve on mint leaves, to be seasoned to taste with *shoyu*.

Kanten with Fruit

SERVES 5

> 2 sticks of *kanten* (agar)
> 3 cups water
> 2 cups diced fresh fruit
> ¼ to ½ teaspoon sea salt

Bring the *kanten* to a boil in the water and simmer, stirring occasionally, for 20 to 25 minutes, or until stringy. Add the diced fruit and simmer for 15 minutes more; season with salt. Pour into a rinsed shallow mold, and chill.

Pumpkin and Chestnut Gelatin

SERVES 5

> 2½ sticks of *kanten* (agar)
> 4 cups water
> ½ teaspoon sea salt
> ¾ pound pumpkin purée
> ½ pound chestnut purée

Bring the *kanten* to a boil in the water and simmer, stirring occasionally, for 20–25 minutes. Season *kanten* with salt and divide between 2 small saucepans. Add the pumpkin purée to 1 pan, bring just to a boil, and pour immediately into a rinsed mold. Add the chestnut puree to the other pan and pour into a separate rinsed mold. Chill. When firm, tap out and serve 1 piece of each kind to each person. For added color serve on maple or chrysanthemum leaves.

Adzuki-Chestnut Gelatin

SERVES 5

> 1 stick of *kanten* (agar)
> 1½ cups water
> Dash of sea salt
> 3 cups *adzuki*-chestnut paste (p. 197)

Bring the *kanten* to a boil in the water and simmer, stirring occasionally, for 20 to 25 minutes. Add a dash of salt and stir in the *adzuki*-chestnut mixture. Bring just to a boil, pour immediately into a rinsed mold, and chill. When firm, tap out, cut into the desired shapes, and serve.

Baked Apples

5 medium-size baking apples, washed
½ to 1 cup *tahini* (sesame butter)
2 or 3 tablespoons *shoyu*
Sea salt

Core apples but leave bottoms of apples intact. Fill apples with 1 or 2 tablespoons *tahini* seasoned lightly with *shoyu*. Sprinkle apples with salt, then arrange in a baking pan containing ½ inch of water. Bake in a preheated 350°F. oven for 20 to 25 minutes.

VARIATION: Peel and quarter 2 apples. Place 1 tablespoon pumpkin purée at the center of each of 5 pieces of aluminum foil, 4 inches square. Embed 1 tender chestnut, several whole peanuts and 1 apple quarter in the pumpkin purée. Gather corners of foil together and twist up to close the packages. Bake in a preheated 350°F. oven for 20 minutes.

Mitsumame *(Fresh Fruit Delight)*   SERVES 5

1 stick of *kanten* (agar)
2 cups water
2 cups diced fresh fruits (apples, melon, etc.)
½ teaspoon sea salt, or 1 teaspoon raw (brown) sugar

Bring the *kanten* to a boil in 2 cups water, then simmer uncovered, stirring occasionally, for 20 to 25 minutes, or until stringy. Pour *kanten* into a rinsed shallow mold, and chill. When firm, dice. Arrange on glass dishes with diced fruits. Serve sprinkled with salt or, for special occasions, with a little raw sugar.

Applesauce

SERVES 5

> 6 medium-size Delicious or Winesap apples,
> peeled and cored
> Dash of sea salt

Quarter the apples and place in a pressure-cooker with just enough water to prevent burning. Add the salt, bring to full pressure, and simmer for 5 minutes. Allow pressure to return to normal. Or grate the apples and simmer in a saucepan for 20 to 30 minutes, seasoning with salt.

VARIATIONS: A. Blend in tender whole chestnuts and/or ½ cup chestnut purée. Simmer together for 5 to 10 minutes.

B. To make apple butter, put the applesauce into a heavy pot and simmer uncovered for 3 to 4 hours, or until thick and deep brown. Season with salt to taste.

Strawberry Cream

SERVES 5

> 1 pint fresh strawberries
> 1 cup mock Béchamel sauce (p. 162)

Rinse the strawberries in lightly salted cold water before removing their small green leaves. Mash with a fork and serve individual portions covered with a salty mock Béchamel sauce.

Watermelon Awayuki

SERVES 5

> 4 cups watermelon juice
> 1 egg white

Boil the juice in a heavy pot until reduced to half the volume. Beat the egg white until stiff. Mix concentrated juice into the stiff white, and divide among 5 serving dishes.

IX. BEVERAGES

BEVERAGES

Try to eliminate artificially dyed and artificially sweetened beverages from your diet at the outset. They are very *yin* and, over the long term, fatigue both body and mind. Gain an appreciation for natural teas and grain coffees, the beverages we recommend for daily use. They are delicious and invigorating.

Bancha Tea

Bancha is a green tea made from the three-year-old growth of leaves and twigs picked from the lower branches of the tea bush. It is a soothing beverage that can be enjoyed by children and adults alike.

Dry-roast the leaves in a heavy skillet over medium heat until browned, shaking the pan and stirring constantly to avoid scorching. Remove from the pan and cool, then store in an airtight jar.

Add 1 to 2 tablespoons of leaves to 1½ quarts boiling water and simmer for 10 to 20 minutes. For a milder and more delicate taste, place the *bancha* into a teapot, add boiling water, and let steep for several minutes. Strain and serve.

To reuse the leaves, boil for 10 minutes, adding a pinch of fresh *bancha*. When a 1-inch layer has formed on the bottom of the pot, discard (or reserve for use in Koi Koku, p. 184) and begin anew.

VARIATION: *Sho-Ban:* Fill a cup with 1 teaspoon *shoyu* and add hot *bancha*. This "yangizing" drink is a remedy for fatigue.

Mu Tea

Mu tea is made from 16 herbs long used in the practice of Chinese medicine. In *Mu* tea these herbs are especially combined according to the principle of *yin* and *yang*. This tea has a particularly strong action upon the stomach and should be brewed weak if served immediately after a meal. Very *yang*, it may be drunk cold during hot weather. Available prepackaged at macrobiotic outlets.

Simmer 1 package of *Mu* tea in 1 quart water for 10 to 15 minutes. The package may be used a second time. For a stronger brew, simmer 1 packet in 3 cups water for 30 minutes.

Grain Tea

Dry-roast brown rice (or any other grain) over medium heat for 10 to 20 minutes, or until rich brown. Shake the pan and stir constantly to prevent burning and insure even heating. Add 2 tablespoons of the grain to 1 quart boiling water and simmer for 10 minutes. Add a pinch of salt (not enough to taste) during brewing. Strain and serve.

VARIATION: *Gemmaicha:* Combine equal parts roasted rice and roasted *bancha*. Place in a teapot and add boiling water. Steep for 10 minutes and serve.

Mugicha *(Barley Tea)*

Dry-roast unhulled barley over medium-high heat, stirring constantly, until almost black. Or oven-roast by spreading the barley out on a cookie sheet and placing it in a 225°F. oven for several hours.

Simmer 2 heaping tablespoons of the roasted grain in 1 quart water for 5 minutes. This is a cooling drink served chilled during hot weather.

Dandelion Coffee

Wash dandelion root and dry thoroughly. Mince, and dry roast in a heavy skillet over low heat. Allow to cool, then grind in a food mill or coffee grinder. Simmer 2 tablespoons in 1 quart water for 10 minutes or more. Add a dash of salt during brewing.

Apple Juice

Chop apples and cook in 1½ to 2 parts water. When tender, mash and strain. Add a pinch of salt. Serve chilled.

Yannoh (Grain Coffee)

Yannoh is a very nutritious coffee made from 5 different grains. Enjoyed at breakfast, it is an excellent source of energy. It is available prepackaged at macrobiotic outlets and natural-food stores.

Use 1 level tablespoon for each cup of water and simmer for 15 to 20 minutes. Add a pinch of salt during brewing. To free the coffee from grounds, strain through cheese-cloth. May be served cold.

Amazake (Sweet Sake)

1 cup sweet brown rice
2 cups water
1½ cups *koji*-rice

Pressure-cook the brown rice with the water for 40 minutes and allow the pressure to return slowly to normal. Cool to lukewarm (140°F.) and add the *koji*, mixing thoroughly. Cover and keep in a warm place (85°F.). In summer the *amazake* should be ready in 5 to 6 hours. Let stand for 2 or 3 days, mixing once or twice each day, and the *amazake* will become even sweeter. When extremely soft and releasing a yeasty aroma, the *amazake* is ready to drink.

To serve, add water for the desired consistency. Try 2 cups water to 1 cup *amazake*. Bring just to the boiling point and add ½ to 1 teaspoon grated gingerroot. Mix and serve.

Kokoh (Grain Milk)

Add 2 heaping tablespoons *kokoh* to 1 quart water and bring to a boil, stirring constantly. Simmer for 20 to 30 minutes, seasoning with a pinch of salt if desired.

Soba Tea

Season leftover noodle broth with *shoyu* to taste. To thicken, add buckwheat flour and heat for several minutes

Umeboshi Juice

Shred 1 or 2 *umeboshi* and bring to a boil in 1 quart water. Simmer for 1 hour, then strain, reserving the liquid. Refrigerate. Serve the liquid cold during the summer for a very thirst-quenching drink. The juice may also be used as a salad dressing or seasoning in place of salt.

BEVERAGES

GLOSSARY

Aburage — fried bean curd

Adzuki — tiny, hard red beans; the most *yang* bean

Amazake — sweet beverage derived from the fermentation of rice

An — a jam, paste or thick sauce

An-kake — a preparation of vegetables topped with a thick *kuzu* sauce

Arai — chilled raw fish

Bancha — green tea made from three-year-old leaves and twigs of tea bush

Biifun — rice flour noodles

Chirimen iriko — small dried fish

Daikon — Japanese white radish from six inches to several feet long

Dango — dumplings

Dashi — basic soup stock, also used in cooking vegetables

Datemaki — rolled omelet

Dengaku — technique of skewering, grilling, and coating vegetables with *miso*

Fu — steamed wheat gluten

Gomashio — sesame seeds and salt table condiment

Gammodoki — a deep-fried cake made of a mixture of *tofu* and vegetables

Goma — sesame seeds

Goma joyu — a mixture of sesame seed paste and *shoyu*

Goma miso — a mixture of sesame seed paste and *miso*

Hatcho miso — a *miso* made from soybeans, salt and water, aged for three years

Harusame — literally "spring rain"; soybean gelatin noodles

Hijiki — a black stringy seaweed

Horenso — spinach

Jinenjo — a wild potato native to Japan

Kabocha — pumpkin

Kampyo — dried gourd shavings

Kanten — agar, a sea gelatin

Kara age — literally "dry-frying"; deep-fried foods without batter

Karinto — a snack made by deep-frying dough

Katsuobushi — dried bonito used primarily in *dashi*

Kimpira — a *nitsuke* of slivered vegetables

Kofu loaf — a wheat-gluten product

Koi koku — whole carp cooked with burdock and *miso*

Koji-rice — seed malt

Kombu — dried kelp; comes in hard sheets

Kome miso — a light *miso* made from rice, soybeans, salt and water

Konnyaku — a translucent cake made from starch of the devil's-tongue plant

Koya-dofu — dried *tofu*

Kurumabu — wheel-shaped cakes of steamed wheat gluten

Kuzu — a vegetable root gelatin

Maki-yuba — strips of soybean-gluten wound into a little cake

Manju — a filled dumpling

Miso	bean paste made with soybeans, salt and grain, fermented by a special enzyme
Miso-zuke	vegetables pickled in *miso*
Mugicha	barley tea
Mugi-miso	a mild *miso* made with barley, soybeans, salt and water
Musubi	rice patties
Nigari	sea brine, used traditionally in making *tofu*
Nitsuke	vegetables sautéed in oil and cooked in a little water
Nori	dried laver, a seaweed
Nuka	rice bran
Oden	traditional Japanese stew
Ohagi	small balls of partially pounded sweet brown rice
Ohitashi	a technique of lightly boiling leafy vegetables
Okonomi yaki	pancakes
Omedeto	grain dish containing *adzuki* beans
Omochi	rice cake
Renkon	lotus root
Sake	rice wine
Satsumaimo	sweet potato
Seitan	pieces of wheat gluten cooked in *shoyu*

Sekihan	rice cooked with *adzuki* beans
Shiitake	dried Japanese mushroom
Shirataki	shredded form of *konnyaku*
Shoyu	natural soy sauce
Soba	buckwheat noodles
Sudare	bamboo mat used for rolling foods
Suiton	dumplings
Suribachi	earthenware mortar with serrated interior
Surikogi	wooden pestle
Takuwan	*daikon* pickled in rice bran and salt
Tazukuri	dried fish approximately 3 inches long
Tekka	a mixture of minced vegetables and miso, sautéed for several hours; used as a condiment
Tempura	batter-fried foods
Tofu	bean curd
Tsukemono	generic term for pickles
Udon	wheat-flour noodles
Umeboshi	small pickled plums
Wakame	long strands of seaweed
Yaki-dofu	grilled *tofu*
Yuzu	citron
Zenibu	a small round cake of wheat gluten with a hole at the center

MACROBIOTIC SOURCE BOOKS

Macrobiotic Guidebooks by Georges Ohsawa (Yukikazu Sakurazawa)

Zen Macrobiotics, Los Angeles, Calif.: Ohsawa Foundation, Inc., 1965

The Book of Judgment, Los Angeles, Calif.: Ohsawa Foundation, Inc., 1966

The Macrobiotic Guidebook for Living, Los Angeles, Calif.: Ohsawa Foundation, Inc., 1967

Cancer and the Philosophy of the Far East, Binghamton, N. Y.: Swan House, 1971

Macrobiotics: An Invitation to Health and Happiness, San Francisco, Calif.: George Ohsawa Macrobiotic Foundation, 1971

Macrobiotic Cookbooks

Abehsera, Michel, *Cooking for Life*, Binghamton, N. Y.: Swan House, 1972

——, *Zen Macrobiotic Cooking*, New Hyde Park, N. Y.: University Books, 1968

Dubawsky, Rebecca, *Cooking with Grains and Vegetables*, Boston, Mass.: Order of the Universe Publications, 1968

Farmilant, Eunice, *Macrobiotic Cooking*, New York, N. Y.: New American Library, 1972

Leadbetter, Jim, *Cooking Good Food*, Boston, Mass.: Order of the Universe Publications, 1969

Zen Cookery, Los Angeles, Calif.: Ohsawa Foundation, Inc., 1965

BIBLIOGRAPHY

Abrahamson, Emanuel Maurice, M.D., and Pezet, A.W., *Body, Mind and Sugar*, New York: Henry Holt and Company, 1951

Butler, Samuel, *Erewhon*, New York: Random House, 1955

Ford Heritage, *Composition and Facts about Foods*, Woodstown, N. J.: Ford Heritage, 1968

Gibbons, Euell, *Stalking the Wild Asparagus*, New York: David McKay, 1962

Goldstein, J. and Goldman, M. C., eds., *Guide to Organic Food Shopping and Organic Living*, Emmaus, Pa.: Rodale Books, 1970

Hauschka, Rudolf, *The Nature of Substance*, London: Vincent Stuart Ltd. 1966

——, *Nutrition*, London: Stuart & Watkins, 1967

Howard, Albert, *The Soil and Health*, New York: The Devin-Adair Co., 1956

Kervran, Louis C., *Biological Transmutations*, Binghamton, N. Y.: Swan House, 1972

Kloss, Jethro, *Back to Eden*, Coalmont, Tenn.: Longview Publishing House, 1939

Longgood, William, *The Poisons in Your Food*, New York: Simon & Schuster, 1960

Rodale, J. I., *Natural Health, Sugar and the Criminal Mind*, New York: Pyramid Books, 1968

Stiskin, M. Nahum, *The Looking-Glass God*, Tokyo: Autumn Press, Inc., 1972

Turner, James S., *The Chemical Feast*, New York: Grossman Publishers, 1970

INDEX

The rice-sheaf crest identifies this book as having
been planned, designed, and produced at Autumn Press, Inc.,
7 Littell Road, Brookline, Massachusetts 02146
Book design and typography by Dana Levy.
The text is set in Monotype Baskerville.